Forest Gardening

Forest Gardening

Cultivating an Edible Landscape

———

Robert Hart

Chelsea Green Publishing Company

White River Junction, Vermont

⁓

Interior design by Merrick Hamilton

Printed in the United States of America
1999 1998 1997 1996   1 2 3 4 5

First Chelsea Green printing, 1996

Originally published in 1991 in the United Kingdom
by Green Books, Ltd. Revised and expanded Green
Books edition published in 1996.

Library of Congress Catalog-in-Publication Data
available upon request.

Chelsea Green Publishing Company
Post Office Box 428
White River Junction, Vermont 05001

To Elena

who loves the Forest Garden

Contents

Foreword

to the North American Edition

I first encountered *Forest Gardening* in the autumn of 1994, while attending a conference in San Francisco for "bioneers"—people from around the globe who are working, with optimism and ingenuity, to preserve the diversity of life on Earth. Sara Stein was speaking there, the author of the influential book *Noah's Garden: Restoring the Ecology of Our Own Back Yards.* Stein explained how she had gone through the process of "unbecoming a gardener," transforming the chemically treated lawns of her suburban home into a living landscape, filled with flowers and herbs, trees and shrubs, birds and wildlife. Australian Bill Mollison was there, too, the iconoclastic Father of Permaculture, and next to his classic books I noticed *Forest Gardening*, a little volume that was being snapped up from a bookseller's stall almost as quickly as the copies could be put out. Clearly, something about this book had struck a chord, and I resolved to find out more about it.

Time passed, as time does, until one day I found myself looking at Robert Hart's book again, this time as the editor engaged to "transplant" *Forest Gardening* and introduce it to North American readers. The task has proved both easy and enjoyable. Many British books on gardening seem disappointing to Americans, since they never adequately address the widely divergent climates found on our continent—from Mediterranean to desert, subtropical to subarctic. Yet *Forest Gardening* offers something very different and very important to home gardeners: an inspiring natural philosophy that introduces us to a new and better way of looking at our gardens, our environment, and our place within both of them.

Bill Mollison has maintained that "Evil is just rigorously applied stupidity—a refusal to know what you know." By the same token, one definition of a genius might be a person who discovers or rediscovers something that all of us already "know," but that we have either forgotten or suppressed in our collective intelligence. Robert Hart's genius is to remind us of the wonderfully rich legacy we have inherited from the Earth, and to propose a system—Forest Gardening—that helps us "live off the interest" of this natural abundance in an ecologically sound way.

Hart saw the sustainable kind of ecosystem management practiced by so-called primitive peoples in the Earth's tropical rain forests as a model that could be used successfully by modern gardeners who live in colder, temperate climes—even those with only a small piece of land. In fact, it is on the small, intensively grown plot that the spectacular productivity of a forest garden becomes most evident. Michael and Julia Guerra, a couple from Hertfordshire, grow a multilevel garden on a mere 400 square feet of space at the back of their house. The Guerras use a combination of forest gardening, permaculture, and organic techniques, and put only four hours of work per week into maintaining their garden. The amount of fresh food they harvest from this small area would translate into fifteen tons per acre, an impressive figure by anyone's standards.

Practical-minded readers may wonder why they should care about Robert Hart's loving description of his Shropshire landscape and its fathomless history, or about matters as seemingly disparate as renewable energy systems, traditional crafts, and tropical agroforestry. To such readers, an acknowledgment is due: *Forest Gardening* is not a how-to manual that will tell you exactly what to plant where in your garden. If it were, it would be largely irrelevant to American gardeners. Instead, the book serves two main purposes. The first is to outline the basic theory and rationale behind the "multistory" forest garden system. The principles of Forest Gardening are eminently sensible and easy to learn. Anyone with a little imagination can read Robert Hart's story of creating his own forest garden and picture their own home landscape as it looks today and as it might look if planted with fruit and nut trees, shrubs with edible berries, and perennial herbs and vegetables. The temperate-zone plants mentioned throughout the text and listed in Appendix One will give interested gardeners a starting place for their own explorations and discoveries.

The second, overarching goal of Hart's book is to present the author's vision of a postindustrial "Green" society, one that uses the best of modern technology (like personal computers and other labor-saving tools), but that at the same time cultivates a new respect both for Nature and for our human abilities. In such a society, we would rediscover the most resilient of our own traditions and skills, passed down from our ancestors. The idea is scarcely a new one. The American Shakers provide one sterling example of how this kind of society might work, drawing from the techniques of both past and present to produce food and other basic necessities in abundance, while at the same time nourishing the human spirit.

In truth, the principles expressed in *Forest Gardening* should resonate strongly with American readers, since in this country we have had such complex emotions concerning our own native forests. In the early years of European settlement, the wilderness represented the mysterious, the dangerous, the Other that had to be cut down and domesticated as quickly as possible so that "civilization" could progress across the continent. This view, of course, ignored that fact that Native Americans managed much of this so-called wilderness long before Europeans ever set foot on the New World, clearing small and temporary garden patches and periodically burning off the understory of the great woods with fire to encourage useful plants to grow beneath the towering trees.

Then there is the other, nobler aspect of our American obsession with the forest. The aspect explored by John Muir, who once said that between every two pines stood the door to the world's greatest cathedral. The aspect embodied by Gifford Pinchot, first director of the U.S. Forest Service, who introduced the famous policy of "multiple use, sustained yield"—a doctrine that, in theory, if not in government practice, is exactly what Forest Gardening is all about. And the aspect epitomized by Henry David Thoreau, who said, in an 1851 lecture to the Concord Lyceum:

> A town is saved, not more by the righteous men in it than by the woods and swamps that surround it. A township where one primitive forest waves above while another primitive forest rots below,—such a town is fitted to raise not only corn and potatoes, but poets and philosophers.

To many people, no doubt, Robert Hart's ultimate vision of a network of forest gardens, slowly spreading across Britain, Europe, North America, and all the world's temperate zones, will appear utopian. But as Oscar Wilde once said, "A map of the world that does not include Utopia is not worth glancing at." And it would be a big mistake to think that the efforts we make in our own gardens have no impact in the world beyond. Gardeners, I have found, are an intensely curious lot, always keeping their noses to the wind to try and sniff out a better way of growing things. Robert Hart's small Forest Garden in Shropshire has already inspired many gardeners in Britain, and now his methods and his example are available to a new American audience. It is tempting to think of one gardener as being merely a "drop in the bucket," but that would be precisely the wrong metaphor to use in this case. No, Robert Hart's *Forest Gardening* is more like the pebble dropped into a still pond, whose influence radiates outward. From a small point in the center, the circles grow wider and wider, until at last that gentle force touches everything in its path.

Benjamin Watson

Diversity is the keynote of the forest garden concept, but it must be an ordered diversity, governed by the principles and laws of plant symbiosis; all plants must be compatible with each other. Most forest gardens are designed primarily to meet the basic needs of the cultivators and their families for food, fuel, fibers, timber, and other necessities, but some also include a cash component.

The forest garden is the most productive of all forms of land use. Most average about half a hectare (1.25 acres) in extent, and this small area can support a family of up to ten people. It therefore offers the most constructive answer to the population explosion. Java, which has a greater concentration of forest gardens, or *pekarangan,* than anywhere else, is one of the most densely populated rural areas in the world. Yet the landscape does not present an urbanized appearance, as most of the villages are built of local materials and concealed behind dense screens of greenery.

The forest garden is far more than a system for supplying mankind's material needs. It is a way of life and it also supplies people's spiritual needs by its beauty and the wealth of wildlife that it attracts.

others. The wide diversity of species ensures that any small invasions of pests never reach epidemic proportions, as they tend to do under monocultural conditions. The large number of aromatic herbs creates a deliciously fragrant atmosphere, and, I am convinced, contributes to the pest and disease-resistance of the other plants. As we eat the herbs and perennial vegetables daily in our salads, the garden makes a significant contribution to our diet throughout the growing season, from the first herbs and wild garlic in March to the last apples in November.

Though I worked out the system for myself, I have since discovered that peasants have been creating similar structures for hundreds or even thousands of years in many parts of the world, especially in tropical areas, where space is limited by population pressure; among isolated communities living on islands and in oases, remote from centers of supply and distribution, where a degree of self-sufficiency is essential for survival. Some of these Forest Gardens, or "Homegardens," as they are more commonly called, are found on the sites of ancient civilizations, such as those of the Maya and Zapotecs in Mexico and Central America, the Benin in West Africa, the Buddhist kingdom of Sri Lanka, and the Hindu kingdom of Java. It must be assumed that those civilizations encouraged a decentralist organization of society, with numerous self-sustaining communities dedicated to all-round human development, as opposed to the empires that imposed uniformity on their subjects and monocultures on the land.

My own first introduction to the traditional homegarden was in an article on Mexico in *Mother Earth,* the former organ of the Soil Association. "Mexico is the pattern of ecology," the author wrote, "and so, in spite of all her natural shortcomings, can teach us a lot . . . The indio's knowledge and practice of plant associations goes much further than ours, which is by comparison elementary. Their *huertos* (orchards) are mostly round the houses . . . they are amazing shambles of banana and coffee bushes, orange and lime trees, towered over by mango and zapote and mamey trees, all wild trees of the indigenous forest whose fruits are delicious and wholesome."

and shelter for livestock, as well as being sources of timber, fuel, fibers, fodder, or food for human consumption. Permaculture (which lays special emphasis on a wide diversity of mainly perennial plants and on landscape design) is a comprehensive form of Agroforestry devised in the early 1970s by Bill Mollison of Australia.

Those who are concerned with the full implications of the ecological crisis which we now face generally agree that urgent steps should be taken to plant many millions of trees. In pondering how this could be achieved, I was haunted by the title of a book by the Australian mining engineer, farmer, and landscape designer, P.A. Yeomans: *The City Forest*. It occurred to me that there was no reason why many of the desperately needed new trees should not be fruit trees planted by the owners of town and suburban gardens, who would gain the bonus of growing nourishing food. If one could persuade 100,000 Londoners to plant just ten fruit trees each, that would be a million trees—quite a forest! And if tree-planting programs were pursued in urban areas around the world, a new world-wide City Forest would arise, one that would go some way towards compensating for the devastation of the tropical rain forest.

I had a vision of mini-forests in millions of backyard gardens. To demonstrate what I had in mind, with my gardener and partner, Garnet Jones, I converted a small orchard of apples and pears into a Forest Garden, comprising upwards of seventy species and varieties of fruit and nut trees, bushes and climbers, as well as herbs and perennial vegetables.

Designed to achieve the utmost economy of space and labor, it is a tiny imitation of the natural forest. Like the forest, it is arranged in seven "stories," with the original apple and pear trees constituting the "canopy" and the other plants occupying the lower tiers. Thus the garden has a well-defined vertical dimension as well as horizontal ones. Now that it has been established for several years, I can affirm that it requires minimal maintenance, as the plants—nearly all perennials—largely look after themselves and are very healthy. The main work involved is that of cutting back plants that try to encroach on

The Mini-Forest

What was Paradise?
but a garden, an
orchard of trees
and herbs, full of
pleasure, and nothing
there but delights.

WILLIAM LAWSON

I have a mini-forest in my backyard garden. It represents a pioneer experiment in restoring a tiny segment of the primeval Long Forest, which once covered a wide area of the Shropshire Hills bioregion. Like the natural forest, it comprises a wide diversity of plants, occupying seven levels or "stories," but, unlike the natural forest, almost all its plants have been carefully chosen to meet human needs. It is, in fact, an attempt to create a model life-support system, which would enable a family or small community to achieve a considerable degree of self-sufficiency in basic necessities throughout the year, while enjoying health-giving exercise in a beautiful, unpolluted, and stimulating environment.

My mini-forest is the culmination of many years' study and practice of the system that has come to be known as Agroforestry or Permaculture, and which many people, including myself, believe has a major role to play in the evolution of an alternative, holistic world order. A Green World. The world of Gaia.

Agroforestry is the generic term for methods of cultivation in which trees are grown in or at the edge of pastureland or in conjunction with crops. The trees are generally regarded as fulfilling multiple functions: conserving the environment, controlling groundwater, providing shade

Forest Gardening

1

≈

Towards a Forest Economy

Editor's note: The words "forest economy" conjure up an image of loggers cutting down trees, which are then sold for cash and turned into pulp and paper, dimension lumber, and a variety of other products. However, this view of the forest as just so much "standing timber" is unbelievably short-sighted. Managed sustainably, a healthy forest can become a perpetual resource, one that provides for many of our basic needs. At the same time, the forest is a living ecosystem: sheltering and feeding wild creatures, conserving water and nutrients, and modifying climate on both the local and planetary level.

This chapter discusses some of the features common to forest garden systems worldwide. It suggests that our current bottom-line approach to forest management at best may be missing the point, and at worst may represent a false economy of the most dangerous kind.

The only basic and comprehensive answer to the colossal harm that our present industrial system is causing to the global environment—harm that could lead to the extermination of all life on earth—is to replace it with a sustainable system, geared largely to the non-polluting, life-enhancing products of the living world.

Bernard Planterose of the Scottish Green Party, in *A Rural Manifesto for the Highlands,* has drawn up a fascinating "greenprint" for restoring the Great Wood of Caledon, which once covered almost the entire Highland region. "The Second Great Wood of Caledon," he writes,

would be no wild and unpopulated place like the first 1000 years
and more ago. Whilst sharing several important biological characteristics of the original it would display many fundamental dissim-
ilarities. The main one being its intensive management by Man—
nurtured, not destroyed: lived in and by, not on. It would be so
well managed in fact as to appear in places almost unmanaged.

It would yield up to its human population a great wealth and
diversity of products as well as providing an incomparably more
hospitable micro-climate and environment than presently
afforded by the bleak and windswept moor.

It would provide a massive new potential of spiritual and aesthetic rewards.

It would fulfill our global responsibilities towards climate
stabilisation and the regeneration of a healthy balance of atmospheric gases.

A recreated forest in the Highlands of Scotland would also take
its place alongside other current initiatives in the world to rein-
habit manmade deserts and would be an expression of solidarity
with developing countries of the Third World.

In total it would provide a rich and sustainable resource for
more people than ever before living in a new harmony with each
other and the land, under new forms of land stewardship which
allow for the growth of more uncompetitive, stable and unex-
ploitative relationships.

The history of Highland ecology shows us that the region has
been naturally dominated by a mixed forest since the last Ice-age,
that it is only in the last 400 years or so that this dominant vegetation type has been artificially replaced by Man with heath or moor.
Ecologists tell us that the present-day natural climax vegetation of
the Highlands should be mixed forest over by far the bulk of the
land mass.

Direct experience shows us that where open moor and denuded peat can only support a few animals, a few plants and

therefore little agriculture, population and employment, a forest can support an abundance of economic activity in proportion to the relative abundance of its biomass and biological diversity.

The Second Great Wood of Caledon would comprise an enormous range of tree and shrub species, providing a correspondingly great range of food (animal and vegetable), fodder, fuel, timber, industrial, craft, and even medicinal products. The Wood might be recreated to comprise the best aspects of forest resource usage current in countries such as Norway, Sweden and Switzerland and from the historical past of the first Great Wood of Caledon itself.

The forest-croft would look a little different from the typical croft we see on the Highland mainland at present but would exhibit many qualities that are enshrined in the original crofting practice . . . It would be intensively managed, serviced by modern appropriate machinery.

Such machinery, Planterose envisages, would include waterwheels, wind generators, solar panels, biomass digesters, and wave and geothermal devices.

Planterose also foresees that:

a wealth of small manufacturing and craft industries would feed off the forest woods. Kitchen utensils, bowls, plates and other household implements would be made from locally cropped woods. Furniture and cabinet-makers would exploit the particular qualities of the woods available in their areas. In the place of today's laminated chipboard and plasterboard there would be good solid Scots pine surfaces and lined walls; warm, insulating and beautiful; not products just a luxury for the wealthy but as the Scandinavians take for granted as part of their forest economy. Other specialist craftsmen would occupy still further economic niches, making musical instruments, boats, toys, tools, charcoal and artworks.

Agroforestry and Permaculture techniques, Planterose considers, would play an important part in the great task of creating a forest economy. He has a vision of "forest gardens" in which would grow an abundance of the hardy fruit trees and bushes, such as apples, black currants, raspberries, and strawberries, which the Scots already know how to grow so well.

The country that already has the most extensive forest economy areas is China. Since 1958, the year of the "Great Leap Forward," China has pursued, wherever feasible, a policy of integrating forestry with agriculture. Forestry, moreover, is no longer regarded as mainly concerned with timber production, but also includes plants producing fruit, nuts, medicines, oils, and many other useful products. Much study has been made of the potentialities of intercropping trees with horticultural crops in compound schemes of an agroforestry nature. The Chinese have long appreciated the special value of multipurpose plants such as the extraordinarily versatile bamboo. In a postindustrial world economy, the bamboo, which can combine the strength of steel with the adaptability of plastics, would replace many nonrenewable resources such as metals and fossil fuels in the manufacture of a wide range of useful products, from bridges to boats, from cooking utensils to curtains, from dams to dust-pans, from lamps to looms, from mats to musical instruments, from paper to drainpipes, from scaffolding to shovels.

From the agroforestry point of view, perhaps the world's most advanced country is the Indian state of Kerala, which boasts no fewer than three and a half *million* forest gardens. The state, a long, narrow strip of land between the Western Ghat mountains and the Arabian Sea, stretches down to India's southern tip. Though it is the most densely populated state in India, much of the land is infertile, acidic, and badly drained. Large parts of the coastline are marshy or comprise mangrove swamps, which are subject to periodical flooding and tidal waves. But the energetic, cheerful people, with a strong instinct for survival, have found constructive answers to most of their problems. And the leading, comprehensive answer is, in many cases, the tiny family forest garden with a wide diversity of plants and livestock and connections with local industry.

Forest-garden-related industries include rubber-tapping, match-making, cashew-nut processing, pineapple canning, the making of furniture, the building of bullock-carts and catamarans, the manufacture of pandanus mats, oil distillation, basket-making, and the processing of cocoa and of coir-fibers from coconuts. Many families are even self-sufficient in energy, running their own biogas plants, which are fed from human, animal, vegetable, and household wastes. The slurry from these plants, combined with crop residues and the use of nitrifying leguminous crops, eliminates the need for bought fertilizers. As an example of the extraordinary intensivity of cultivation of some forest gardens, one plot of only 0.12 hectare (0.3 acre) was found by a study group to have twenty-three young coconut palms, twelve cloves, fifty-six bananas, and forty-nine pineapples, with thirty pepper vines trained up its trees. In addition, the smallholder grew fodder for his house-cow. Most gardens throughout the state have canopies of coconuts, towering over a multilayered structure of different economic plants. The name Kerala, in fact, means "Coconutland."

Residents along the coast make full use of the amazing qualities of the various mangrove trees, which constitute "forests of the sea." Mangroves have evolved unique biological structures, which enable them to survive conditions that no other plant would tolerate: constant immersion in salt water and oxygenless, waterlogged mud. In some trees, aerial roots descend from the branches, and "prop" or "stilt" roots spring out from the trunks, arching down into the mud. These roots pump air into the submerged roots. In other trees the aeration process is performed by vertical roots projecting above the mud. Many mangroves have seeds that float and germinate in salt water; in one tree, the seeds germinate while still attached to the tree. Mangrove wood is extremely heavy and makes the most highly prized firewood. It has an exceptionally high calorific content; mangrove charcoal burns at white heat.

Because of an equitable land distribution system, inaugurated in the 1930s under the influence of Gandhi, most Keralese families have a bit of land of their own. And about half those families have converted their plot, however tiny—many are no bigger than English suburban gardens—into a forest garden, towered over by coconut palms.

Because of these family forest gardens, most people in Kerala are to some extent self-sufficient in the basic necessities, above all food. Therefore, poor as they are, they are far better nourished than most other Indians. They can enjoy the two basic essentials of a nourishing diet: fruit and green leaves. Most Indians never see their national fruit, the mango, vast quantities of which are exported, fresh or in the form of chutney. But the Keralese grow their own mangoes in their own forest gardens, together with some sixty other nourishing food and fodder plants, medicinal herbs, and spices.

The Keralese forest gardens are very intensively planted, on several levels, like the natural forest, so that their cultivation, the processing of their products, and looking after livestock provide full-time healthy occupations for most members of the families involved, which average six to eight people.

The way of life these forest gardens provide is secure, healthy, cooperative, constructive, and creative. There is very little need for money; the Keralese work, not primarily for cash, but for the all-round self-fulfillment of themselves and their families. This is true freedom. The family forest garden is the basic unit of society; it provides practical education for the children and happy living, largely free from bureaucratic, political, or economic constraints.

Forest garden systems are characteristic of the rainforest belt around the world, from Indonesia to Sri Lanka, from Tanzania and Nigeria to Central America. Since time immemorial, people have been entering the rain forests, not to destroy them, but to utilize their vast resources in sustainable ways to satisfy essential human needs. In the process, they have gained an encyclopedic knowledge of the properties of rainforest plants and maintained those that were most valuable. Beneath the protective canopies of the tall rainforest trees, they have grown plants that, experience has shown, best meet their personal and economic needs—plants such as cassava and maize, pineapples and bananas. This is the best way to conserve the environment: not to preserve bits of forest and other so-called scenic areas as static museums or parks or recreation areas, but to *develop* them in the best sense of the word: to utilize their vast and wonderful resources in constructive, sustainable ways for the satisfaction of human needs. Science has hardly begun to explore the full potentialities of plant life. Only about one percent of rainforest plants have been subjected to exhaustive scientific analysis.

It is only in the last twenty years that Western science has begun to take an interest in the tropical forest garden. Until then, if Western administrators or agronomists were aware that such things existed, they dismissed them as haphazard conglomerations of plants. But when the International Council for Research in Agroforestry (ICRAF) was founded by a group of Canadian scientists at Nairobi in 1978, it began to make a close analytical scrutiny of the forest garden and found that, far from being haphazard, it was often a precise, multistoried structure put together by people who had an intimate knowledge of the properties, products, and habits of growth of the plants involved.

2

Unity and Diversity

How many of us ever stop to ponder that well-worn Latin phrase found on U.S. coins? E pluribus unum. From many, one. This pithy little maxim defines a healthy ecosystem as neatly as it does a robust and stable republic, as a vigorous forest is home to a great diversity of plant and animal species. Yet this forest represents much more than the sum of its constituent parts.

In nature, the continual exchange between individual life forms demonstrates that there is competition at work (as Darwin recognized), but also an unmistakable cooperation. Plants in a natural setting create niches in which other plants can thrive, or draw nutrients from the air and from the deep subsoil, thus "nursing" and enriching their neighbors. Competition and cooperation thus work in concert, and together they form the dynamic soul of the forest garden.

Symbiosis—"Living Together," or mutual aid—is the basic law of life. Evolution is a holistic process, the development of ever more complex, integrated organisms, involving a spiritual element which ensures that the whole is more than the sum of its parts. The living cell is a miracle of coordinated, cooperative activity. One of the first living beings to colonize a barren or devastated landscape, such as a rock-face or an area struck by a volcanic eruption, is a microscopic lichen. This is a symbiotic organism, a tiny green alga enveloped by a fungus. By photosynthesis the alga creates carbohydrates from air and water, using the energy of the sun, and feeds the fungus, which, in return, gives the alga shelter and protection.

Another symbiotic association involving fungi is found very widely among the higher plants, from orchids to trees. This association is a *mycorrhiza*, a mass of fine fungal threads, like the molds that give character to fine cheeses, which envelops and, in some cases, enters plant roots. The purpose of this beneficial invasion is to supply the plant with phosphorus, an essential plant nutrient and a constituent of the nucleic acids that carry genetic information. In return the plant feeds the fungus with sugar and nitrogen. Many familiar woodland fungi, such as the decorative red and white fly agaric—favorite seat for garden gnomes—are involved in this process.

The roots of leguminous plants—members of the Fabaceae, or Bean Family—and a few other plants, including alders, also develop associations with soil bacteria that extract nitrogen from the air. The bacteria supply the plants with nitrogen, and in turn the plants make their surplus nitrogen available to other plants, their neighbors and successors. The whole process is highly complicated, with the bacteria passing through a series of transformations. Starting as minute specks, or *cocci*, they develop tails like tadpoles, with which they wriggle through the soil in response to the stimulus of a root exudate. A colony is formed near the tip of a root hair, and this excretes a substance which causes the root hair to curl. At the bent tip the bacteria make their way through the cell walls into the root, where they undergo further transformations, from rods back to *cocci*, and rapidly multiply. This causes the formation of a root excrescence, or nodule—the "factory" where the process of nitrogen fixation takes place. The bacteria receive energy for this process and for growth from the plant, which sends out vascular strands from its root; these grow alongside the nodule and pass sugar into it. The nodules involved in nitrogen fixation are pink, and it is interesting to note that the chemical constitution of the pink pigment is almost identical to that of hemoglobin, the substance which colors the red corpuscles that transport oxygen in the blood of animals and humans.

A problem common to all plants is that of perpetuating their species and bringing forth healthy offspring. Nature (Gaia) has evolved innumerable answers to this problem, some of amazing ingenuity, and many of them involve the cooperation of insects, birds, bats, and other animals. The two main aspects of the problem are: (1) how to ensure the strength and adaptability of the young plants through the introduction of "new blood" from other plants (though some plants are self-fertile), and (2) how to disperse seeds over a wide area, so that they do not suffocate each other and are not starved for light by growing in clumps in their parent's shade.

Sexual reproduction in flowering plants is carried out by pollination, the process by which the male pollen is transported to the stigma, the receptive female surface that is connected to the ovary by the style. While some plants rely on wind or water for pollination, the majority employ various devices to enlist the help of insects. The principal attraction offered is "nectar," an energizing sugar solution which is so located inside the flower that insects, in striving to reach it, brush their bodies against the pollen-manufacturing anthers. In continuing their search for nectar, the insects carry the pollen on their bodies to other flowers, where it is deposited on the stigmas. Some flowers have highly specialized relationships with particular insects, to such an extent that botanists speak of "coevolution" of the two orders of life. Much of the individual beauty of flowers is attributable to their different answers to the problem of attracting specific insects and making use of their particular anatomical features, such as long tongues or long proboscises or particular behavior patterns. In some cases pollination is an extremely complicated process. The sexual organs of the Brazil nut flower, for instance, are protected by a heavy lid, which can only be lifted by an exceptionally strong female bee of one particular species. This bee depends for her existence on the courting activities of the male bee of the same species, who arms himself with scent from a rare orchid in order to make himself sexually desirable. Because human beings have been unable to take advantage of these highly specialized conditions, which are only found in the wild Amazonian rain forest, they have failed in all their efforts to grow Brazil nuts commercially, and the nuts are still gathered by Indians and rubber-tappers.

Birds and other animals are also instrumental in the dispersal of seeds. For this purpose many plants offer the attraction of a juicy fruit, in which the seed is imbedded. The animal, after eating the fruit, obligingly deposits the seed, complete with a coating of manure, at some point conveniently remote from the mother plant. Other plants seek the assistance of animals by covering their seeds with sticky hairs, which adhere to the animals' coats.

These examples of cooperation between plants and plants as well as plants and fauna are well established and have been subjected to rigorous scientific research. However, there must be many interactions in nature that science has so far failed to recognize. Of potentially great economic importance is the widespread traditional lore of companion plants, which claims that many plants affect their neighbors by stimulating their growth or warding off pests and diseases. Many of the plants involved in this lore are highly aromatic. Science admits that the purpose of plant scents is to attract beneficial insects and deter predators; most people know for instance, that lavender, when placed in a clothes drawer or closet, deters moths. Therefore it seems reasonable to accept that these same benefits may be conveyed to the plants' neighbors. It is also admitted that some plants help to fertilize other plants by excreting root exudates, such as saponin. There can be no doubt, in fact, that there is a continuous interchange of minerals, nutrient fluids, and water within the root sphere.

In the temperate forest, with its deep, rich soils, the root system burrowing down to the underlying rocks, from which it extracts minerals and in which it finds anchorage, is the main powerhouse of the whole vast organism. Every plant has a different biochemical composition and therefore, by its root excretions and decay, makes its individual contribution to the fertility of the whole. Living organisms in the topsoil, from bacteria to earthworms, also help to build up fertility while maintaining the soil's circulation system, by which water, oxygen, minerals, and radiation are kept constantly flowing. By contrast, in the tropical rain forest, with its far shallower soils, most of the fertility buildup takes place on the forest floor and up the stems of plants, where a vast horde of "decomposers" ensures the almost immediate recycling of every waste product. The "wheel of life," transforming matter into energy, turns far more rapidly under tropical than under temperate conditions. This, however, means that the tropical forest, with all its exuberant vitality, is a far more fragile organism than the temperate one. A temperate forest, once felled, has a vast reservoir of energy in its root system and rich soils that enables it to regenerate; but when a tropical forest has been burnt or bulldozed, all its above-ground energy is lost, and the thin, infertile soils are rapidly transformed by sun and rain into lifeless concrete.

The forest is not a mere haphazard conglomeration of plants and animals but an enormously complex, self-sufficient, self-recycling, self-fertilizing, and self-watering organism, which takes nothing from outside itself, but confers innumerable benefits on all forms of life. It absorbs the "greenhouse" gas, carbon dioxide, at a daily rate that has been reckoned to be the equivalent of a 150-foot-high cylinder on the surface of each leaf; at the same time, the forest gives off life-giving oxygen. With its architectural framework of trees, it provides niches and "nurse conditions" for animals of all sizes. The oak, the most ecologically hospitable of all temperate trees, has been described as "the monarch of the forest," but it does not dominate the other life forms. Rather, it is the great giver. Its trunk and branches provide niches for birds, small mammals, insects, and grubs; its deep roots draw up water and minerals from the subsoil and make them available to other plants, transpiring water through its abundant foliage to make rain. It injects calcium into soils deficient in this vital substance. No wonder the oak was worshipped by the Druids as a symbol and manifestation of the Earth-Mother, Bridya or Gaia, the great giver of all good.

The forest has its own vast circulation system, equivalent to the circulation of blood, lymph, and nerve impulses in the human body. Through this system pass endless streams of water, sap, and other fluids, of gases, aromas, and magnetic radiations, of forces and information. The force that raises tree sap high above ground, known as "vertical pressure differential," depends on the complexity of the tree's cell structure; it is a force that may exceed a quarter of a ton per square inch, and may operate at speeds in excess of two-thirds of an inch per second. The exchange of information between animals represents a kind of "circulation," too, and it ranges from mating calls to the dances by which scout bees indicate sources of nectar to their fellow workers. Undoubtedly there are innumerable interactions like these that science has not yet discovered.

Though the forest provides a highly stable environment for its in-dwelling life for thousands of years—if humans allow it to—this environment is not static. It is continually evolving, with the stronger, coarser plants, especially trees, providing "nurse conditions," secure niches within which more complex, more sensitive organisms, may safely develop. This is the law and process of ecological succession, by which Gaia—or her agents—facilitates the emergence of organisms still more fitted to win the battle for survival.

Because, though the forest may convey an impression of all-pervading peace and harmony, and mutual aid is the dominant note, it is also a continual battleground, a scene of incessant conflicts between predators and prey, parasites and their victims, encroachers and encroachees. To meet these challenges, living organisms have shown extraordinary ingenuity in developing an amazing range of weapons and devices of defense and offense. These include systems of camou-flage and deception; thorns, claws, and fangs; and the secretion of poi-sons. In some cases symbiotic mechanisms are employed; for instance, some tropical trees "employ" armies of ants to protect them against defoliating insects, rewarding their defenders with secure niches in their trunks and a diet of sugary sap.

The organisms that have been most successful in evolving into higher forms of life have been those that have not concentrated on the development of offensive weapons, but have accepted the challenges of antagonism, transmuting them into inner strength, powers of resis-tance, health, wholeness, and self-sufficiency. The organisms that have attained climax status in ecological succession have not merely found ways of overcoming the hazards of antagonists and environment, but have utilized them to their own advantage.

The forest is the scene of incessant dynamic happenings, positive and negative, harmonious and competitive: fighting and courtship, mating and feeding, socializing and display. By miracles of natural alchemy, Gaia and her agents have evolved innumerable forms, rhythms, colors, structures, devices, movements, scents, sounds, and adaptations, some of extraordinary ingenuity, many of great beauty. One cannot resist the conclusion that creative intelligences of a very high order are at work, continually seeking ever more refined and practical solutions to life's basic problems, but also determined to create beauty for its own sake. One day even human beings, intent on destroying the environment on which they depend and absorbed in their own narrow, greedy aims, will discover that beauty is a biological necessity.

A forest, like other ecosystems and landscapes, may comprise a number of distinct bioregions. A bioregion is defined as any area, small or large, that has a clearly recognizable identity. Many factors contribute to this identity: geological structure, soil, climate, types of vegetation, history, culture, "atmosphere," and magnetic and spiritual forces. Some of the world's most notable bioregions can boast well-known "regional" writers, painters, musicians, and craftspeople who, by their art, have interpreted the bioregional "soul" as manifested by its human inhabitants. Among outstanding examples of links between art and earth are the novels of Hardy and the landscape of "Wessex," the paintings of Constable and the landscape of the Essex-Suffolk border, and the operas of Janácek and the Moravian forest. In many parts of Europe, Asia, and Latin America, village communities can be recognized by the costumes, songs, and dances of their inhabitants, many of them inspired by features of the environment. The patterns and plants of permaculture plots, forest gardens, and other forms of land-working should also reflect the character of their bioregions. Those who work them are most likely to benefit if their diets consist largely of the plants that contain the minerals and other nutrients peculiar to local soils, and if they subsist as much as possible on local resources, thereby giving jobs to their neighbors and minimizing the polluting effects of mechanical transport. Such people—rooted or "hefted," to use the Scottish term, to their bioregional soils—enjoy a sense of psychological security unknown to restless city-dwellers.

Both the Highland clan and the Native American tribe are examples of bioregional organisms. The relationship of a member of a clan or tribe to her or his *duthus* (the Gaelic term for communal land) has an intense and poignantly beautiful quality. The essence of Amerindian religion lies in the effort to unify soul with soil, the human psyche with the rocks and rivers, the trees and wildlife of the natural environment.

3

Health and Wholeness

Just as a healthy forest is made up of many species, so a healthy diet should include as wide a variety of natural whole foods as possible: fruits, nuts, vegetables (especially green, leafy ones), and herbs.

At present in the industrialized world, we rely on a perilously small number of cultivated plants to feed ourselves. Not only does this lack of variety threaten our food supply, but the intensive monoculture approach requires us to farm large tracts of land in unsustainable and destructive ways. What's more, an unnaturally limited diet can negatively affect our health and thus all other aspects of our lives.

A multilayered forest garden, even on the small scale of an individual backyard, ensures an ever-changing harvest of absolutely fresh, organic food throughout much of the year. Growing and harvesting food that is nutritious and "alive" not only provides us with more energy, but contributes to an overall sense of well-being and self-reliance that nourishes the spirit as well as the body.

One of the supreme problems facing humanity today is the vast amount of suffering caused by avoidable disease.

Any living organism, from a plant to a human being, in a state of positive health, has marvelous self-healing and self-adjusting mechanisms. It immediately recognizes antagonistic factors, whether poisons, pests, or disease germs, and takes steps to eliminate them. One of its outstanding characteristics is that the fluids, whether blood, sap, lymph, or glandular secretions, that constitute a large proportion of its total substance are in constant free circulation. Therefore one of the main physical causes of all disease is any clogging of the bodily channels that allows a buildup of antagonistic factors. Another characteristic of truly healthy organisms is that they are predominantly alkaline in their makeup. Therefore, another major cause of disease is the consumption of foods and beverages that tip the bodily balance towards acidity. It so happens that most human diets throughout the world consist predominantly of cereals and foods and beverages of animal origin, which tend, in the long run, to have clogging and/or acidifying effects. Therefore, in order to build up lasting positive health, it is essential to adopt a diet that is eliminative and alkaline. Such a diet should consist of at least seventy percent fresh or sun-dried fruit and green vegetables. Fruit sugars are among the best of all brain foods, energizing and rejuvenating the body, while the green pigment chlorophyll has a chemical composition similar to that of human blood. Dr. Max Bircher-Benner, the pioneering Swiss nutritionist, wrote eloquently about the health-promoting qualities of chlorophyll, which, by its unique ability to create carbohydrates by harnessing the power of the sun, is the basis of all physical life. It contains a large number of vitamins and—contrary to general belief—a valuable protein. These make it an efficient creator of red blood cells, a normalizer of blood pressure, and a healer of wounds. One of Bircher-Benner's maxims was: "Never let a day pass without eating green leaves."

The "forest garden diet" comprises the widest possible variety of fresh fruit and greenery, derived not only from vegetables but also from cultivated and wild herbs. It thus approximates the "sallets" that were regularly consumed in seventeenth-century England, the age of the great herbalists. Many visitors to my home learn from experience that this diet is not only satisfying but can be surprisingly delicious. The strong flavors of many herbs, and even "weeds," lose their harshness when chopped up with other foods and served with a drop of fruit juice and/or tofu mayonnaise. Tasting sessions are a popular feature of visits to Highwood Hill. One of the garden's specialities is experimenting with uncommon food plants.

My whole life has been a struggle against ill health in my family and myself, and for me the forest garden has been part of the culmination of that struggle.

It has never been merely a negative struggle, against weakness, fatigue, nervous debility, and pain, but from childhood I have sought to transcend my own and my family's problems by working out a science of positive health, a holistic way of life, that might in time benefit many others as well as ourselves.

The essence of life should be continuous creativity: in working out creative and comprehensive solutions to one's problems, one rises above them. They become smaller, less tormentingly insistent, until, perhaps, in time, one realizes they have just faded away.

One way in which I have sought to rise above my problems has been—literally—by climbing hills and mountains. During my last holiday abroad I explored a remote Swiss valley from end to end, and there I first encountered the peasant ethos of proud self-sufficiency. During one phenomenally hot summer, the glacier at the head of the valley had partially melted, causing a disastrous flood. A subscription had been organized throughout the country to help the stricken inhabitants, but when the money reached the town hall of the valley's principal village, the people asked that it should be given to others "less able to help themselves."

In his study of Chinese yoga, *The Secret of the Golden Flower,* the great Swiss psychologist C.G. Jung wrote:

I always worked with the temperamental conviction that in the last analysis there are no insoluble problems, and experience has so far justified me in that I have often seen individuals who simply outgrew a problem which had destroyed others. This "outgrowing" revealed itself on further experience to be the raising of the level of consciousness. Some higher or wider interest arose on the person's horizon, and through this widening of his view, the insoluble problem lost its urgency. It was not solved logically on its own terms, but faded out in contrast to a new and stronger life-tendency. It was not repressed and made unconscious, but merely appeared in a different light, and so became different itself. What, on a lower level, had led to the wildest conflicts and to emotions full of panic, viewed from the higher level of the personality, now seemed like a storm in the valley seen from a high mountain top. This does not mean that the thunderstorm is robbed of its reality; it means that, instead of being in it, one is now above it. *(English translation by Cary F. Baynes; London: Kegan, Paul, 1945, p. 88.)*

Having thus transcended the problem, one is able to transmute its negative elements into something wholly positive. This fundamental psychological process is the secret of all great art. Thus Beethoven was able to transmute the traumatic discovery that he was becoming deaf into the *Eroica* symphony, that crucial landmark in the history of music. Musicologists have argued about the identity of the "hero" whom the symphony was "about," but Beethoven himself was the true hero: a Beethoven who had learned to transcend his personal problem by identifying himself with humankind's struggle for freedom.

In taking over Highwood Hill, I resolved that the creative enterprise of building up a small organic farm was to be a major comprehensive and constructive answer to my own and my family's health problems. It was to be the alchemical *opus*, in the course of which the leaden burdens of our physical and mental shackles were to be transmuted into the gold of health and beauty.

'What is a medicinal herb?

It is a plant containing "secondary" products that play no identifiable part in the metabolism of the plant itself, but seem to be intended by Nature—by Gaia—for the healing of animals, of human beings, and—possibly, in some cases—of other plants. These "secondary" products are highly complex chemicals. They include:

alkaloids, which are known to affect the human nervous system;
anthraquinones, which are purgatives and also dyes;
bitter principles, which stimulate the secretion of digestive juices;
cardiac glycosides, which can increase the power of the heartbeat;
essential oils, which are aromatic, antiseptic, and strengthen the
  immune system;
flavones and flavonoids, which stimulate and strengthen the circu-
  latory system;
mucilages, which soothe the whole system and reduce inflammation;
phenolic compounds, which are antiseptic and reduce pain;
saponins, soaplike substances, which reduce inflammation and are
  used as purgatives; and
tannins, which have an astringent effect and aid the sealing of
  wounds.

Despite all the scientific research that has gone into them—research
that has led to the production of a number of well-known drugs—
herbs still have a mysterious fascination for me. I have been growing,
studying, and using them since my first days at Highwood Hill. They
can be divided into two categories: those that, in their natural state, are
woodland plants, and therefore tolerate shade, and those that naturally grow on heaths or in grassland and therefore require full sunlight.

Among shade-tolerant herbs and perennial vegetables growing in
the forest garden are ten varieties of mint, including eau-de-cologne
mint *(Mentha piperita citrata),* which has the most delicious scent of
any plant I know; two varieties of balm *(Melissa officinalis),* with its
lemony scent and taste, a plant much valued by herbalists for psychological effects in relieving anxiety and raising the spirits; three varieties of sorrel, another plant with lemon-flavored leaves, an ingredient
both of traditional salads and of the French *soupe Ö l'oseille;* tansy, a
vigorous plant with gay, golden flowers, a pungent odor and an acrid
taste; lady's-mantle, a groundcover plant with frilly leaves, esteemed
by the Arabs and throughout Europe for its effectiveness in treating

feminine ailments; three types of celery: wild celery *(Vallisneria americana)*, sweet cicely, and lovage, a giant herb that may reach heights exceeding nine feet; comfrey, formerly known in country areas as "knit-bone," another extremely vigorous plant containing a potent mucilage which can aid the healing of fractures; good King Henry, known in Eastern England as "Lincolnshire asparagus," a member of a very interesting family of dual-purpose plants, which also includes the Peruvian quinoa, and which combines the virtues of vegetables and cereals; and *Rosa rugosa*, a tall and vigorous member of what is probably the most loved of all plant genera, prized equally by medieval herbalists and modern nutritionists for the high vitamin C content of its large, tomato-shaped hips, and whose crimson flowers inject a startling note of vivid color into the prevailing greenery.

Among sun-loving herbs are several species of *Artemisia*, including wormwood and southernwood, plants with pungent odors and extremely acrid tastes, which have long been valued by herbalists for the treatment of digestive troubles; rue, with striking blue foliage and a sickly sweet smell; marjoram, with its florets of subtle purplish pink; fennel, with its gold umbellifer flowers set off by feathery "bronze" foliage; Biblical hyssop with purple, strongly aromatic flowers, which benefits the eyes and helps to regulate the circulation of the blood; borage, with its heavenly blue flowers, beloved of bees, which is said to instill courage into the human heart; catnip, another herb with bluish flowers beloved of bees—and of cats, who find it literally intoxicating; rosemary, the favorite herb of Juliette de Bairacli Levy, who describes it as "a supreme heart tonic"; an uncommon purple broom *(Cytisus atropurpurea)*, used by Spanish gypsies for making perfume; lavender, another scent-making plant, whose powerful aroma wards off insect pests and benefits the nerves; goat's-rue *(Galega officinalis)*, a tall herb with white pea-flowers capable of promoting milk secretion in all mammals, and soapwort, a plant with flowers of pinkish white, notable for its store of saponin, which not only brings medicinal benefits to the skin but is also a detergent, still used for washing delicate fabrics, such as old tapestries. One of the choicest spots in the whole garden is a bed of soapwort, hyssop, and southernwood, framed by a peartree, a crabapple, and two buddleias, beloved of butterflies, with, as its backdrop, a distant view of the wooded slope of Wenlock Edge.

Of all the drugs commonly prescribed by Western medicine, at least fifty percent contain ingredients of plant origin. Moreover, research is continually in progress to analyze fresh plants for their healing potential. Modern science therefore fully endorses the traditional view, going back to ancient Egypt, and probably to prehistoric times, that the plant world is a vast repository of precise and effective remedies for most of the ills of humankind. Where herbalists disagree with conventional medicine is in maintaining that safer and, in the long run, more effective results can be obtained from consuming plants whole rather then in the form of extracts. Plants are complex and intricately balanced organisms containing a wide diversity of hormones, enzymes, and other vital substances, whose negative effects are neutralized by positive ones. If, therefore, a plant extract is consumed alone, there tend to be undesirable side effects that may lead to complications.

For quick results in emergencies, antibiotics may sometimes be necessary. The practice of herbalism is essentially part of a positive, holistic, health-building process, whose results tend to be slower and less sensational than those of orthodox medicine, but which tend to have a more lasting effect on overall health. Human beings are what they eat and drink—and think. Our systems are made of the foods and beverages that we consume and the thoughts that we allow into our minds. Moreover, there is a constant interaction between physical and mental factors: they affect each other. By what we eat and think we help to control the construction of our most vital organs, including the brain, heart, liver, glands, nervous system, and eyes. An engineer building an elaborate and sensitive machine such as a computer or spacecraft, takes the utmost care to select the most appropriate materials, whether metals, timber, or plastics, to ensure strength and endurance, resilience, and reliability. If, therefore, we wish to obtain and maintain lasting health in all our organs—more intricate and complex than those of any manmade machine—and if we wish to avoid chronic illness, there can be no doubt that we must include in our diets a wide diversity of the plant materials that experience has shown have the most beneficial effects on the different components of our systems.

In the sixteenth and seventeenth centuries, when England experienced a notable flowering of genius in several spheres—literature, music, science, religion, philosophy, medicine, and herbalism—it is significant that a standard dish was a "sallet" or "salmagundy" comprising a wide variety of ingredients, including herbs, whose healing and prophylactic effects were well understood. Intelligent, life-loving people practiced the advice of the contemporary Swiss philosopher and physician, Paracelsus: "Make food your medicine and medicine your food."

The consumption of chlorophyll-rich green plants, especially when eaten raw and fresh from the soil, has been proven to confer many benefits on the human system. It promotes the formation of red blood cells, improves circulation, normalizes blood pressure, heals wounds, and even helps to protect the body against airborne pollution and radiation. Moreover, perennial green plants, such as many herbs, are particularly rich in minerals, which their deep roots extract from the subsoil.

Among these essential minerals is iron, one of the main constituents of red blood cells, where one of its functions is to form an association with oxygen, which we breathe in from the air with our lungs. Oxygen is one of the six essential elements of living matter, the others being carbon, hydrogen, nitrogen, sulphur, and phosphorus. The function of oxygen is purifying and transformative. With the aid of iron, it courses through the blood and is carried to every part of the human body, burning up blood sugar and waste products and converting them into energy. Oxygen is therefore the main fuel of the body-machine. When it is deficient, owing to a shortage of iron in the diet, then anemia sets in, which is characterized by listlessness, fatigue, headaches, bad memory, and low blood pressure. An abundance of dietary iron is therefore essential for nursing mothers and growing children. Iron also helps to control the circulation of the blood, acting as a built-in thermostat, keeping us relatively warm in cold weather and cool in hot weather. It gives us vitality, strength, and endurance. Among the best sources of iron are whole cereals (not refined cereals), apples, pears, plums, grapes, apricots, bananas, raisins, dates, figs, nuts, carrots, onions, turnips, lentils, honey, watercress, spinach, and other green vegetables.

Another basic necessity for healthy blood is an abundance of vitamin C, the best source of which is fresh, raw fruit and vegetables. It had long been known that sailors, deprived of fresh fruit and vegetables during long sea voyages, tended to suffer from scurvy, a disease characterized by anemia, spontaneous bleeding, and slow healing of wounds. Captain James Cook was the first to realize the cause of scurvy and the best way of preventing it. He ordered that his ships should be provided with abundant supplies of oranges and limes, and, under his influence, the practice was started of including lime-juice in the rations of the Royal Navy, a practice which led to British people being known in America as "limeys." One of the most important functions of vitamin C is to strengthen the blood's wonderful armory of protective devices, the phagocytes and antibodies that destroy invading disease germs. Bircher-Benner stated that, for optimum health and lasting youthfulness, the body should be "saturated" with vitamin C, but this can only be done by consuming large quantities of fresh, raw fruit and vegetables every day. Vitamin C is the most vulnerable of all the vitamins; it is destroyed by unnatural chemical substances and also by cooking and storage; moreover, unlike other vitamins, it is not stored or manufactured within the body's tissues. This is why we need daily supplies.

Another vitamin that is essential for healthy blood is vitamin E. It is essential for the free circulation of the blood: it dissolves blood clots, and therefore helps to prevent coronary thrombosis, that major killer in our Western civilization. It is also beneficial in the treatment of high blood pressure, varicose veins, and heart trouble. It is the major fertility vitamin, found in the seeds of vegetables and cereals, especially wheat germ, and in oils derived from seeds, such as peanut oil and sunflower oil, and also in green leaves. It is the most important vitamin for nursing mothers.

Another mineral which is essential for good blood circulation, by ensuring that the heart functions efficiently in its work as pump, is iodine. Iodine is one of the main foods of the thyroid, the tiny gland in our throats that exerts a key role in controlling many of our body's vital functions, including metabolism, energy production, growth, reproduction, nerve currents in our muscles, and the growth of skin and hair. It is interesting to note that the Japanese, a very healthy race, ensure a steady supply of iodine and other minerals in their diets by consuming large quantities of seaweed, the constituents of which are almost identical to human blood; in fact, Japanese doctors often use an extract of seaweed as a substitute for blood plasma. The Japanese have thousands of seaweed farms, many of them employing girls as skin divers, who harvest the weed under the waves. The rest of us are largely dependent on fruit, vegetables, and cereals, which extract iodine from the soil. This, however, is an unreliable source, as some soils, especially in limestone areas such as Derbyshire and parts of Switzerland, are iodine-deficient. People in such areas are prone to goiter, an enlargement of the thyroid caused by lack of iodine. Goiter has been largely eradicated in Switzerland through the use of iodized table salt. Apart from seafood, good sources of iodine are garlic, onions, soybeans, pineapple, pears, strawberries, tomatoes, celery, lettuce, oats, spinach, beets, and wheat. If iodine deficiency is suspected, kelp tablets seem to be quite effective. Another way of ensuring an adequacy of iodine in the diet is by applying seaweed fertilizers and seaweed foliar sprays to one's own fruit, vegetables, and herbs, as I do myself.

Among minerals that are essential to the brain and nerves, the most important is phosphorus, of which the best sources are whole cereals, nuts, and most vegetables, especially peas and beans. A diet that is deficient in these vital ingredients can affect the intelligence—and also the character.

Another mineral essential to the nervous system is calcium. It helps the transportation of nerve impulses and promotes the sensitivity of the nervous system to stimulation; shortage of calcium leads to tension, irritability, and cramps. Calcium, phosphorus, and potassium are the three most important minerals concerned with building the body of the growing child. Calcium is a vital constituent of bones and teeth.

The motive power for many of the body's complicated mechanisms is provided by the enzymes: tiny, highly specialized chemical catalysts that exist in every cell. Enzymes are above all transformers, and they act by causing fermentation. They perform the extraordinary feat of transforming the food we eat into entirely different substances, such as blood, bones, nerves, hair, and fingernails—a feat that the world's greatest chemical genius is incapable of duplicating. Enzymes are also at the heart of every chemical action in the body, including those involved in growth, nerve impulses, and the movements of muscles. While some enzymes are manufactured by the body, most are dependent on minerals in the food we eat, including iron, potassium, manganese, copper, and zinc. The best sources of these and other minerals are raw fruit, vegetables, nuts, sun-dried fruits, and wholegrain cereals. We also imbibe complete enzymes from plant cells. It is an interesting fact that many plant foods contain the precise enzymes that are necessary to digest them.

Consumption of refined sugar, sweets, and soft drinks tends to neutralize the effects of calcium; this is why so many children today suffer from tooth decay. The best source of calcium, both for children and adults, is generally considered to be milk, but some nutritionists have reservations about milk as an ideal food, except for mother's milk in the case of a baby. Milk is a highly specialized food (it is a food, not a beverage, as it coagulates in the process of digestion), designed by nature to promote the development of young mammals. Each species has a different milk. Human milk has five times more brain-forming substances than cow's milk, which is adapted to the needs of a bulky, slow-moving, and not very intelligent animal. Moreover, milk, milk products, and all other forms of animal fat cause, in the adult, a gradual clogging of the system with cholesterol, which eventually leads to arthritis, heart disease, and other chronic illnesses characteristic of Western civilization. It is significant that the Chinese, Japanese, and Koreans drink very little cow's milk and eat very little meat because they are short of agricultural land and can't afford to waste it by putting it down to grass, when it can be used so much more productively for growing crops. Instead, they eat enormous quantities of soybeans and soy products and drink soy milk. Soybeans are a good source of calcium, as are citrus fruits, figs, whole grains, and nuts. Soybeans also provide what is probably the best of all proteins, as they are the only foodstuffs known that contain the full complement of twenty-two amino acids, of which complete proteins consist.

Proteins and water are two primary substances of which our bodies are made, so a good supply of proteins is essential for growing children. Adults need a smaller proportion of proteins in their diet—just sufficient to make up for the continuous wearing process in their tissues. Nutritionists consider that it is best for adults to avoid overburdening their systems with excessive proteins, if they wish to retain their fitness, energy, and youthfulness. Nutritionists of the Bircher-Benner school strongly oppose the notion that only animal proteins—meat, cheese, etc.—are "first-class," while vegetable proteins—such as beans, lentils, nuts, cereals, mushrooms, and green leaves—are "second-class." In fact, they believe the reverse to be the case. The green leaf contains a protein of particularly high value.

The cells of the stomach are strengthened by vitamin A, which is also essential for the strength and health of other vital organs, especially the eyes, skin, bones, teeth, nerves, and all mucus membranes. The adrenal glands, which pump energy-giving hormones into the system in emergencies, need an abundant supply of vitamin A and also of vitamin C if they are to function efficiently and not let us down in times of crisis. Vitamin A also affects the breathing; if it is in short supply, we are liable to complaints affecting the lungs and bronchial tubes. The best of all sources of vitamin A is raw carrots. During the Second World War pilots of night-flying aircraft were given raw carrots to strengthen their eyesight. Other good sources are apricots, rose hips, peaches, oranges, pineapples, tomatoes, green vegetables, whole cereals, and vegetable oils.

Another source of energy in emergencies is glycogen, or animal starch, which is stored as granules in all the tissues, but especially in the muscles and liver. The glycogen in the liver is the body's principal energy reserve. It is mobilized when needed by conversion into glucose, which enters the bloodstream, giving us the "shot in the arm" we need in order to face up to difficulty or danger. The best source of glycogen is an abundant supply of vegetable carbohydrates, those basic substances manufactured by green plants with the aid of the sun's energy in the course of photosynthesis.

The only comparable process to photosynthesis in the case of human beings is the manufacture of vitamin D through the effect of ultraviolet rays from the sun on fat in the skin. Vitamin D exerts a major influence on the growth and hardening of bones and teeth. A deficiency in childhood leads to rickets and tooth decay. As the teeth are the hardest bones in the body, tooth decay may be a warning of more serious disorders affecting the more delicate internal organs, and, apart from visits to the dentist, measures should be taken to build up general health. These should include taking every opportunity to enable the child to enjoy the effect of sun on his skin, thus accumulating valuable stores of vitamin D. The process of manufacturing vitamin D in the skin is assisted by green plants, cereal germ, and yeast. The principal food sources of vitamin D are generally assumed to be milk and eggs, but it is also found in sunflower oil, peanuts, and mushrooms.

When I remark that we live on a mainly raw vegan diet with no animal products and only one gluten cereal—rye—people exclaim, "What on earth do you eat?" In fact we enjoy an extremely varied diet. Our daily salads comprise the widest possible diversity of fruit, including dried fruit, vegetables, herbs, nuts, and fungi, including mushrooms and yeast extracts, as well as vegetable oils. In addition I cook, minimally, roots, pulses, and cereals as well as certain vegetables, such as cauliflower, that are somewhat indigestible if eaten raw. I avoid the gluten cereals—wheat, barley, and oats—because gluten, the protein that these cereals contain, as its name implies is a gluey substance that tends to clog the system. Rye has the least gluten of any of the gluten cereals and contains strengthening factors that make it the favored cereal of the hardy people of northern Europe. We eat it in the form of Ryvita and rye bread. The other cereals we eat are rice, millet, buckwheat, sesame, and quinoa.

Anyone who has any doubts as to the enormous variety of foods that can be included in the daily salad should peruse Joy Larkcom's fascinating and beautifully illustrated book, *The Salad Garden*. To her the creation of a salad is a work of art, from the sowing of seeds in carefully worked-out associations, to giving aesthetic effects to the concoctions of dishes, ornamented with flowers and variegated leaves. She doesn't despise wild plants, even "weeds," some of which contain robust nutritional factors that are absent from more delicate cultivated plants. Incidentally, the best way to deal with coarse leaves, such as those of nettles and comfrey, I have found, is to boil up a saucepanful of potatoes, adding the leaves when the potatoes are just cooked. Cutting the leaves up with the potatoes is sufficient to remove the roughness and sting, and the result is a surprisingly tasty variation on the traditional British dish known as "bubble-and-squeak."

4

~

Personal Pilgrimage

~~~~~~

In this restless modern age, when relocation to new homes, new jobs, and new landscapes every few years has become almost routine, most of us no longer feel a sense of "rootedness," of truly being native to a place. This is especially true of city-dwellers and suburbanites, who often have little chance to interact with non-human nature on a daily basis, learning to recognize its intimate and local character. Robert Hart's own search for a home has led him to a small farm in Shropshire, and his experience speaks to anyone who longs to find a home place in this era of transients.

The journey homeward is not only a physical and spiritual process, but an adventure in time itself. Seeing the past, the present, and even the future of a landscape and its people—simultaneously and on many layers—is a state of mind known as "ceremonial time," and this capacity is recognized and valued by many of the Earth's indigenous peoples. In this chapter, Robert Hart demonstrates that rare quality of vision, harking back to the age of Romans, Celts, and Saxon Christians, who worshipped both God and nature. Yet Hart's view also reaches forward, to a greener, more integrated world—a world in which the forest once again sustains humanity, and vice versa.

~~~~~~

$\mathcal{M}$y own pilgrimage, which led to the realization of the forest garden concept, started in a rather primitive wooden bungalow raised on stilts above one of the smallest of the Norfolk Broads. It could be regarded as a descendant of the prehistoric Swiss lakeside dwellings. Running beneath its entire length, except for the veranda, was the boathouse, and, when some of the supporting piles were found to be rotten and needed renewing, a giant Norfolk wherry was piloted into the boathouse by a local giant—Nat Bircham, the odd-job-man—and the whole bungalow was raised while the work of sinking new piles went ahead. My mother laid out the garden on Japanese lines, with purple *Iris kaempferi* surrounding a sculptured figure known as the Alder Girl. A humpbacked Japanese wooden bridge made by a local craftsman linked the garden to a small marshy wood, known in Norfolk as a "carr," with a path leading to a summerhouse, also on stilts, overlooking the large neighboring broad. The garden, wood, broads, and river teemed with wildlife: wild yellow iris, marsh orchids, flowering rushes, electric blue dragonflies, swallowtail butterflies, otters, herons, great crested grebes, and bitterns, which kept us awake at night with their "booming." In the winter the garden was usually under floodwater, and I remember seeing my mother's beloved crimson roses blooming beneath the ice. One of the principal local industries was reed-cutting, and our bungalow was roofed with reed thatch. For the first time in my life I felt I was becoming an initiated member of a regional ecology.

In fact my first introduction to the study of ecology and organic growing came from reading a book by a member of an old Norfolk family, H. J. Massingham, the country writer whose prolific works are now enjoying a revival of interest. Following a near-fatal accident which led to his losing a leg and the use of an arm, Massingham found solace during the Second World War by building up a garden behind his cottage in North Buckinghamshire, and by dedicating himself to self-sufficiency and wholeness of living. Described in his masterpiece *This Plot of Earth,* he regarded the garden as a model of a new civilized order, freed from the aberrations which lead to war and the destruction of the environment. Covering just one acre, it was an ordered jungle comprising a bewildering variety of fruit trees and bushes, vegetables, herbs, and even two cereals, oats and maize, all interspersed with flowers and organically cultivated. Enjoying meals of home-grown produce throughout the year and mentally nourished by the ever-changing beauty of his environment, Massingham cured himself of chronic ailments, such as catarrh, which had formerly afflicted him, and found himself able to do twice the amount of intellectual labor he had done before his accident.

Norfolk was the first stage in the long process by which I, a Londoner born and bred, have gradually sunk ever deeper roots in the English countryside.

My forebears originated in beautiful and historic rural areas but all, for various reasons, converged on London. My father was of Lowland Scots and Spanish Basque descent. Robert Hart the First, my great-grandfather, was a steel engraver, a skilled craftsman who came from Melrose in the well-wooded Tweed valley, one of the cradles of Celtic Christianity, from which missionaries carried the Christian faith through much of Saxon England before the arrival of Augustine. I have one of Robert's finest engravings: a portrait of John Evelyn, the "seventeenth-century St. Barbe-Baker," whose great work *Silva* led to the planting of millions of trees in an England denuded by the "great bravery of building" and shipbuilding during the Tudor and early Stuart periods. Robert had a passion for history and, in particular, for the story of humankind's agelong struggle for freedom. He named his two sons George Washington and John Hampden and his three daughters after ladies who had all met violent deaths in the cause of freedom: Boadicea, Lucretia, and Virginia; the last being a Roman plebeian maiden who was slain by her father to prevent her from being raped by a patrician.

On the Basque side my ancestor Nicasio María Serafín de Jauralde was a freedom fighter himself. The son of a Pyrenean landowner, he became caught up in the siege of Saragossa during the Peninsular War and later took part in an abortive revolution against a reactionary king, Ferdinand VII, only to be taken prisoner by the king's French allies. After escaping from a French prison camp, Nicasio made his way to London, where he maintained himself by teaching the guitar—then a fashionable instrument—and married one of his pupils. On the accession of a more liberal monarch, he returned to Spain, only to be caught up in a civil war and again forced to flee. His wife carried their baby on muleback across the Pyrenees. Eventually he settled in London as head of a Spanish financial delegation, to be succeeded by his son, another Nicasio, who served in the Spanish government service for the phenomenal period of seventy-two years, retiring at the age of eighty-eight.

Among my mother's ancestors were a family named Lacon, who were first recorded as living in a village of the same name in North Shropshire in the twelfth century. In the Tudor and Stuart periods they seem to have been great foresters, as one of their estates, Kinlet, close to Wyre Forest, was once famous for its trees, and another, Willey, still has some magnificent trees that may well be 400 years old, as well as a remnant of the royal forest of Shirlett, part of the primeval woodland that once covered most of South Shropshire. In the tower of Willey Old Hall is a priest's hole leading to a vast underground vault, which might well have housed the whole local population of Roman Catholics at time of religious persecution, as the Lacons were ardent Catholics. Another of my mother's ancestors was Thomas Pear of Spalding, Lincolnshire, one of the engineers who drained the Fens.

After leaving Norfolk we spent over two years house-hunting from bases in Sussex and the Hardy country. The most attractive of our temporary homes was an old mill-house in a village between Sherborne and the great Iron Age hill fort of Cadbury Castle, reputed to be Arthur's Camelot. I found that Cadbury Castle, among the first of many hill forts around which I have since roamed, exuded an overwhelming "atmosphere." One of the essential factors in the process of sinking spiritual roots in the countryside is the development of sensitivity to the spirit of place. I would define "atmosphere" as a sense of communion with the human beings whose emotions have left an imprint on the area where they lived and loved and suffered. In many historical sites I have felt a warm sense of kinship with the men and women who strove to survive in the frontier conditions of Celtic Britain and Saxon England. I felt an intense desire to reconstruct their way of life—at any rate in my mind—and it occurred to me that we in the twentieth century have much to learn from them. Above all, the tight-knit comradeship of men and women living in forest clearings, their villages stockaded to keep out wild animals and human marauders, was far preferable to the "couldn't-care-less" individualism that prevails in our urban and suburban non-communities.

Studying landscape archeology, I learned to recognize indications of the structures both of the Celtic civilization, which was presided over by the *acropolis* of the hill fort, and of the Saxon village community. In both ways of life, self-sufficiency was the keynote. Trade routes, following ley lines (alignments of powerful earth energy), packhorse tracks, or ridgeways, were practically the only contact with the outside world, bringing in the few necessities, such as salt, that the villagers could not produce themselves. The later Saxon village community, when situated in an undulating area, was a three-tier structure with summer grazings on the hilltops, open fields of grain on the slopes, and meadows for hay, calf-rearing, and winter keep in the valleys. The most important building in most villages after the church was the mill. This could be either a windmill or a watermill. Most often it was used for grinding grain, but, in more recent times, it might be a "waulking" mill for fulling cloth, or a sawmill, or it might be used to drive a machine such as a trip-hammer. A watermill often involved an elaborate system of leats, weirs, and ponds, the maintenance of which was the responsibility of the whole village. These waterworks played an important part in the control of flooding.

An indispensable part of the village community system was the patch of wild woodland, which was carefully maintained on a sustainable basis for the supply of timber and fuel, the trees being coppiced or pollarded. The wood, hedgerows, and wastelands were also valued for their wild foods and medicines. It is obvious that our forebears of the Saxon and medieval periods had an encyclopedic knowledge of the properties of wild plants, comparable to that of the forest and desert Indians of the more remote parts of the Americas today. Remnants of this knowledge can be found in such books as *Food for Free* and *Plants with a Purpose* by Richard Mabey, as well as in many modern herbals.

This vast fund of traditional knowledge bore fruit in the works of the famous school of English herbalists in Tudor and Stuart times, from William Turner, the "Father of English Botany," to Culpeper and Coles.

While staying in the Sussex village of Bosham near Chichester I heard a series of BBC talks by John Seymour, the well-known writer and organic pioneer, known as the "Guru of Self-Sufficiency," in which he described how he and his wife Sally had carved a miniature organic farm out of five acres of remote Suffolk heathland. I was badly bitten by the self-sufficiency bug. Lifting up my eyes to the South Downs, I resolved to look for a small upland farm where I could strive to achieve a degree of self-sufficiency myself. After extensive searching I found what I was looking for: a beautiful old red sandstone farmhouse in a secluded West Somerset backwater on the lower slopes of the Brendon Hills west of Lydeard St. Lawrence.

The area had been eloquently described by H.J. Massingham in *Wisdom of the Fields* after his stay on one of the small family farms characteristic of the area during the momentous months following D-Day in 1944. For Massingham, the contrast between the carnage taking place in France and the peace of this remote corner of rural England was overwhelming. This peace was, for him, not a mere absence of strife in an idyllic landscape, but a positive sense of secure and harmonious living, rooted in the earth and maintained by all-round human development and the cooperative ethos—cooperation not only between human beings but also between people and nature. "This is a home for the family farmer," he wrote. "Of such a life as he leads among the tossing foothills self-sufficiency is the structure and neighbourliness the buttress . . . The interchange of voluntary labour occurs at the peak periods throughout the year—above all at harvest time."

For Massingham, the special significance of the Lydeard St. Lawrence experience lay in the fact that he saw in its farmers the spiritual descendants of the yeomen who, in the seventeenth and eighteenth centuries, had been regarded as the backbone of England: sturdy, freedom-loving, and hard-working with wives as industrious as themselves, skilled in the arts and crafts of self-sufficiency. The archetypal

yeoman was William Cobbett, who, at the beginning of the nineteenth century, waged a lone rear-guard action in his writings and
speeches as a Member of Parliament against the forces let loose by the
Industrial Revolution, which he saw striking at the root of the ecological agricultural system and way of life.

My own small farm was approached by a steep, narrow lane with
high banks on both sides, so that in summertime, when the hedges on
top of the banks were in full growth, it practically became a tunnel.
The farm comprised an almost precipitous pasture field of five acres,
from the top of which one could gain a distant view of the Bristol
Channel, and three acres of orchards and soft fruit. Having let the field
to a local farmer for grazing, I concentrated on the fruit as well as on
sowing vegetables. Intent on following the organic system, one of my
first actions was to build seventeen compost heaps at strategic points,
the largest of which I named "Dungery Beacon," after Dunkery Beacon, the highest point of nearby Exmoor.

My main cash crop was black currants, which I manured with seaweed from Dunster Beach. After harvesting them I took the currants
on my trailer across the Quantocks to a jam factory at Bridgwater.
Some of the bushes had been interplanted with plums, which I
learned was a traditional association in the Southwest, as both sets of
plants were believed to encourage each others' growth and neutralize
each others' pests and diseases. This was my first introduction to the
lore and science of plant symbiosis.

Throughout my career on the land, I have been fortunate in my contacts with old-fashioned country workers, from whom I have learned
more about the true arts of growing plants and tending livestock than
I could ever have learned at a horticultural or agricultural college. As
some of the old craftsmen knew, the best way to learn skills is simply
to watch a skilled and experienced craftsman at work and imbibe the
feel of his actions. So when my gardener, Mr. White, earthed up two
rows of cauliflowers with a mattock—a tool that is a Somerset speciality

and known locally as a "biskey"—I felt I was being initiated into a new realm of rhythm and of plant care. The mattock is perhaps the most ancient of all tools, going back to the Stone Age, and though it is largely obsolete in Britain, it is still used throughout Africa. When wielded by an experienced hand it becomes an invaluable, multipurpose tool for breaking up stiff ground, planting, hoeing, weeding, earthing-up, and, as I learned later, for irrigating.

My tutor in beekeeping, Mr. Rowe, was an indomitably cheerful little man who drove a horsedrawn cart and led an arduous life cultivating three and a half acres of precipitous, terraced hillside, every square inch of which was covered with a wide variety of fruit, vegetables, and fodder crops, providing sustenance for himself, his wife, a flock of goats, and poultry. I couldn't have had a better introduction to traditional self-sufficiency.

Somerset was a brief interlude in my quest for self-sufficiency. The farmhouse proved too large and inconvenient for my mother to manage, so regretfully we sold Dean's Farm and resumed our search for a more suitable home. One day we found ourselves looking down on a small stone cottage nestling in a fold of Wenlock Edge, the heavily wooded limestone ridge which runs for some twenty miles across South Shropshire, and we felt we had reached our final destination. I had been drawn towards the quiet and—in places—wild Welsh border countryside of Shropshire, with its strong Celtic atmosphere, ever since reading the poems of A.E. Housman and the novels of Mary Webb shortly after leaving school. I can't help feeling also that my Lacon ancestors had exerted some sort of magnetic pull. They had once been a potent force in the very neighborhood where we decided to settle, owning an estate called Wilderhope in Hopedale and a reputedly haunted, moated manor house called Thonglands in Corvedale, both a few miles from our new home.

The cottage occupies what is obviously a very ancient inhabited site. It stands by a spring of deliciously pure water, which would obviously have been a focus for settlement for early colonists, seeking homes in the Long Forest, which once covered a wide area from Hope-

dale to the Stiperstones. It also stands at the meeting point of three ancient causeways: a prehistoric packhorse track, passing along a "hollow-
way" at places up to forty feet deep and leading to a packhorse bridge
in the village at the bottom of the hill; a track leading to a remote
shrunken village called Middlehope in Hopedale, which once boasted
a Norman castle; and a Roman road, part of whose surface we uncovered. This seems to have been part of the line of advance of a Roman
army based at a fort called Wall Town near Cleobury Mortimer, when
attacking the forces of Caractacus, the British leader, whose headquarters were at the great hill fort named after him, Caer Caradoc, whose
top I can just glimpse above a line of hills to the west. "My" Roman
road, it seems, was later extended to join Watling Street, the road
which runs from London to Viroconium, known as the "Birmingham
of Roman Britain," and then turns southwest to end at the Roman fort
of Kenchester, near Hereford. In Corvedale, it seems my road passed
by a Roman quarry at Bouldon, which once supplied green roofing
tiles for Viroconium.

In a paddock above the cottage is a circular earthwork. Shortly after
arrival, I invited a horticultural adviser from the Ministry of Agriculture to help me lay out the farm, which runs to just over twenty acres.
Standing on the vantage point of the earthwork, the adviser suddenly
remarked, "This area shows the outline of a motte-and-bailey." This is
a kind of fortification erected by the Normans of which many remains
can be seen in this much-fought-over frontier land. The motte is a circular mound that was once surmounted by a wooden keep, and the
bailey a rectangular enclosure, originally stockaded, stood adjacent to
it. In the adviser's opinion, the circular enclosure would have contained the motte, while the bailey stretched from the cottage in the
form of a long rectangular patch of about an acre, which had obviously
been artificially raised. Later, however, a visiting archeologist suggested
that the circular mound had been the site of a Celtic monastery—a
ring of log huts with a small chapel in the middle—while a depression
to the south of the "bailey" might have been a monastic fishpond, fed
by two streams which now disappear into a sump.

While the "bailey" was to become the main focus of my activities at Highwood Hill, for the early years I concentrated largely on livestock: poultry, goats, sheep, and cattle, as well as nine hives of bees. My first cattle were a bunch of Ayrshire heifers, which I bought from Sam Mayall of Harmer Hill, North Shropshire, one of the leading organic farmers of the day. These I had artificially inseminated and sold after calving as dairy heifers at Shrewsbury Market. Later I switched to the Channel Island breeds. The Jersey makes the ideal house cow for the small farmer. Apart from giving the richest milk, she is small, neat, docile, intelligent, and friendly and can be treated as a pet, though the Jersey bull can be bad-tempered and unreliable. However, I found the rearing of dairy heifers both too emotionally exacting and too time-consuming, and as I wanted to devote more time to fruit and vegetable growing, my last cattle were a small herd of single-suckling Welsh Blacks—the hardy, shaggy, long-horned breed which the ancient Britons drove into the fastnesses of Wales when retreating before the advancing Romans. I became very fond of these primitive denizens of the British countryside, and gave them all Welsh names such as Myfanwy, Arianwen, and Melangell, the latter named after the Celtic patron saint of wildlife. As a very sturdy calf recently weaned by her mother at the age of nine months, Melangell, when suddenly startled— possibly by a wandering hen—made a dramatic leap over a fence and a water-tank. I can still see the startling spectacle of the hairy black doodlebug flying through the air.

As in Somerset, so at Highwood Hill I have been fortunate in securing help, advice, and instruction from old-fashioned countrymen with a wealth of practical experience. When I first took up livestock rearing I had the assistance of three brothers, Harry, Victor, and Geoff Tipton, whose grandfather, a famous local character named "Boney" Higgins, had occupied my cottage when he was first married, and lived to be almost a hundred in another cottage that he built himself at the edge of a wood just above. "Boney" was a mighty wielder of the scythe and two-handled saw and also a mighty consumer of cider made by his nephew, who was an itinerant cider-maker like the hero of Hardy's novel *The Woodlanders*. He also helped to build the little railway which used to pass the bottom of my land and which his grandsons helped to demolish.

Geoff Tipton, who had started his farming career as a three-horse wagoner at the age of twelve, was once described as an "animal magician" because of his seemingly miraculous powers of transforming undersized, sickly, unthrifty animals, whether calves, lambs, or kittens, into beautiful beasts, with the gleam of life in their eyes and the gloss of health on their coats. I once bought six "cade" (orphan) lambs from him that he had brought up on the bottle. They developed into enormous dignified ewes, who looked like grizzly bears when sitting on their backsides to be shorn, and who flatly refused to be "worked" by my border collie, but stamped their feet at him.

I got great enjoyment from my animals. In general they seemed happy, contented, and very healthy under my 100 percent organic regime. Intimate, cooperative contact with another order of life, as in hand-milking or helping a calf into the world, is a profoundly satisfying and moving experience. This is attested by the beautiful milking croons that Hebridean herd girls used to sing to their "kyne" to keep them still while milking and to promote the flow of milk. My first initiation into an ecological experience was gained when riding in a London park, when I discovered the possibility of telepathic communication with my horse via its deeply expressive ears, which seemed like radio antennae capable of being attuned to one's unspoken thoughts. Such experiences immensely enrich one's life. The ultimate ideal, in a more truly ecological society, would be for human beings generally to develop intimate relationships with animals that are leading entirely free and natural lives in the wild, like those between Joy Adamson and the lioness Elsa and between Horace Dobbs and his dolphin friends.

The humanitarian and economic arguments against exploiting animals for food and other products became, for me, inescapable. This realization began to dawn when rearing dairy heifers. The separation of the newborn calf from its mother, which is an essential factor in commercial milk production, became a more and more unbearably pathetic experience. That is one reason why, though a vegetarian, I switched to single suckling, even though the end product of single suckling is beef. Eventually I disposed of all my livestock. For me it was the only way. Because I was so fond of all my animals, even the hens, the prospect of their eventual slaughter became more and more intolerable. Moreover, at this time of widespread hunger and starvation in the Third World, the rearing of big livestock such as cattle is an unforgiveably wasteful form of land use. The growing of crops, above all tree crops, is a vastly more productive way of using agricultural resources, which, in many countries, are rapidly diminishing in relation to the growth of populations.

For me the idea of a system of land use capable of supplying all basic human needs, consisting mainly of trees and other perennial plants with no livestock component, was a case of gradual evolution. While I was writing my first book, *The Inviolable Hills,* Eve Balfour, one of the pioneers of the organic movement and founder of the Soil Association, who wrote the preface, sent me an article that I found more exciting than any detective story. The author, James Sholto Douglas, described a new system of land use that he was operating in the Limpopo Valley of southern Africa, which I felt had worldwide implications. Called Three-Dimensional Forestry or Forest Farming, it was pioneered by a Japanese, Toyohiko Kagawa, who will surely come to be acknowledged as a universal genius on a par with Leonardo da Vinci. Christian evangelist, scientist, novelist, poet, linguist, political reformer, and one of the founders of the Japanese trade union movement, Kagawa's concern with the total human condition was comparable with Gandhi's. In the 1930s the focus of his concern switched to the plight of Japan's mountain farmers, who were finding their livelihoods threatened by soil erosion caused by deforestation—a problem that has since spread to many other parts of the world. While studying at Princeton, Kagawa had come across J. Russell Smith's classic *Tree Crops—A Permanent Agriculture,* which emphasizes the value of the tree as a multipurpose organism, providing not only food and a host of other useful products, but also protection for soils and water supplies.

Inspired by this book, Kagawa managed to persuade many of his country's upland farmers that the solution to their erosion problem lay in widespread tree-planting, and that they could gain a bonus from this if they planted fodder-bearing trees, such as quick-maturing walnuts, which they could feed to their pigs. Thus the three "dimensions" of his 3-D system were the trees as conservers of the soil and suppliers of food and the livestock which benefited from them.

Impressed by the vast potentialities of "3-D," Sholto Douglas, after meeting Kagawa in Tokyo, carried out a number of experiments in various parts of southern and central Africa, in conjunction with UNESCO, to test the applicability of the system to different soils and climatic conditions. Among trees that he found particularly useful were several leguminous bean-bearing trees, especially the carob and mesquite, which fertilize the soil for the benefit of grass and other plants by the injection of nitrogen, as well as providing food for people and animals.

While collaborating with Sholto Douglas in the preparation of the book *Forest Farming*, which has been widely read around the world, I gave much thought to the possibilities of extending the system to temperate countries such as Britain. Observing the habits of my own cattle, it occurred to me that the traditional multispecies English hedgerow, which I saw being browsed throughout the year, even in the depths of winter, fulfilled some of the functions of Kagawa's and Douglas's fodder-bearing trees. Moreover, after reading *Fertility Pastures* by Newman Turner and *Herbal Handbook for Farm and Stable* by Juliette de Bairacli-Levy, I realized the value of hedgerow and pasture herbs, not only as adding minerals and other nutrients to the animals' diet, but also as agents for the prevention and cure of disease. Some traditional English farmers believed, I am sure correctly, that if a cow felt she was sickening for some disease, she would seek out the requisite healing herb.

On the basis of these findings, I developed my own "3-D" system, which I called OPS—Organic Perennial Subsistence farming. That involved "cultivating" my hedgerows by encouraging the growth of plants that contained substances particularly nourishing for cattle, such as the elder, wild rose, and hazel, and sowing some of the many perennial pasture herbs recommended by Newman Turner, such as chicory, ribwort, yarrow, and sheep's parsley.

But my primary aim was self-sufficiency, so I extended my system beyond livestock farming to include trees and other plants—mainly perennial—which would contribute to the health and welfare of human beings. In time, after I had adopted a vegan diet and for other personal reasons, the plant component completely replaced the animal one, and, after making a study of companion planting, I renamed my system "Ecological Horticulture" or "Ecocultivation." I then discovered that other people were working along similar lines in other parts of the world and that the generally accepted generic term for all such systems was "Agroforestry." So I adopted that term for my own.

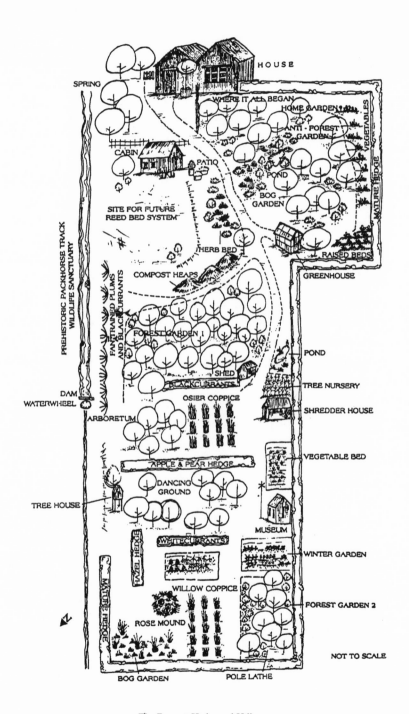

The Farm at Highwood Hill

5

~

The Wenlock Edge Project

$\mathcal{M}$y small farm, which stretches up to the edge of the woods that clothe the top of Wenlock Edge, was originally carved out of the open fields of the medieval village community. A relic of the original enclosure was a long, narrow paddock bordering a stream, which was called "The Slang," a name for one of the strips into which the open fields were divided. The communal lands were equitably laid out to enable each of the villagers to have his share of the different types of land that the parish comprised: grain fields, upland pastures, and lowland meadows. In certain lights the strip-pattern can be clearly discerned on my largest field.

In laying out Highwood Hill, as I called the farm after one of the woods above it, I originally designated five small pasture fields and two orchards, in one of which I kept a flock of free-range hens as the cash-component. These were eventually taken over by a community.

My self-sufficiency efforts were concentrated on the "bailey," which is a tongue of land of about one acre, beside and behind the cottage, and the adjacent depression, which the archeologist surmised had once been a monastic fish-pond. While this was mainly occupied by a plastic tunnel for winter vegetables, I divided the bailey into a garden of herbs and perennial vegetables, which meant digging up the lawn; a black currant plantation; a tiny orchard of apples, pears, and damsons; and a large vegetable garden. The small orchard, about one-eighth of an acre, was to become my model forest garden.

The small garden of herbs and perennial vegetables lay literally outside the kitchen door, on the southwest side of the cottage—an ideal position. It was a suntrap, protected from north and east winds, and the person preparing a meal could nip out, just before serving it, to pick a handful of fragrant greenery, fresh from the soil, to add to salad, soup, or stew. We found many uses for the plants that grew there. Lovage, that statuesque plant which can grow over eight feet tall, can be used as a piquant substitute for celery, to which it is related. Lemon-balm, eau-de-cologne mint, and peppermint can give an original tang to fruit salads. Sweet cicely can reduce the tartness of stewed gooseberries or black currant pie. Good King Henry, a wild form of spinach, also known as "Lincolnshire asparagus," can be added to stews, as can the young leaves of dwarf comfrey—one of the few herbs that continue to put out leaves during the winter. The leaves of sorrel, with their mild lemon flavor, and wild garlic, with its not-so-mild reminder of its cultivated cousin, make an interesting substitute for lettuce in salads.

From the first, these exciting plants inspired experiment. I realized that perennial herbs, with their deep roots tapping the minerals in the subsoil, could make an invaluable contribution to nutrition over and above their curative and prophylactic powers. I tried passing them through the juice extractor together with our homegrown apples, pears, and black currants, to produce delicious non-alcoholic "liqueurs." Peppermint, eau-de-cologne mint, and other herbs, added to apples, plums, damsons, and dried apricots—the whole pressed through a colander after stewing—produced uncommon jams, "cheeses," and chutneys. Moreover, honey from our own hives, the inhabitants of which were particularly attracted to the bluish flowers of balm and comfrey, added yet another dimension of nourishment and flavor. A range of "Herb and Honey Products," which I developed, included *Rejuce*, a herbal slimming drink, and attracted the attention of a director of a newly formed health-food manufacturing company, which I was invited to join. Unfortunately the time did not seem ripe for its activities and, after a short period, it folded up.

But I continued to work—or rather not-work—our herb garden. The plants, I found, could look after themselves very nicely, thank you. All they needed was a dressing of straw or compost in the winter, and every spring they faithfully reappeared, sending out fresh shoots and leaves for months on end. Pests and diseases were conspicuous by their absence.

My creative faculties were also attracted to another traditional aspect of these fascinating plants: their reputed ability to extend their vigor, health, disease resistance, and pest resistance to neighboring plants. At the far end of the bailey Harry and Victor Tipton laid out a large garden of conventional vegetables. Among these I planted rows of apple mint, borage, and other herbs—and the vegetables seemed to like them. They grew well, even though the herbs rapidly became rather too rampant. I saw cabbages struggling manfully through mini-jungles of borage. Borage, though an annual, is an avid self-seeder and, in its second year, the vegetable garden seemed to shimmer in the electric-blue haze of its ever-present flowers.

Another experiment I made in the vegetable garden was a system of "organic irrigation." I got a local engineer to make an adjustable valve that could be fitted to the pipe from which the spring emerged beside the cottage. To this was attached a length of alkathene piping extending to the far end of the vegetable garden, which was on a gentle slope. Taps were fitted at intervals of about twenty yards. Channels were then dug by mattock from top to bottom of the vegetable garden, on both sides, and between the rows of vegetables. In order to water a double row of vegetables, all that was necessary was to turn on the nearest tap and direct the water to the vegetables by mattock, smoothing and hardening the channel bottoms. Water was also switched from channel to channel by means of small dams of compost or manure. That was where the "organic" element came in, as particles of compost or manure were washed down the channels, to which was added liquid seaweed. The whole area was thus, in time, thoroughly fertilized.

The task of clearing the channels of loose mud and molehills and constructing new channels was greatly facilitated by the force of water gushing from the taps. The mattock was used as a multipurpose tool:

while digging channels, one also hoed, weeded, and earthed up the vegetables. The whole system was beautifully simple, easy, and cheap.

However, in comparing the garden of conventional vegetables with the garden of herbs and perennial vegetables, it was obvious which one demanded the least work. In growing annual plants one can't avoid the arduous and fiddlesome chores of digging, raking, preparing seedbeds, sowing, transplanting, thinning out, hoeing, weeding, watering, and fertilizing. But the herbs and perennial vegetables, once established, needed little or no watering or fertilizing, because their deep roots drew up water and minerals from the subsoil, for the benefit of themselves and each other, and they did not even need hoeing and weeding, as they quickly spread over the whole surface of the soil, suppressing all competitors, while their intricate tangle of roots maintained a porous soil structure. All they did need was periodic thinning-out, to prevent them from encroaching on each other, but, as they constituted an important part of our daily diet, a fair proportion of the thinnings found its way into the kitchen.

Pondering on the contrast between the two gardens, it came to me that, if one could devise an integrated system of land use consisting mainly of perennial plants—fruit and nut trees and bushes together with perennial vegetables and herbs—as well as a diet based on this mix, the task of achieving self-sufficiency would be vastly simplified. This is how I discovered agroforestry.

The decisive event which enabled me to work out a demonstration of how agroforestry could be applied in the conditions of Western, largely urban, civilization, where in general only small plots of land are available for self-sufficiency enthusiasts, was the advent of Garnet Jones. Living in the village at the bottom of the hill, he is a Celt of magnificent physique, who comes from an old yeoman family in the wilds of Mid-Wales. While his whole nature is steeped in traditional country lore and his roots are deep in the soil, he has an alert and lively mind, receptive to new ideas. A true yeoman, he can turn his hand to a wide variety of practical tasks, and, having also worked on the railway, he shows something akin to genius as an engineer. He is of the stuff of the countrymen who, torn from the soil, pioneered the Industrial Revolution in the Ironbridge Gorge area of Shropshire and elsewhere in Britain. His enthusiastic participation in the Wenlock Edge Project has been intensely stimulating, while his muscle-power and brain-power have been invaluable. The creation of the project has been a partnership between us.

The project now comprises a number of sectors:

1 The main *Forest Garden,* literally the centerpiece.

2 The *Ante (Anti) Forest Garden* (AFG), so called because it comes before (ante) the main forest garden and contains plants requiring full sunlight and/or acid soil, which are therefore antagonistic (anti) to forest garden conditions.

3 The *Homegarden,* an area about twenty meters square immediately adjacent to the house, containing fruit, vegetables, and herbs, which, for some mysterious reason, is exceptionally productive. So-called because "homegarden" is the term by which most tropical forest gardens are known.

4 *Where It All Began,* a strip of economic plants surrounding an old 'Improved Fertility" pear outside the back door—a tiny microcosm of the whole project.

5 The *Patio Garden,* a small assembly of plants in tubs, designed to demonstrate that even town-dwellers with only small paved yards can enjoy some of the benefits of the Forest Garden.

6 The *Wildlife Sanctuary,* a prehistoric packhorse track, possibly a stone axe trading route, which constitutes a very deep cutting or "hollow-way" along the garden's northern boundary. As it contains some magnificent old trees, it can be regarded as a strip of ancient, natural forest. It is left completely undisturbed and is scheduled as a Prime Site of Conservation Interest.

7 The *Osier Coppice,* cut once a year for basketry.

8 The *Arboretum,* containing specimen trees of special interest, including Shagbark Hickory *(Carya ovata),* which has been described as "the most valuable nut-producing species in the

USA"; Silver Maple *(Acer saccharinum)*; Arolla Pine *(Pinus cembra)*; Maidenhair Tree *(Ginkgo biloba)* and Dawn Redwood *(Metasequoia glyptostroboides)*, two "living fossils," typical of the vegetation that created the coal measures 100 million years ago; Antarctic Beech *(Nothofagus antarctica)*, probably the most southern tree in the world; Red-Twigged Lime *(Tilia platyphyllos rubra)*; Red Oak *(Quercus rubra)*, an American species noted for its brilliant autumn coloring; Service Tree *(Sorbus domestica)*, which bears small edible fruits known as "chequerberries," German Walnut *(Juglans regia,* var. 'Buccaneer"), an early-fruiting variety, and White Mulberry *(Morus alba)*, which produces both edible fruit and leaves which are used for feeding silkworms.

9 The *Circle-Dancing Area,* a small open space surrounding the Massingham Oak, where dancing takes place during seasonal festivals. It is overlooked by the *Tree House,* built partway up a living ash, which constitutes an irresistible attraction for children. Also nearby is the *Ecological House,* a small cabin built very expertly by Garnet (who also built the Tree House), which is lit by a wind generator and contains a small collection of interesting examples of craftwork from several parts of the world.

10 The *Winter Garden,* a number of beds and a mound, mostly unshaded, designed for winter vegetables.

11 *Forest Garden No. 2,* a small multistory plantation surrounding the Kagawa Plum.

12 The *Bog Garden,* a plantation of reeds and other plants requiring damp conditions, irrigated by Garnet's waterwheel in the Packhorse Track.

The main Forest Garden has contained over 100 species and varieties of plant in its very limited area—about that of a large town garden—but some have not been fully adapted to the conditions and have died off. At present the number of species and varieties is at least seventy and others are being added every year. Like the natural forest, it is a largely self-regulating, developing ecosystem that requires minimal maintenance.

The "stories" comprise:

1 *Canopy:* standard or semidwarf fruit trees;
2 *Low-tree layer:* fruit and nut trees on dwarfing rootstocks and bamboo;
3 *Shrub layer:* currant and gooseberry bushes and Rosa rugosa;
4 *Herbaceous layer:* herbs and perennial vegetables;
5 *Vertical layer:* climbing berries, nasturtiums, runner beans, and vines, trained up trees, over fences, and over a shed;
6 *Groundcover layer:* creeping plants such as Rubus species;
7 *Rhizosphere:* shade-tolerant plants and winter root vegetables.

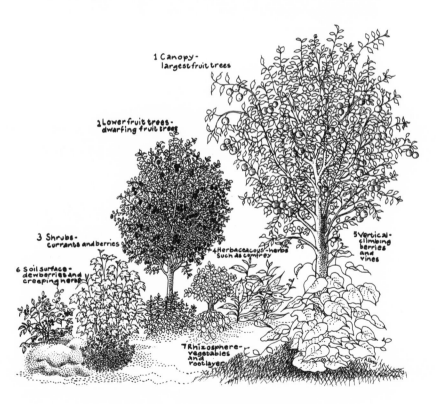

Temperate forest garden, with seven stories

The system is:

self-perpetuating, because almost all the plants are perennial or active self-seeders, such as borage and cress;

self-fertilizing, because deep-rooting trees, bushes, and herbs draw
upon minerals in the subsoil and make them available to their
neighbors, and because the system includes edible legumes,
which inject nitrogen into the soil, and mineral-rich plants such
as buckwheat, which inject calcium;

self-watering, because deep-rooting plants tap the spring veins in
the subsoil, even at times of drought, and pump up water for the
benefit of the whole system;

self-mulching and *weed-suppressing,* because rapidly spreading
herbs, such as mints and balm, soon cover all the ground between the trees and bushes and thus create a permanent "living
mulch";

self-pollinating, because the trees are carefully selected to be mutually compatible or self-fertile, and because the flowering herbs
attract pollinating insects;

self-healing, because the scheme includes a number of aromatic
herbs, which undoubtedly deter pests and disease germs and
exhale healing radiations; and

resistant to pests and disease, because of the aromatic plants, and
because any complex comprising a wide spectrum of different
plants does not allow the buildup of epidemics such as affects
monocultures.

This forest garden model, which could be reproduced even in
smaller areas, and in town gardens and wastelands, could, when well
established, enable a family to enjoy a considerable degree of self-
sufficiency for some seven months in the year, in the very best foods
for building up positive health.

The Ante (Anti) Forest Garden, with its annual vegetables, sun-
loving herbs, and strawberries, as well as some fruit trees and bushes,

is conveniently situated immediately outside the back door—one minute's walk from the kitchen. And, in approaching it, the first sight that meets one's eyes is Where It All Began: my first experiment in companion planting or plant symbiosis. It consists of a small 'Improved Fertility" pear closely surrounded by black, white, and red currants and herbs. I can never remember the little pear tree or the currants failing to give bumper crops, a sign that they seem to enjoy each others' company as well as that of the herbs. A tiny area, yet intensely productive, year after year.

Just inside the gate is another mini-plantation: the Patio Garden, designed to demonstrate to the town-dweller that it is possible to have a forest garden even if one has no garden at all, but only a paved yard. It comprises plants in tubs and trained up a trellis. Most of the plants are lime-haters, so they wouldn't thrive in ordinary soil anyhow. Growing in ericacious (or "heath-soil") compost and peat, they include four blueberries and a witch-hazel. There is also a dwarf 'Lilliput' apple and an ornamental gooseberry as well as the—to me—inevitable herbs. Two dwarf roses enhance the gaiety of the scene.

Nearby are two further "anti" beds, containing plants that would not enjoy forest garden conditions, because, in their native state, they grow in treeless bogs, heaths, and grassland. The bog-garden comprises peat spread over a plastic sheet to restrict drainage; it contains cranberries and other *Vaccinium* species as well as a flowering rush and Siberian iris. The sun-loving herb garden comprises typical downland plants, such as thyme, marjoram, yarrow, and rue, growing in a light soil, also mixed with peat.

Another device of interest to the town-dweller with very restricted space is the mound-garden (see page 54). Originating in China, like so many other down-to-earth practical ideas, mound planting has been taken up with enthusiasm in Germany, where it is called *Hugelkultur*. Unlike the raised-bed system, which involves double-digging, you start the mound by making a trench about one foot deep. This is piled up with woody material, such as small branches, hedge cuttings, and prunings, to make a firm but highly porous core, enabling air, water,

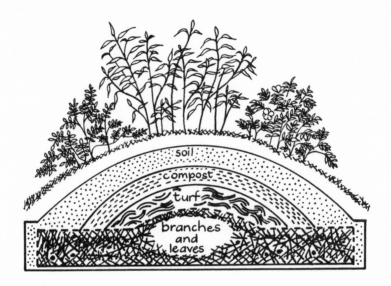

Rose-mound showing layers

and sunshine to circulate freely. This framework is then covered with sods, placed grass-side downwards, followed by a layer of compost, the whole being topped with soil. Plants are grown both on the top and sides of the mound, so that the space-saving advantages are obvious. It should be said, however, that the mounds gradually sink, so that they have to be periodically renewed. The AFG contains three such mounds.

Along the north boundary of the AFG is a "Bouché-Thomas" hedge, consisting of apple trees planted diagonally so that they grow into each other and so create a rigid fence (see page 55). I first learned about this system in an article by the gardener of Caldey Island monastery, off South Wales, where the system was formerly used to provide windbreaks for asparagus.

Approached through the wrought-iron "Arch of Gaia," created by my next-door neighbor in the valley, who lived with his wife and a multitude of dogs and cats by the packhorse bridge, the arboretum contains a wide variety of trees, as well as the ecological house "Cookery Nook," with its wind generator and a waterwheel, which will be described in more detail in later chapters.

As with my animals, so I have developed warm personal relationships with many of my trees. Until I came into intimate daily contact with a large concourse of young trees, with a wide diversity of shapes, colors, sizes, habits, and uses, I never realized how fascinatingly individual trees can be. In early spring it is a daily thrill to watch the ways in which different trees spring into new life. Some of my most valued trees—which are not necessarily the most valuable—have been named after people to whom they have been dedicated: people, some famous, some obscure, who have influenced my life and thought.

The practice of tree dedication began when a couple, David and Stella Griffiths of Middlesbrough, who showed an interest in my agroforestry experiments, expressed a wish to plant four trees in memory of their parents. They asked me to choose the trees that I considered most suitable, and I bought from a local nursery four wild cherries—

Bouché–Thomas hedge

a species that will for ever be associated with Shropshire through A.E. Housman's lines:

> Loveliest of trees, the cherry now
> Is hung with bloom along the bough,
> And stands about the woodland ride
> Wearing white for Eastertide.

The cherries were planted in the AFG, as the arboretum had not then been started.

Pride of place in the arboretum must go to the English oak commemorating H.J. Massingham, that eloquent defender of the English rural tradition to whom I owe so much.

Other trees and their dedicatees include:

Atlas Cedar *(Cedrus atlantica):* Richard St. Barbe Baker and his great scheme for Sahara reclamation;

Southern Beech *(Nothofagus antarctica):* Edward Adrian Wilson, naturalist, doctor, and antarctic explorer, who died with Scott;

Western Red Cedar (the totem pole tree, *Thuja plicata):* Chief Seathl, whose ecological-ethical philosophy is relevant to some of the profoundest problems of today;

Shagbark Hickory *(Carya ovata):* Tsikatsitsiakwa (known as "Katsi"), a Mohawk maiden who established a Permaculture group in New York State;

'Shropshire' Damson *(Prunus insititia):* Mary Webb, the novelist, a Shropshire damsel;

Sugar Maple (*Acer saccharum*): Helen Nearing, whose classic on self-sufficiency, *Living the Good Life,* was written in collaboration with her husband Scott;

Red-Twigged Lime *(Tilia platyphyllos rubra):* Blanche Cazalis, a charming Parisian artist who introduced me to *Tisane de Tilleul,* lime-flower tea;

Chestnut *(Castanea satira),* 'Marron de Lyon': Claude Monet, my
most beloved of landscape painters;

Scots Pine *(Pinus sylvestris):* Marjory Kennedy-Fraser, collector
and arranger of Hebridean folksongs;

Giant Fir *(Abies grandis):* Leos Janácek, the composer who put his
beloved Moravian forests into his opera *The Cunning Little
Vixen;*

Arolla Pine *(Pinus cembra):* Rainer Maria Rilke, the German-
Czech poet to whose tower retreat in Switzerland I made a pilgrimage during my last holiday abroad;

Walnut *(Juglans regia),* 'Buccaneer' (a German hybrid): Johann
Wolfgang Goethe, universal genius, whose pioneer botanical
work revealed the *Urpflanze,* the primal plant;

Japanese Red Cedar *(Cryptomeria japarica):* Toyohiko Kagawa, another universal genius, who originated Forest Farming;

Apple *(Malus domestica),* 'Court Pendu Plat' (said to go back to
Roman times): Virgil, epic poet who also created an agricultural
masterpiece, the *Georgics;*

Apple, *(Malus domestica),* 'Flower of Kent': said to be the tree that
inspired Isaac Newton's Theory of Gravity;

Monkey Puzzle Tree *(Araucaria araucana*—from Chile): Victor
Jara, the Chilean folksinger martyred in 1973;

Himalayan Whitebeam *(Sorbus cuspidata):* Murlidhar Devidas
Amte, whose heroic struggles on behalf of leprosy sufferers, of
Indian aborigines, and their rainforest home have been of truly
Himalayan proportions.

6

~

Plant Life: Its Infinite Potentialities

~~~~~~

The modern science of plant breeding has introduced a whole host of valuable and beautiful new varieties to the world. Yet it is important that we recognize that the selection and "improvement" of useful plants by humans has been going on, quietly and ubiquitously, for millennia, even before the era of settled agriculture.

Scientists cannot create genes; they can only manipulate what God, or nature, has provided. In recent years, geneticists have toyed with putting fish and pig genes into vegetables, though the wisdom and ethics of such shuffling remain debatable. What should be indisputable, however, is that we need to preserve the unique genetic legacy that is contained within every wild species and in traditional or "heirloom" plant varieties, thereby maintaining a broad genetic diversity.

Within the forest garden there is room to grow a wide range of plants, from home-garden standards such as apples and gooseberries to little-known perennial vegetables that include sea-kale and good King Henry. Local growing conditions and the gardener's personal tastes will make each forest garden unique, but in this chapter Robert Hart shares a few of his own favorite varieties. Far from being a prescriptive list, these recommended plants represent a starting-point for every gardener's lifelong voyage of discovery.

~~~~~~

There is incredible generosity in the potentialities of Nature. We only have to discover and utilize them." So wrote E.F. Schumacher in his foreword to Forest Farming.

Of some 300,000 known species of plants, only some 150 are grown regularly and to any considerable extent to meet human needs. Largely for commercial reasons, the plant production in Western or Westernized countries has been mainly reduced to a small number of standardized staples, grown under monocultural conditions and subjected to a wide range of chemical treatments. Today we rely on a mere twenty species to provide ninety percent of the world's food needs, and over half of humankind's calorific intake is supplied by just three grasses: wheat, rice, and maize. For this highly restrictive form of food production only eight percent of the world's soils are considered suitable.

Thus there is a staggering neglect, not only of useful plants but of areas where useful plants can be grown, as indigenous peoples know. Areas such as the rain forests, with their vast diversity of plants whose uses are known or remain to be explored, are ruthlessly destroyed, to be replaced by pastures designed to provide a single food product— beef—in infinitesimal quantities compared to the productivity of the natural forest. The wastefulness of "orthodox" agriculture and horticulture is unspeakable. Because it "pays" best to specialize in only one product at a time, all other plants are neglected or destroyed. In exploiting a tropical forest for the sake of a single timber, such as mahogany or teak, all other plants, and even up to eighty percent of the timber trees themselves, are abandoned. Modern plant-breeding techniques have evolved the possibility of still further increasing the range of useful plants available, but many "improved" hybrids can only flourish if heavily dosed with chemical fertilizers and sprays and copious irrigation, which puts them beyond the reach of all but the richest farmers and landowners. Hence the failure of the much-heralded "Green Revolution" to solve the heartbreaking problems of food shortages in the Third World.

Over the years, on this small sector of a chilly Welsh Border hillside, we have successfully grown 200 to 300 species and varieties of useful plants, from exotic vegetables in the AFG to unusual trees in the arboretum, with a solid core of Old Reliables, mainly concentrated in the forest garden, to ensure a degree of self-sufficiency throughout the year. I have even experimented with two "miracle plants" that could play key roles in feeding the Third World. These are amaranth, a vegetable-cereal much prized by the civilizations of the Incas and Aztecs, and the winged bean *(Psophocarpus tetragonolobus)*, which originated in Papua New Guinea. Amaranth belongs to a small and highly select "club" of plants, whose powers of photosynthesis are more efficient and potent than those of the majority. Photosynthesis, the process by which chlorophyll, the green pigment in plants, combines carbon dioxide from the atmosphere with hydrogen from water to create carbohydrates, is the basic process on which all physical life depends. The carbohydrate content of amaranth seeds is comparable to that of conventional cereals but the protein and fat content are higher. Moreover amaranth also has leaves comparable in nutritional value to those of spinach. The winged bean, a leguminous plant with the nitrogen-fixing, soil-improving qualities of most members of its tribe, is edible in its every part: seeds, pods, flowers, leaves, and stems; it even has tubers, with four times the protein content of potatoes.

A common quality of both amaranth and winged bean is their ability to thrive in both tropical and temperate climates, though the winged bean grows much larger in the tropics, where it can become a vegetable colossus with tendrils thirty feet long. Both plants are especially suitable for mixed cropping procedures, such as agroforestry, so they can become constituents of land-use systems that are vastly more productive than monocultures.

I myself have grown amaranth and winged beans in conjunction with some of the many fascinating salad vegetables introduced by Joy Larkcom and others from the continent of Europe and the Far East. The vegetable garden, I believe, should be as decorative as the flower garden; in fact, a number of flowering herbs make "good companions" for vegetables, and should be interspersed among them. In some cases the flowers themselves, including those of pot-marigold (calendula), bergamot, nasturtium, and borage, are edible and greatly add to the appetizing appearance of salads. Some of the many chicories now available are attractive both for their sky-blue flowers and for their leaves. The Italian 'Rossadi Treviso' chicory, for example, starts green but transforms itself in the autumn into a pyramid of crimson, sharply pointed leaves. 'Grumolo', a very hardy chicory from the mountains of Piedmont, hugs the ground as a tight rosette during the winter but in spring forms a tall, narrow pagoda.

To economize time, labor, and money, I favor vegetables that are perennial, such as sorrel, good King Henry, Egyptian or tree onions, wild garlic, sea kale, and cardoon; that readily self-seed, such as land cress, spinach, and Japanese edible chrysanthemums *(shungiku);* or that resprout after cutting, such as some lettuces, some brassicas, 'Sugarloaf' chicory and Chinese cabbage. My favorite super-hardy winter vegetable is 'Pentland Brig' kale, or borecole, which used to be known in its native northeast of Scotland as the "green doctor," because people believed that those who regularly consumed it never needed medical attention.

Perennial vegetables, together with edible and medicinal herbs, constitute the "herbaceous story" of the forest garden, while root vegetables occupy the rhizosphere. The root mound is host to a number of vegetables suitable for forest conditions, including Hamburg parsley, which tolerates shade, and winter radishes, which come into their own when perennial plants die down.

The remaining "stories" of the forest garden mainly comprise fruit and nut trees and bushes, together with wild strawberries and *Rubus* species, such as the strawberry-raspberry *(R. illecebrosus)* and dewberry, which hug the ground.

No epicurean dish served at the most exclusive restaurant can compare with fresh fruit, organically grown without chemicals, picked from one's own garden.

Perhaps the most delicious of all edibles is the true greengage, which is said to have been introduced into Britain from the mountains of Central Asia in ancient times, probably by medieval monks. Though a vigorous tree, it seldom crops well, but there are other gages which, while perhaps lacking the "Oriental" scented flavor of the original wild species, taste almost as good. One of these is the 'Early Transparent' Gage, described as "a connoisseur's fruit of the highest quality." Another is 'Denniston's Superb', of which I planted several specimens in my main orchard. These have grown into large. hardy, trouble-free trees that seldom fail to give an abundant crop of honey-sweet fruit.

In many parts of Britain it should be possible, if one has a reasonably large garden, to enjoy one's own outdoor fruit every month of the year, from the first gooseberries, which ripen at the end of May, to the latest apples, which ripen in February and can be stored till June.

To extend the picking season as long as possible, one should try to buy at least three varieties—early, midseason, and late—of the fruits of one's choice. This is also desirable in the case of most trees, for the sake of cross-pollination. Almost every fruit tree needs another tree of a different variety—sometimes two others—for pollination; even those trees that are self-fertile tend to crop better if there are other trees of different varieties in the neighborhood. Moreover, the complementary trees must blossom at approximately the same time.

Like other fruit, plums are divided into categories according to their times of ripening, from July to October. The best flavored of the earlies is claimed to be a recently introduced variety call 'Opal', which regularly produces large crops of juicy red-purple fruit. A reliable old variety that is prolific, hardy, and has good resistance to frost is 'Czar', whose black-purple fruit, however, is only considered suitable for cooking. Though I love to experiment with rare and choice fruits, it is good to have a solid nucleus of hardy standbys that won't let you down. Another example of these comes in the next time-category, mid to late August; it is 'Purple Pershore'. The best known of all British plums, 'Victoria', comes into the same categories of time and reliability, though it is susceptible to silver-leaf disease. The September plums include an epicurean variety, 'Kirke's Blue', which is, however, a light cropper. The latest of all plums in another of my solid standbys, 'Marjorie's Seedling', which can be picked as late as December, provided there are no sharp November frosts. The damsons are also late-ripening and very hardy; when fully ripe, they are surprisingly sweet and can be eaten raw. The two best, which can be grown as hedges, are 'Farleigh' and 'Shropshire Prune'. All plums and damsons, including the "cookers," are delicious eaten raw if left to stand for an hour or two with a covering of honey.

Apples are divided into six categories according to time of ripening. An apple is ready to pick when the stem swells and the fruit comes away after a slight twist. One of the best of the earlies is 'George Cave', a small crisp apple that crops well and is sometimes ready before the end of July. Moving on to early October, I find my 'Spartans' have a wine-rich flavor that matches their purple hue—far superior to shop Spartans. Slightly later is my favorite apple, 'Sunset', a small crisp apple from the 'Cox's Orange Pippin' stable—hardier and, to my mind, even more fragrant than its more famous relative. Later still are two recent introductions from East Malling, the finest fruit-breeding station in the world. They are 'Jupiter' and 'Suntan', a cross between 'Cox' and 'Court Pendu Plat'. An old apple, dating back at least to 1720, is 'Ashmead's Kernel', a russet type that was once voted the best of all apples for flavor. Possibly the best keeper of all is a cooking variety, 'Annie Elizabeth', which can be stored till June.

Pears can be divided into two categories: the richly scented, juicy, but rather delicate French epicurean varieties, such as 'Jargonelle' and

George Cave apple tree with scaffolding to support fully fruited branches

'Doyenne du Comice', and the more down-to-earth English varieties, such as 'Improved Fertility', 'Hessle', and 'Conference'.

All bush and cane fruits, except blueberries, are suitable for the forest garden, because all will tolerate some shade. Along the fence above the Packhorse Track are fan-trained plums interplanted with black currants. Along a short mound is a hedge of 'Ben Sarek' black currants, a recent introduction by the Scottish Crop Research Institute. They produce fruit as large and sweet as grapes. From the same Institute comes a midseason raspberry, 'Glen Cova'. Next to it is the very latest in autumn-fruiting raspberries, which form compact bushes which don't need staking. It is 'Autumn Bliss', a hybrid produced by East Malling—after years of endless patience—combining an Arctic raspberry, the American wild raspberry, and no fewer than six old British varieties.

Raspberries are among the constituents of the forest garden's "vertical story." They are trained along the fence above the "monastic fishpond," together with cultivated blackberries and hybrid raspberry-blackberry crosses: tayberry, boysenberry, and loganberry. Over two sheds are trained a Japanese wineberry and a hardy Brant grapevine *(Vitis vinifera,* 'Brandt'), while another Brant vine is trained up an old damson tree. In the summer other trees are also entwined with nasturtiums and runner beans, whose flowers add gaiety to the greenery. A small greenhouse contains a "strawberry vine" *(Vitis vinifera,* 'Fragoia').

I have also experimented with a number of fruit trees and bushes—some rare, some common, all fascinating—whose nutritious products will never find their way into the shops. For me the most beautiful of all small trees are the ornamental crabs, some of which have bright red leaves. All have edible fruit, the best flavored and largest of which are those of 'John Downie'. Crabapples are of special value in a forest garden setting, as they are good pollinators of ordinary apples. A genus of small trees which also has great potentialities for forest gardens is *Sorbus,* the best known species of which is the rowan, of which I have an "edible" variety. I write "edible" in quotes, because the fruits are little less tart than those of the ordinary wild rowan, but they add an intriguing flavor to sweet fruit salads. "Intriguing" is also the word for the flavor of the berries of another *Sorbus* species, the whitebeam, while the berries of a rare English native, the wild service tree, have been described by Richard Mabey as having a unique taste with "hints of tamarind, sultana, apricot, and damson."

Among berries of North American origin, those most valued by the Indians of British Columbia belong to a small tree or bush, variously called serviceberry, juneberry, shadbush, or Saskatoon berry, of which I have two specimens. When ripe, the berries are reddish purple to dark blue and vary considerably in size, texture, and taste. There is a wide scope for breeding improved varieties, as has been done with blueberries and cranberries. A large bush, called in Britain "Worcesterberry," was once thought to be a blackcurrant-gooseberry cross, but it is now known to be a wild American gooseberry. Its small berries—deepest purple, almost black—are deliciously sweet. From the Far North of Canada as well as Scandinavia comes another much valued fruit, the cloudberry, which puts forth exquisite magenta blossoms as early as February, to be followed by berries like large orange raspberries. Also from the Far North comes the Siberian gooseberry, an *Actinidia* species related to the kiwi fruit, two specimens of which, a male and female (essential for fruit production), have been trained over the trellis surrounding the Sanctuary. In China, the native *Actinidia* is greatly valued as a multipurpose plant. Its fruits are especially rich in vitamin C; its seeds yield an oil which can be used as a substitute for sesame oil; its flowers yield scent; its leaves, rich in starch, protein, and vitamin C, are used for fodder; its roots have medicinal virtues; its fibers can be used for fine papermaking, and its abundant resin can be used in the manufacture of paper, dyes, and plastics.

Just as George Washington Carver, the largely self-educated son of slave parents, showed extraordinary ingenuity in tapping the potentialities of the peanut, for which he found over 300 uses, as well as the soybean—and thus introduced both products into world commerce—so the Chinese have skillfully uncovered many uses for their own plants. I have two bamboos, which I hope will some day send out edible shoots.

On one of the mounds is a Japanese *Rosa rugosa,* with large meaty hips the size and shape of small tomatoes. Rose hips are said to be the richest of all sources of vitamin C. The Rosaceae is a large and tremendously productive family of plants, one which includes most of our wild and cultivated temperate fruits. One member of the family that originated in North Africa, and of which a specimen grows in AFG, is the azarole, a hawthorn with quite palatable fruit shaped exactly like miniature apples. Nearby is a "family" apple tree: three compatible varieties of apple growing on a single rootstock (see below). This is a very convenient method of introducing diversity into a small garden. I also have a "family" pear and a "family" plum. A fruit tree which does not belong to the Rosaceae is the mulberry, of which I have two specimens, one black and the other white, the tree used for breeding silkworms.

Hazelnuts, the only nut trees grown commercially in Britain for their fruits, constitute part of the "low-tree story" in the forest garden,

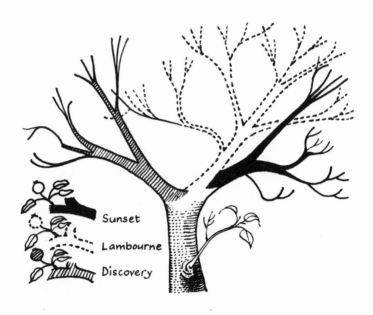

Sunset

Lambourne

Discovery

"Family" apple tree

while there is a short hedge of mixed varieties, including "Harry Lauder's Walking Stick" *(Corylus contorta)*, near the end of the aboretum. I am also experimenting with other species of nut trees suitable for the British climate. These include the butternut and shagbark hickory from North America, a German hybrid walnut that fruits sooner than the English walnut, and a French chestnut, 'Marron de Lyon', which produces nuts larger than the sweet chestnut commonly grown in England. The arboretum also possesses a Swiss Arolla pine that can produce edible kernels. Other nut-bearing pines capable of being grown in Britain include the Italian Stone pine, source of the pine nuts sold in health-food stores, which was first introduced into Britain by the Romans to supplement army rations.

Sweet chestnuts are sometimes known as a "tree cereal," because in the south of France they are occasionally ground into flour to make bread and cakes. A small specimen of another "tree cereal" grows in the forest garden. It is a honey locust, one of a number of bean-bearing leguminous trees, which include also the carob and mesquite, grown in Mediterranean climates. The honey locust is a poor and irregular bearer in the British climate, but there is little doubt that more productive varieties could be bred. In the tropics other "tree cereals" include sago palms, bananas, breadfruit trees, and jackfruit trees. The worldwide reliance on a few staple cereals as basic factors in human diet, with all the uncertainties and expense involved, could be reduced if more use were made of cereal equivalents grown on trees.

Protein deficiencies—a very serious problem in many parts of the Third World—could be remedied by far more widespread growing of mushrooms and other edible fungi. I have grown mushrooms in a small hut in the arboretum and in containers in the house, as well as oyster mushrooms and brown-capped mushrooms in the greenhouse. The *shiitake*, an epicurean fungus that grows on dead trees, has for centuries been cultivated in the Far East. The cultivation of edible fungi is very popular in Germany, where experience indicates that it would be a very suitable constituent of agroforestry systems. Many Germans grow fungi on logs in orchards, taking advantage of the shade provided by the trees. Blackberries are also said to be suitable "nurse crop" for many types of fungus.

The possibilities are almost infinite. A vast abundance of plant foods and cultivating techniques awaits thoroughgoing research and application. Moreover the know-how exists to make up for the deficiencies of nature by modern breeding techniques, such as genetic manipulation and tissue culture. Improved varieties can be produced with qualities such as better cold hardiness and disease resistance. A search is continually in progress to rediscover the wild ancestors of cultivated crops, so that their genes can be utilized to reinvigorate their descendants.

If only the know-how could be equalled by the will-to-serve, by compassion for human suffering caused by hunger and deficiency diseases, there is no reason why fully balanced diets consisting largely of plant foods should not be made available for hundreds of millions of undernourished people in the West as well as in the Third World.

7

~

Design and Maintenance

〰〰〰〰〰〰〰〰〰〰〰〰〰〰〰〰〰〰〰〰〰〰〰〰〰〰〰〰〰〰〰

In his landmark book, The One-Straw Revolution, *Japanese farmer Masanobu Fukuoka argues in favor of a "do-nothing" agriculture, one that focuses only on those tasks that are absolutely necessary to ensure natural order and balance. "When you get right down to it," he writes, "there are few agricultural practices that are really necessary."*

A forest garden requires thoughtful planning at its inception, and lots of work to get it planted and well established. Yet as the garden's trees, shrubs, and herbaceous perennials mature, less and less effort is needed to maintain what has become, in effect, a largely self-regulating system. Rather than having to do all of the tilling, raking, seeding, transplanting, and other tasks required in an annual garden, a forest gardener need only perform regular maintenance—simple tasks that soon become an enjoyable extension of ordinary walks and daily observation of plants in the garden. Judicious pruning or weeding keeps plants in balance with one other. Mulching deeply with organic materials enriches the living soil, conserves moisture, and suppresses weeds. Harvesting is probably the most time-consuming task in the forest garden—and picking fresh, delicious food for the table on a daily basis is the one chore that almost no one finds onerous or tiresome.

〰〰〰〰〰〰〰〰〰〰〰〰〰〰〰〰〰〰〰〰〰〰〰〰〰〰〰〰〰〰〰

The Wenlock Edge Project is a minimal maintenance system. Garnet and I are very busy men who have no time for the High Art of Horticulture. For those who choose to practice that art numerous textbooks and manuals are available. Those who can't bear the sight of a weed or a gate tied up with string would do well to steer clear of Highwood Hill.

The First Principle governing all our decisions and activities has been Down-to-Earth Utility. And yet, strangely enough, that principle is not incompatible with beauty and delight.

The design and laying out of the project have been inspirational and pragmatic, a step-by-step process of development rather than working from a mathematically detailed blueprint. I would compare the result to a landscape sketch by Constable as opposed to one of his finished academic masterpieces. And, for that very reason, the whole setup has, I believe, a more "natural" appearance than the formal garden; it blends better with its environment.

D.H. Lawrence, writing of the "sculptured hills and softly, sensitively terraced slopes" of Tuscany, stressed the naturalness of their beauty, "because man, feeling his way sensitively to the fruitfulness of the earth, has moulded the earth to his necessity without violating it." This has been my aim.

Large trees and other conspicuous objects constitute focal points in the design. At the junction between the forest garden and the AFG stands an ancient twisted damson with a triple trunk, up which I have trained a Brant grapevine. Between the cottage and six rows of raspberries rises the stately form of an edible rowan (mountain-ash), resplendent with orange-red berries in the autumn. Beneath its shade is a small pond and bog garden. Along the northeastern boundary of the AFG runs the Bouché-Thomas apple hedge (see page 55). Close to the southeastern boundary is a row of small but interesting trees or large bushes: a juneberry and an azarole, an edible hawthorn of Mediterranean origin. Between the forest garden and the arboretum stands the Arch of Gaia, festooned with roses, beside a black-currant hedge. At the other side is the Sanctuary, a small enclosure containing a frog pond and a *Sorbus* 'Joseph Rock', which produces whitish berries. The northeastern boundary of the forest garden, above the packhorse track at its deepest point, comprises a trellised fence, with fantrained plums interplanted with black currants and with gooseberries in front. The southwestern boundary, also a trellised fence above the "monastic fishpond," has raspberries, blackberries, and hybrid berries, such as loganberries. In the arboretum, between the osier coppice and an apple-and-pear hedge, the main focal point is provided by the striking reddish form of the dawn redwood, *Metasequoia glyptostroboides,* a "living fossil," typical of the vegetation that flourished 200 million years ago and that created the coal measures. Incredibly, and like its nearby cousin, the maidenhair tree or ginkgo, its ancestors had managed to survive in China alone, where it was discovered in a remote forest in 1941.

Liquid seaweed is the only spray ever used in the project. Its effect is not to kill pests or disease germs but to build up the plants' own powers of resistance. At the same time, seaweed, whether in liquid or granular form, is a first-class soil conditioner. Extremely rich in minerals and trace elements, originally washed into the sea from the land via rivers and streams, seaweed also has the ability to release minerals that have been "locked up" in the soil through compaction. We spray once or twice a year on a dull but rainless day—spraying in full sunlight has the effect of "scorching" leaves.

While establishment of the project has involved a lot of digging and other hard labor, maintenance, as I have said, has been minimal. In fact it grows less from year to year, as the trees and other perennial plants that have decided to stay, grow stronger, more deeply rooted, more stable and secure, and thus better able to withstand the onslaughts of pests, disease germs, and weeds. The entire ground surface of the forest garden, except the part set aside for root vegetables, becomes more and more densely covered with a "lining mulch" of herbs, perennial vegetables, and *Rubus* plants.

Within this mulch certain weeds are tolerated. I agree with F.C. King, the humble gardener of genius—who lived and worked in Wordsworth's county of Westmoreland, where he originated the No-Digging system—that weeds can have an important controlled role to play in productive horticulture. With their deep roots drawing up minerals and water from the subsoil and their amazing adaptations for survival under adverse conditions, there is evidence that some weeds have beneficial, symbiotic effects on neighboring plants, to which they impart something of their health, strength, and vigor, but of course they must be kept in check. Some weeds are also of direct benefit to human beings, as sources of food, medicines, and other useful products, such as dyes. I try to gain an intimate knowledge of the properties of every plant in the complex, tame and wild, consulting Richard Mabey's *Food for Free* and *Plants with a Purpose*, as well as several herbals. Among weeds that we eat are dandelions and nettles (warmed just sufficiently to remove the sting). Both are recognized to have outstanding nutritional qualities. For optimum health it is desirable to make one's diet as varied as possible, as every food has its own individual mix of vitamins, enzymes, proteins, and other nutrients. Some weeds are a valuable source of minerals and trace elements.

To suppress unwanted weeds, I spread straw thickly between the plants. In the forest garden this has to be done as soon as possible after the perennial herbs reappear in the spring. It is important to pack the straw tightly under fruit bushes and other large plants, to prevent weeds such as couch grass, buttercups, and bindweed—and, I must confess, mints—from growing up inside the plants. After adequate mulching, plants tend to grow freely and suppress competitors themselves. However, I periodically find it necessary—especially after a rain, when weeds can readily be pulled up by the roots—to embark on a crawl-and-claw expedition through the undergrowth. Armed with a stout pair of gardening gloves, the most tenacious weeds can be clawed out from the interstices of valued plants. The fragrance of the ever-present herbs makes this an enjoyable and satisfying task.

To deal with weeds in the vegetable beds I find a mattock is the most effective tool.

The trees in the arboretum are planted in old pasture. To deal with weeds here I find constant cutting is reasonably effective. Even the most stubborn weeds such as docks and hogweeds tend to give up the struggle after a time, especially if cut in June and July when most of the vitality is in the tops, and when the roots tend to wither.

Weeding loses most of its daunting prospect as a back-breaking chore if carried out as a regular routine in connection with other work. During twice-daily picking sessions, when fruits, vegetables, and herbs are gathered fresh for meals, I pull up most of the more obtrusive weeds in my path, adding them to the mulch. Picking in the forest garden is part of the process of pruning surplus growth and cutting back plants that encroach on their neighbors.

One way in which weeds can make themselves most useful is as a protective screen against birds during the fruit-ripening season. When gooseberries and currants start changing color I refrain from pulling up bindweed and goosegrass in order to conceal the fruit from my feathered friends, who carefully time their nesting so that there is an abundance of juicy morsels with which to feed their fledglings. Apart from the weeds, anyhow, in the dense foliage of the forest garden, most fruits are far less conspicuous to the eyes of marauders than in the open conditions of conventional monocultures.

One year in the AFG I also made protective screens to protect vegetable seedlings, not only from birds but also from slugs. It was after an entire generation of seedlings in the arboretum had been wiped out that I decided to make a comprehensive study of the likes, dislikes, and habits of my slimy friends. I was determined to get even with them at all costs—except by the use of poisons. In this conservation project, poisons of any kind are taboo, even poisonous plants. Poisoned slugs can lead to poisoned birds, moles, and hedgehogs.

Sir Albert Howard, one of the pioneers of the organic movement, regarded pests and disease germs as "censors" of less-than-perfect health in plants, animals, and soils. Any organism in a state of positive health has the ability to resist pests and diseases. At Howard's Indian agricultural research station, his cattle rubbed noses over the fence with cattle suffering from foot-and-mouth disease, and remained unharmed. It is said that a positively healthy plum tree can even resist bullfinches. The reason for this is in the immune system, which nature provides for all organisms, including humankind. Pests, germs, and viruses are not the basic cause of disease; they are nature's method of destroying unhealthy tissues. They are attracted to acid substances; all organisms in a state of positive health, including soils, are predominantly alkaline.

There is little doubt that slugs are a symptom of acidity in the soil. Soil on which uncomposted farmyard manure has been spread is a breeding ground for slugs. Therefore the first line of defense against them is a covering of lime. This not only sweetens the soil but also tickles their sensitive tummies, which they don't like. Wood ash and soot perform similar functions. Watering the soil with liquid seaweed also has an alkalizing effect. Calcified seaweed meal has the additional bonus of tiny shells, which also deter slugs.

Slugs also dislike strong smells. Many aromatic herbs, such as the various mints, tansy, and balm, deter slugs and other pests and disease germs from attacking not only themselves but also their plant neighbors. The trouble with planting them between vegetables, however, is that they are extremely invasive; they are as vigorous as the worst weeds.

The best way to protect vegetable seedlings and transplants, I have discovered, is a herbal mulch, consisting of sprigs of aromatic plants, which I spread between the rows. This not only deters slugs and other pests, but also screens the young plants from the wind, shades them from excessive sunlight, and breaks the force of heavy rain. It also suppresses weeds and improves the soil, keeping it damp and preventing compaction. As it decays it feeds the young plants.

The herbal mulch also has a camouflaging effect. A bed of tender, young greenery can be irresistibly attractive to mischievous birds and mice, but, when surrounded by a many-colored "barbed-wire screen," the young plants are less conspicuous.

The final weapon in the campaign against slugs and other pests is constant hoeing. This not only breaks up clumps of earth, under which slugs love to hide, but also, by aerating the soil and removing obstacles to growth, including weeds, hastens the young plants' growth. "Keep them moving" is the watchword. The young plants soon acquire the vigor needed to enable them to resist pests and diseases themselves.

The final tip is, as far as possible, to choose plants with a natural immunity. Greedy slugs love brassicas, which are greedy feeders, requiring lots of manure. But more and more members of the chicory-endive family (genus *Cichorium*) are appearing in seed catalogs. These are attractive, hardy plants with a wide variety of shapes and colors—some even develop red and variegated spears in the autumn—which originate from France and Italy. They are excellent substitutes for brassicas and lettuces throughout the year and, in my experience, they are almost completely immune to slugs.

In the forest garden the main tasks are cutting back plants that seek to encroach on their neighbors, and pruning, so far as this is necessary. Even horticultural experts disagree as to how much pruning is really essential, apart from the obvious fact that dead and diseased twigs and branches should be cut out. Dr. W.E. Shewell-Cooper, founder of the Good Gardeners' Association and prolific writer on all aspects of horticulture, writes in *The Compost Fruit Grower:* "Pruning should be regarded as a necessary evil rather than an operation that invariably does good. Pruning creates wounds, and wounds may easily be the open sesame to disease."

The apple and plum trees in the large orchard, which I planted when I first came to Highwood Hill, have not been properly pruned for years, and yet many of them continue to give bumper crops. It is true that some of the fruits are undersized or blemished; they would be scornfully rejected by the eagle eyes of a supermarket manager. But how far superior in flavor, and therefore, I'm convinced, in nutritional value, to his glossy, uniform, and lifeless specimens!

If one has the time and inclination to prune, it can be a very satisfying form of artistic creation. Most gardening books make it seem a daunting and bewildering task, but once you have mastered a few basic facts and principles, it is mostly a matter of common sense.

The first fact you must learn is how each tree bears its fruit, whether on new or old wood, or, in the case of apples, whether a tree is spur- or tip-bearing. Then, if you constantly bear in mind the aims of the operation, you can work out their application for yourself. The main aims are:

1 To allow sun, air, and rain equal access to all parts of the tree or bush. The two best shapes for this are the pyramid and the "open-center" or "goblet" shape.
2 To cut out dead, diseased, or weak unfruitful branches.
3 To prevent branches from rubbing against each other and so breaking their "skins" and causing wounds, through which disease organisms can enter.
4 To ensure regular bearing by seeing that there are roughly equal quantities of fruit buds each year. If this is not done, one is liable to get gluts followed by barren seasons.
5 In the case of cordons, espaliers, and fan-trained trees, to ensure they are trained according to the desired patterns of growth.

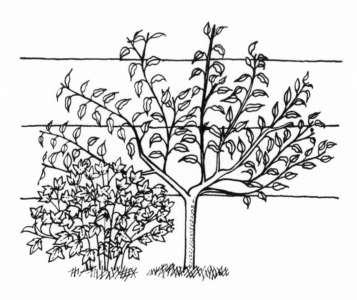

Fan-trained plum tree with black currant bush

The most basic rule of pruning is: "If in doubt, don't." It is far better to underprune than overprune, especially in the case of plants in their first, tender years.

Once a year, when the herbaceous plants in the forest garden die down in the late autumn, the leaf litter is supplemented by a deep layer of compost, straw, and grass cuttings. This is necessary to build up the fertility of the soil and also to protect the plants and soil organisms from frost. As in the natural forest, the soil should be permanently covered. Many vegetable gardeners are devotees of the "bare fallow" during the winter. They dig over their beds roughly and leave the clods to be broken down by the frost, creating a fine tilth for seeding in the spring. But the frost also kills the living organisms, such as earthworms and beetles as well as myriads of microfauna, or drives them to take shelter deep in the subsoil. As these are the main agents of fertility, the fine tilth, attractive though it may look, is largely deprived of nutrients, and these have to be added, in the form of compost, manure, or fertilizer, at the time of seeding. Therefore, to my mind, the whole garden, AFG as well as forest garden, should be permanently covered throughout the year, either with plants or mulch. Mulching is not only less toilsome than hoeing and weeding, but also avoids the necessity of disturbing the soil structure. When the time comes for planting or seeding, all that is generally necessary is to rake off the mulch material and then rake over the soil underneath.

8

Water and No Water

Water is the great limiting factor for any agriculture, and indeed for almost all forms of life on Earth. With it we flourish; without it we die.

Ironically, humans have become far too adept at utilizing the relatively small percentage of fresh water that is available on this ocean planet. Huge dams impound and divert rivers for the sake of industrial agriculture, leaving only a trickle to flow downstream. Groundwater in many agricultural areas is either polluted by chemical runoff or drawn down to dangerous levels through overirrigation, as is now the case with the gigantic Oglala Aquifer that lies beneath the Great Plains.

There is a better way. Throughout the world, examples abound of cultures who have worked with nature to make the most of limited freshwater resources—from the terraced hillsides of Indonesia to the chinampas, or "floating gardens" of Mexico. Trees themselves can help make water available in an otherwise dry and inhospitable landscape. In fact, planting forests is one of the best ways to reclaim barren lands and to literally make the desert bloom.

*T*here is much evidence that this small farm was originally carved out of the Long Forest, which once clothed much of South Shropshire, by men and women from the mixed Celtic Christian monastery at Much Wenlock, which, in the seventh century, was presided over by St. Milburga, daughter of the king of Saxon subkingdom of Magonsaeta. Those pioneers certainly had an eye for water. Just below the circular earthwork, which, I am convinced, was the site of their monastery, rises a spring, whose delicious water we still customarily enjoy, through it sometimes runs dry in times of drought. In the center of the five-acre field, once called "Middle Stocking," another spring rises from a perfect example of a *knickpoint,* the geological term for the lowest point of a hillside contour, where the slope flattens out and where the groundwaters tend to meet to form a spring.

The keen eyes of P.A. Yeomans, the Australian mining engineer, farmer, and conservationist, trained in landscape assessment, intuitively recognized in the "knickpoint" the clue to his Keyline System of land reclamation. He renamed the knickpoint the *keypoint* and called the contour which passes through it the *keyline.* The essence of his system is contour-plowing parallel to the keyline with a non-inverting chisel plow invented by himself. This has the effect of creating thousands of small channels, which cause the groundwater to spread across the slope instead of converging on the keypoint. The circulation of mineral-carrying water so brought about has the effect of releasing stores of fertility "locked up" by soil compaction. The result, as Yeomans triumphantly proved on his farm at Yobarnie, New South Wales, can lead to the regeneration of land condemned by agricultural experts as "irredeemable," after it had been baked as hard as concrete by a forest fire.

The Keyline System might have great significance for rainforest areas, whose thin "lateritic" soils have also been concretized by the twin forces of tropical sun and tropical rainfall, after the forest had been burnt to death to provide brief pastures for "hamburger ranches." In fact, Keyline would seem to provide a good chance of restoring those degraded soils and making them productive once more.

Yeomans developed his system into a comprehensive method of landscape architecture, applicable to any reasonably large undulating area. One refinement was the building of a series of small reservoirs along the contours, which could be temporarily dammed for sheet irrigation. Another was the planting of shelterbelts of trees to distinguish the Keylines.

The idea of landscape design seems to be deeply rooted in the Australian consciousness, as the people's ancestors not so long ago were involved in opening up virgin territory. Bill Mollison, also an Australian, makes landscape design the centerpiece of his system of Permaculture, which he first conceived in the early 1970s at the same time as I was, quite independently, working out my own system of Organic Perennial Subsistence Agriculture or Ecocultivation. In *Permaculture One*, written by Mollison and David Holmgren, the authors say:

> Permaculture is a word we have coined for an integrated, evolving system of perennial or self-perpetuating plant and animal species useful to man. It is, in essence, a complete agricultural ecosystem . . . Perhaps we seek the Garden of Eden, and why not? We believe that a low-energy, high-yielding agriculture is a possible aim for the whole world.

I couldn't agree more.

In his book *Permaculture Two*, Mollison speaks with authority and passion about a problem that is dominating ever-growing sectors of the earth's surface: how to rehabilitate arid lands. Referring to Australia's vast empty spaces, Mollison affirms:

> I must state that, in my opinion, based on real examples sighted, the "dead center" is a myth. Not only will many important vegetables and tree crops grow in deserts, but the native vegetation, where not overburnt or overgrazed, is, in itself, a great resource. Water lies close underground in many places . . . Growth in desert soil is phenomenal if water is available.

Listing a number of systems for trapping, conserving, and utilizing every available drop of water, Mollison shows that a large number of trees and other perennial plants can be induced to grow in areas typically regarded as barren wastes. These include figs, olives, and grapes, the three staples of arid and eroded areas in the ancient Mediterranean, as well as mulberries, date palms, oranges, lemons, carobs, mangoes, cashew nuts, jujubes, and pomegranates.

In his great book, *Permaculture: A Designer's Manual,* Mollison describes in exhaustive detail numerous techniques for the reclamation of deserts and other arid lands—techniques that may well have to be applied in Britain and other European countries, as well as much of the rest of the world, if drastic steps are not taken to reverse the Greenhouse Effect.

Mollison paints a fascinating picture of the desert garden, as found in Central Australia, from which we in Britain may have much to learn if summer droughts continue. The garden is integrated with the house, for which it provides shade, shelter, and climate amelioration. The roof may be covered with soil and planted with ice-plants, succulents, and hardy desert species. This roof garden cools the house in summer, when watered, and insulates it from winter cold. Trellised vines on the walls have a similar effect. Hedges of tamarisk, white cedar, paulownia, or bamboo screen the house from cold winds. Arbors are formed adjacent to the house, in which strawberries, black currants, gooseberries, and herbs are grown, deeply mulched to retain moisture. Lean-to greenhouses provide winter greens, peppers, and tomatoes, as well as spices and other flavoring plants such as ginger, turmeric, and vanilla. All wastewater from the house is fully utilized. Sewage and "greywater" from baths and sinks is conveyed to perforated pipes beneath the garden. Sludge from septic tanks is conveyed to planting holes, covered with soil and then planted with dates, figs, citrus trees, or mulberries. If the house is situated on a frost-free hillside, tropical plants such as guavas, papayas, and mangoes, sheltered by trees such acacias and paulownias, may grow successfully, being irrigated by a wind pump. If possible, the house is built near a water runoff area, such as a rock, and care is taken to see that all the water is absorbed into sand-lots or "swales"—contour ditches designed to trap water and release it gradually into the soil.

The staple plants of the desert garden are drought-tolerant species, able to survive on minimal watering, such as dates, olives, avocados, apricots, bananas, sweet potatoes, cucumbers, and melons. However, most tropical and temperate vegetables can be grown in small beds, soaked every three to ten days, and shaded by slats, vines, or leguminous trees. The legumes inject nitrogen into the soil. Other companion plants are used, including marigolds, gladioli, and wallflowers, so that the desert garden can be gay with color.

Many irrigation devices have been used in the past—and are still being used—to ensure that gardens and orchards in arid lands are places of beauty and fecundity. A notable example is provided by the elaborate water works created by the Moorish cultivators in southern Spain, which included dams, aqueducts, reservoirs, sluices, tunnels, and siphons.

In the Far East many upland areas have been terraced with incredible skill, to ensure that every available drop of water is utilized for growing crops. Alfred Russel Wallace, the famous Victorian biologist, who conceived the theory of natural selection independently of but contemporaneously with Charles Darwin, recounts in this book, *The Malay Archipelago*, his astonishment at the system of cultivation that he discovered on the Indonesian island of Lombok, from which at that time almost all Europeans were excluded:

I rode through this strange garden utterly amazed, and hardly able to realize the fact that in this remote and little-known island . . . many hundreds of square miles of irregularly undulating country had been so skillfully terraced and leveled, and so permeated by artificial channels, that every portion of it can be irrigated and dried at pleasure . . . Here were luxuriant patches of tobacco; there cucumbers, sweet potatoes, yams, beans or Indian corn . . . The banks which bordered every terrace rose regularly in horizontal lines above each other, sometimes rounding an abrupt knoll and looking like a fortification, or sweeping round some deep hollow and forming on a gigantic scale the seats of an amphitheatre. Every brook and rivulet had been diverted from its bed, and instead of flowing along the lowest ground were to be found cross-

ing our road half-way up our ascent, yet bordered by ancient trees
and moss-grown stones so as to have all the appearance of a natural channel, and bearing testimony to the remote period at which
the work has been done. As we advanced further into the country,
the scene was diversified by abrupt rocky hills, by steep ravines,
and by clumps of bamboos and palm trees near houses and villages; while in the distance the range of mountains of which Lombok peak, eight thousand feet high, is the culminating point,
formed a fit background to a view scarcely to be surpassed in
human interest or picturesque beauty.

A system of water control that was developed over 2,000 years ago
in one of the harshest arid areas in the world, that of the Negev Desert,
has been successfully revived by an Israeli professor, Michael Evenari.
The system was originated about 200 BC by the Nabateans, builders of
the famous rock-hewn city of Petra. It comprises an ingenious complex of runoff channels, small dams, trenches, terraces, and cisterns,
designed to gather up the meager rainfall—three to four inches a
year—and concentrate it in a single growing area. Evenari refined the
system to the extent that he created microcatchments, each designed
to irrigate a single tree or bush: olive, pomegranate, peach, apricot,
fig, almond, grapevine, or saltbush (used for fodder). Yields from this
modern version of an ancient system were extraordinarily high, and
so impressed a German relief group that they translated the system to
a heavily eroded area of Bolivia. There, in a strange "lunar" landscape
of gullies and dome-shaped mounds, they recreated Evenari's microcatchments into forms that were nicknamed by the local inhabitants
medias lunas, 'half-moons'. Each of these comprises a small rainfall
collection area, with an earth wall on the downhill side to prevent
erosion. In each half-moon two saplings are planted: leguminous
trees bearing high-protein beans, intended to provide food, fodder,
and firewood, while improving the fertility of the soil by injecting nitrogen. The retention of moisture in the soil has had the effect of attracting the colonization of wild plants, and is hoped that a train of

ecological succession has been set in motion, the culmination of which will be a dense climax forest, like that with which the area was originally clothed.

More and more it is being recognized that the tree provides the master key to the reclamation, fertilization, and regeneration of arid lands. Where large numbers of trees are planted there is no need for elaborate irrigation schemes. Such schemes, with their associated big dams, often involving the drowning of hundreds of square miles of fertile land, may lead to ecological disaster. The irrigated soils tend to become heavily salinated and therefore incapable of growing crops, while the reservoirs become silted up and lose their utility. Trees, on the other hand, with their complex root systems, create their own irrigation channels in the soil, through which pass pure, life-giving streams of water, laden with subsoil minerals, which nourish other crops.

No country in the world understands the value of trees as does China, which, in recent decades, has planted countless millions for the reclamation of deserts; for shade, shelter, and windbreaks; and for the control of water, to halt the cycle of floods and droughts, which has been one of the banes of China's history.

Trees can be used not only for the restoration of arid lands but also for the prevention of flooding. One of the main causes of floods in many countries, not least Britain, is the felling of forests and the draining of marshes in upland catchment areas where most rivers and streams have their sources. This means that there is little absorption of precipitation in those areas. Storm water races down the denuded slopes, and rivers and streams become suddenly swollen and burst their banks.

Forests not only make rain my transpiring groundwater into the atmosphere, but they also absorb rain through their roots and then release it gradually into the groundwater system, so that "flash floods" are rare in a forested area. The simplest and most effective way to stop flooding, therefore, is to restore tree cover to upland catchments. Marshes in the same areas could, I suggest, be transformed into economically viable wetland permacultures.

A large and very remarkable "forest garden" called *Sol y Sombra* (Sun and Shade), including some 150,000 economic trees and shrubs, has been created by Beth and Charles Miller high up in the hills near Santa Fe, New Mexico. In this arid area rainwater is harvested by more than 100 "swales." Sewage and greywater is treated by a reedbed system, comprising four gravel beds and two ponds, planted with reeds, rushes, and bog flowers.

In recent years a number of systems for treating wastewater by natural, biological techniques have been developed in many parts of the world. These systems are highly compatible with agroforestry principles:

1 They make use of plants and bacteria to purify and detoxify potentially harmful material, transmuting it into useful resources, including energy and fertilizer.
2 They help to conserve the environment, creating beauty and attracting wildlife.
3 They are largely self-sustaining, requiring minimal maintenance.

A feature incorporated into many of these systems is the "flowform," a series of concrete basins carefully sculpted to impart rhythmic, pulsing movements to the water, which, it is claimed, help to oxygenate it and enhance its ability to support the purifying organisms.

The reeds and rushes, which often play a key role in water-treatment systems, have many traditional uses. Richard Mabey in his *Plants with a Purpose* writes: "It is the common characteristics of the stems of reeds, rushes and sedges that make them so useful and adaptable. They are long and straight, always lightweight and often hollow. The grouping of tough fibers round the outside of the stems makes them pliant, durable and easy to work. They are ideal, therefore, for weaving or bunching into hardwearing articles like baskets or mats . . . In Nevada, the Paiute Indians weave rush cradleboards for their babies and, with a real understanding of the natural waterproofing of a

Forest Gardening

plant that spends its life up to its knees in the wet, makeshift boats."
The reedmace, *Typha latifolia,* often erroneously called "bulrush,"
is a plant with a multitude of uses. The familiar long brown spiky flowers, which give it its American name of "cattail," can be cooked and
eaten. The seeds are also edible and yield an edible oil. The pollen is a
first-class source of protein, and the young shoots can be eaten like asparagus. The core of the rhizome contains more carbohydrate than
potatoes and as much protein as maize or rice. Of all wild plants, the
reedmace has been described as the most useful emergency food
source. But the leaves and stems also yield fibers that are used for weaving and have potential value for papermaking. Mexican studies have
shown that woven reedmace leaves, when coated with plastic resins,
are as strong as fiberglass.

At this time, when the threat of the Greenhouse Effect looms over
the lives of all of us, a special study should be made of temperate
plants that require a minimum of watering, comparable to the studies
made of drought-resistant plants in the tropics. The common characteristics of such plants seem to include:

1 Small or waxy leaves, which reduce evaporation;
2 Hairy leaves that retain moist air, keeping them cool;
3 Hollow stems, used for storing water (onions and thistles);
4 Ability to survive in shallow grassland or on rocky slopes
   (thyme, marjoram, and yarrow);
5 Deep roots, which extract water from the subsoil.

Among tactics which I employed to combat the severe drought in
England in 1995 were heavy mulching to preserve the moisture in the
soil and drastic pruning and weeding to minimize stress in the more
valuable plants.

9

Stored-Up Sunshine:
Energy Yesterday and Tomorrow

All energy derives ultimately from the sun: fossil-fuel deposits created millions of years ago from plants and animals; wind and clouds and weather patterns; or the alchemy of plant photosynthesis: "The force that through the green fuse drives the flower/Drives my green age," in the words of Dylan Thomas.

As we enter the Post-Industrial Age, we must come to terms with the consequences of our over-reliance on ancient fossil fuels (global warming, pollution, oil wars) and return to a current solar economy, one that uses and stores the sun's present-day energy efficiently and locally to power our homes and energize our lives. Such a solar culture is already taking shape in many developing countries, and improved technology in photovoltaics, solar thermal, wind power, and other applications promises all people a cleaner, less wasteful, and more ecological energy future.

*I*ronbridge Gorge in Shropshire was the birthplace of the Industrial Revolution. Little can the Quaker ironmasters who originated it have foreseen the devastating effects on the whole world of the forces that they set in motion, the powers that they unleashed.

If the appalling damage that industrialism has done to the environment is to be reversed, a great new comprehensive initiative must be set afoot, comparable in vitality and intensity to the Industrial Revolution itself. But all true progress is a spiral, not a straight line; the new must grow out of the old and include elements which, to some extent, are reversions to older patterns. The Post-Industrial Society, which some far-sighted "Greens" proclaim, can find ideas and inspiration from a study of the processes which led to our own present problems.

Before the Industrial Revolution, and for some time after, Shropshire, with its many streams and rivers, had, like many other parts of Britain, relied mainly on water as a source of power. Watermills had been used for grinding corn, for fulling (shrinking) cloth, for sawing wood, for making paper, and for blowing bellows in blast furnaces. A number of old mills and mill-houses still exist. Anyone with an eye for landscape and some knowledge of milling techniques can detect signs of the ponds and weirs, dams, leats, and millraces, which the milling operations entailed. Regular, disciplined activities were required to keep the often elaborate milling landscapes in good order. As mills were sited at regular intervals on almost every waterway, however small, the water-control network must have done much to prevent flooding.

When my brother and I gave up livestock farming, we spent some six months thoroughly exploring the South Shropshire countryside in our ancient Land Rover and on foot. We saw many relics of Shropshire's industrial past and talked to some people who remembered them in operation. What we saw and heard gave much food for thought.

Bouldon is one of Corvedale's many dead or shrunken villages. It lies about five miles to the east of Highwood Hill, on the far side of Wenlock Edge and on the Roman road which crosses my land. It contains an old watermill, with an impressive outside wheel below a stretch of grass that was once the millpond. About half a mile to the east, on the Clee Brook, is a high weir, like a mini-Niagra Falls. The farmer who lives behind the mill-house told me that he could remember the wheel being used to grind grain; before it could operate, the water had to be switched from the weir and conveyed along an elaborate system of leats to the millpond. Before it was used to grind grain, Bouldon mill had served as adjunct to a blast furnace land as a paper mill. Now this once important industrial village is a tiny rural backwater. Still more remarkable is the total ruralization of the Willey estate near Broseley, which once belonged to my mother's ancestors, the Lacons, and which, during the seventeenth and eighteenth centuries, was an important arms manufacturing area. At Willey Wharf on the Severn the world's first ironclad ship was launched. Now Willey is mainly remarkable for its magnificent trees and for a small remnant of the once extensive primeval Shirlett Forest. The former furnace ponds have been converted into ornamental lakes.

Many people, myself included, would like to see parts (at least) of the former mill network restored; not perhaps for its former purposes, but as a sustainable, clean, nonpolluting means of generating electricity: a system that, far from contaminating and defacing the landscape, would with the assistance of trees, help to maintain the circulation of water, which is the lifeblood of the landscape.

I don't suggest that electricity generated by waterwheel should be fed into the National Grid, but it is a possible source of light, heat, and power for small communities striving for self-sufficiency. Other, more sophisticated mechanisms, developed within the last two centuries, should also be considered, provided that adequate water is available. These include the turbine, the hydraulic ram, and the air compressor.

While the principle of the turbine was originally conceived by Hero of Alexandria in 100 B.C., the first effective models date back to the middle of the last century. One of the earliest, most primitive versions, called the "hurdy-gurdy," was developed by miners during the California Gold Rush of 1849. It consisted of a simple pulley with flat plates bolted to the rim. The pulley was caused to spin by water from above dropping onto the plates. In the succeeding 140 years many types of turbine have been developed, using propellers and other devices, to provide power for grain-mills, pumps, sawmills, metal-working machinery and, above all, to generate electricity. They vary in size from monstrous units requiring big dams and incorporated in giant hydroelectric projects to tiny "micro-hydros" that can be assembled by any do-it-yourself enthusiast for home power generation.

The hydraulic ram, a kind of "water-hammer" used to raise water above the height of its source, was invented by John Whitehurst, a Cheshire brewer, in 1772. But the version that is still widely used today owes its effectiveness to the invention in 1798 of the automatic pulse valve by Pierre Mongolfier of hot-air balloon fame. While the ram is most commonly used as an automatic, low-maintenance pump for supplying water from hill streams to remote farmhouses, it has also been used for compressing air for rock drills.

A still simpler device that the ram, with no moving parts, the hydraulic air compressor or "trompe" was first developed in medieval Catalonia to act as an automatic bellows for an iron furnace. For a brief period it was revived at the beginning of the present century in the United States. The National Academy of Sciences in Washington in *Energy for Rural Development* (1976) suggests that the compressor should be:

> resurrected for further study and possible use in hilly terrain where ample water is available. The ability of the device to operate day and night, with its simple storage of energy in the form of compressed air in tanks or caves, makes it an interesting and potentially fruitful problem to investigate. The compressed air could be piped to sites to drive reciprocating engines or turbines that, in turn, could power production machines or electric generators.

Of special significance in the agroforestry context is the use of biomass for energy production. *Biomass* is the generic term for all forms of organic, carbon-containing material, living or dead, including garbage and sewage.

A number of methods can be employed for extracting energy from biomass sources:

> 1 *Burning.* The simplest method, employed since before the dawn of history, is the burning of wood, peat, and cattle dung.

Incredibly, this is the principal or only method still used for cooking and heating by over half the world's population. It is extremely inefficient, owing to the large amount of heat lost in the air.

2 *Pyrolysis.* This involves baking the raw fuel in the absence of air. It can produce combustible solids, liquids, or gases. Charcoal has been made by this method for hundreds of years.

3 *Gasification.* The heating of biomass under pressure in the presence of air and steam to produce combustible gas.

4 *Pelletization.* The manufacture of "briquettes" from materials such as sawdust to produce coal substitutes.

5 *Bacterial digestion.* The production of methane or biogas from sewage, garbage, and organic wastes generally.

6 *Fermentation.* The production of ethanol, butanol, and acetone by the processing of plants with high contents of sugar or starch, such as pineapples, potatoes, maize, cassava, sorghum, sugar beet, and sugar cane.

7 *Extraction of energy-rich products from plants.* For example, palm oil and olive oil.

Large quantities of ethanol have been produced over the years from Brazilian sugar cane plantations. As a motor fuel, ethanol can be used in conjunction with gasoline in a proportion of about one to five, but where engines have been redesigned, hydrated ethanol can be used alone. However, ethanol can cause corrosion of some metal alloys and deterioration of some plastics.

Biogas is an energy source very extensively used in a number of countries, notably China. Millions of Chinese peasants use small do-it-yourself digesters to convert human, animal, and plant wastes for home cooking, heating, and lighting. The residue is a virtually odorless, disease-free liquid used as fertilizer.

The special importance of biogas lies in the fact that it is a way of utilizing objectionable materials that are available everywhere and that in most countries, are not utilized, as they should be for creating energy, but are instead disposed of in ways that seriously pollute the environment, especially inland waterways and the oceans.

In the natural forest *all* biomass residues are recycled to form compost, which feeds and energizes the plants.

The raw materials of biogas can include, not only human, animal, and plant wastes, but also the most objectionable and troublesome of weeds, such as water hyacinth, which in many tropical and subtropical regions clogs vast areas of inland waterways and lakes.

In *Making Aquatic Weeds Useful* (National Academy of Sciences, 1979) it is stated:

In a pioneering effort of great significance, researchers at the National Aeronautics and Space Administration (NASA) are working on converting water hyacinth and other aquatic weeds into a biogas rich in methane. Methane is the main ingredient in natural gas, which is used worldwide as fuel and is a major item in international trade. The recovery of fuel from aquatic weeds . . . has interesting implications, especially for rural areas in developing countries. As many developing nations have apparently inexhaustible supply of aquatic weeds within their borders, this potential energy source deserves further research and testing. Aquatic weeds are converted to biogas by capitalizing upon one of nature's processes for decomposing wastes—decay by anaerobic bacteria. Methane-producing bacteria are common in nature (for instance, in the stagnant bottom mud of swamps, where they produce bubbles of methane known as "marsh gas"). If they are cultured on water hyacinth in a tank, sealed to keep out all air, they produce a biogas composed of about 70 percent methane and 30 percent carbon dioxide. The high moisture content of aquatic weeds is an advantage in this process. It is needed for fermentation. This is one method of aquatic weed utilization that does not require dewatering—a big advantage. . . .

Based on NASA's findings, it appears that the water hyacinth harvested from one hectare [2.5 acres] will produce more than 70,000 cubic meters of biogas. Each kilogram of water hyacinth (dry-weight basis) yields about 370 liters of biogas with an average methane content of 69 percent and a calorific (heating) value when used as a fuel, of about 22,000 kJ/m3.

These amazing figures, based on just one of the many possible ingredients of biogas, indicate its vast unused potential.

If mineral-neutralizing aquatic plants were added to city sewage, that would probably be the answer to those who object that sewage sludge is unsuitable for conversion into fertilizer, not only on account of its content of heavy metals and pernicious micro-organisms but also because it contains harmful industrial chemicals.

Another water-loving plant, the willow, is being grown in large numbers in Sweden, Northern Ireland, and the Somerset levels as a quick-maturing source of biomass fuels. Willows do particularly well in Ireland's moist climate and boggy soils, and leading horticuluturalists believe that "energy forests" could do much to revitalize the country's rural economy. The original aim of research initiated in 1973 at the Horticultural Centre at Loughall, County Armagh, was to find "superwillows" that, by coppicing, would form a regularly renewable source of pulp for papermaking. But the energy crisis of 1974 caused the research team to change their priorities. They came to the conclusion that willows could form a valuable source of relatively cheap energy in the form of chips, pellets, or briquettes. In a three-year trial with greenhouse tomatoes, it was found that the cost of heating with willow chips was only one-third the cost of conventional fuel oils. Using trees carefully selected by Long Ashton Research Station in Bristol, it was found that yields of up to twenty-five tons per hectare per year could be achieved. Other applications for the willows include fuel for domestic wood-burning stoves, ethanol to replace lead as a high-octane enhancer in gasoline, and vicose to be used in combination with flax or other fibers in Northern Ireland's textile industry.

From this vision of "The Wind in the Willows" it is only a short conceptual step to the subject of wind generators.

For nearly a thousand years windmills played an important part in the economy of Britain and other European countries. It has been reckoned that a single traditional windmill used for grinding grain, with a 25 meter rotor made from wooden spars and canvas, could do the work of more than 200 people. Towards the end of the nineteenth century much research was done into the possibility of improving windmill efficiency, and in the 1890s Denmark successfully produced windmills designed specifically for the generation of electricity. By 1908 several hundred small wind-power stations were in existence, each one capable of generating five to twenty-five kilowatts of electricity. In the 1930s the Soviet Union built the world's first large wind turbine, capable of generating up to 100 kW. In the following years a number of large experimental machines were built, but it was not until the energy crisis in the 1970s that governments and other official bodies began to take a serious interest in wind generators. In 1975 a prototype 100 kW wind turbine began operation at Sandusky, Ohio; it had been designed by NASA, the National Aeronautics and Space Administration. The first multimegawatt wind turbine in North America was commissioned in 1979 at Boone, North Carolina. Today a wide array of wind generators is available: experimental and practical, of all shapes and sizes, suitable for large-scale projects or for domestic use. The Rutland Windcharger, which I had installed to supply light for the small cabin that houses my craft museum, is a highly efficient, small, but tough and durable machine, mass-produced at Corby, Northhamptonshire. It is extensively used in several parts of the world as a source of power for lights, radio, TV, and other utilities in mobile homes, boats, farms, remote buildings, and even an Antarctic research station. For remote sites, Northumbrian Energy Workshop Ltd. of Hexham supplies a composite package comprising a wind generator, micro-hydro turbine, and photovoltaic module. In the United States, several companies—among them Real Goods Trading Corp. of Hopland, California—design and sell site-specific renewable energy systems for the home.

The photovoltaic module or cell is one form of "active" solar device for converting sunlight into electricity. The first modules were developed in 1954 at Bell Laboratories in the US during research into silicon chips. Basically all that is involved is a single crystal silicon cell, which generates electricity when exposed to sunlight. Such cells were used to power instruments aboard early space satellites.

A form of solar generator that is more familiar to the general public is the "panel," used to heat water, which can now be seen on the south-facing roofs of many houses. The panel is usually made of stainless steel and faced with glass. The inside surface is usually matte black, designed to absorb solar radiation and transform it into heat. The heat is transferred from the surface of the panel into cavities or pipes within the panel, which are filled with air, water, or an oil-based fluid. The liquid or air is passed through a normal plumbing circuit into a spiral element, which heats the water in a well-insulated storage tank.

A type of solar generator that would fit well into a home permaculture system is the solar pond, first developed in Israel. A typical solar pond is six to ten feet deep with conical sides and a flat, blackened bottom. It is filled with layers of brine of increasing concentration, the densest at the bottom containing as much as twenty percent salt. Sunlight absorbed by the brine can yield temperatures as high as 100°C (212 F). Loss of heat is prevented by the salt gradient, which suppresses thermal convection, and ponds can effectively store heat for months. The heat is removed by drawing brine from the bottom of the pond through heat exchangers or by circulating a heat transfer fluid through submerged coils. In Israel, solar ponds are used to drive heat engines for production of electricity. They can also be used for district heating systems.

"Passive" solar heating relies on the architectural design of a building, which is so devised as to capture, store, and distribute the sun's radiation. The ancient Greeks were the first to develop solar architecture, designing buildings with open, south-facing porticoes, which permitted low winter sunshine to penetrate to the living areas, while providing shade in the summer. The heat was absorbed by dark stone floors and thick masonry. Buildings were insulated to prevent drafts. The Greeks actually built several solar cities. The Pueblo Indians of the southwestern United States also built several solar hill towns in the eleventh and twelfth centuries. One of the most sophisticated was Acoma, which had three terraces running east to west, built in tiers for maximum exposure to the winter sun. The roof of each tier was layered with straw and other materials to insulate the houses from the full blaze of the summer sun.

In the hills of Mid-Wales today, David Huw Stephens is developing a solar village called Tir Gaia, at Rhayader. The design of the model "Survivor House" is fascinating in the extreme. It combines both passive and active solar features. On the roof is a greenhouse, with rainwater tanks to provide water for the plants and house. The tanks will absorb radiant solar heat during the day and help to keep the greenhouse frost-free at night by reradiation of the heat. On the south side of the house is a solar panel to provide hot water, and below the foundations are water cylinders to transfer heat from the solar panel to the soil and thus create subterranean heat storage. Large south-facing, double-glazed windows admit solar energy to the main living room, which is on the first floor. The walls have absorbent surfaces that convert solar radiation into convecting warm air. North-facing walls are "super-insulated" and the down stairs bedrooms have insulating shutters, which are closed at night to reduce heat loss. Outside the front door, referring to the produce of the rooftop greenhouse, hangs a notice: "Home-Grown Bananas."

In the UK, remarkable and comprehensive display of sustainable and nonpolluting devices for producing and saving energy can be seen at the Centre for Alternative Technology, Machynlleth, Mid-Wales. In the US, Real Goods Trading Corporation has recently opened its Solar Living Center in Hopland, California, which not only serves as the company's headquarters but incorporates many renewable-energy and sustainable-building strategies, including the highly effective straw bale construction method.

10

~

The Thinking Hand:
Skills of the Craftsman

~~~~~~

Most of us work for an hourly wage in order to buy objects or services that we need (or are told that we need) from other people who work for an hourly wage. This, we are told, is modern economics. But the accumulation of possessions cannot make up for a fundamental lack of control and creativity in our lives. Supporters of the "simple living" movement have long since recognized this truth, and today their numbers are growing.

Learning a craft can transfer our focus from possession to expression. Traditional craftwork may seem quaint and anachronistic in this era of mass production. But the crucial manual skills, such as working in wood, metal, clay, or glass, remain far too important to relegate to "living history" museums.

When we think about the value of work, let us emulate the American Shakers rather than the British Luddites. The Luddites feared technology and smashed textile machinery in the years between 1811 and 1816. The Shakers, meanwhile, were inventing labor-saving devices—what today we might call "intermediate" or "human-scale" technology—not to supplant or devalue human work, but to make work more graceful and more enjoyable. To the Shakers, work was a form of worship; naturally, they strove to make it joyful instead of burdensome. Whatever our vocation, we have much to learn from their spirit and ingenuity.

~~~~~~

A permaculture/agroforestry scheme, as a holistic organism designed to sustain and foster whole human beings, should incorporate craftwork of various kinds, so that it supplies as many as possible of the diverse needs of those who run it, In the traditional rural community there were no "closed shops," no union rivalries, but there was complete integration between craftsmanship, husbandry, and forestry. The true peasant was a versatile all-rounder, who could turn his or her hand to almost any country task and was capable of facing up to almost any emergency. H.J. Massingham, in *The English Countryman,* writes:

> From times immemorial, the practice of a craft was the part-time or seasonal occupation of the husbandman, while the craftsman almost invariably had a "close" or holding of his own, the hurdler an acre or less of coppice, the basket-maker an osier-bed, the straw-plaiter a plot of corn, the potter a stake in the claypit, the mason or waller a share in the quarry.

To my great regret, I have never found time to practice any rural crafts—writing and teaching have been my crafts—but I have been closely associated with the work of craftsmen who have contributed to my farm and garden. Whenever possible, I have employed skilled private individuals from the neighborhood or further afield in Shropshire, rather than faceless firms in distant towns or cities. At the same time, in an incessant urge to sink roots every more deeply into my ancestral countryside, I have tried to seek out traditional crafts and vernacular styles throughout the county.

The main focus of my studies has been two highly contrasted regions: Ironbridge Gorge and Shropshire's "Middle West," the wild country immediately adjacent to Wales, between the Stiperstones with their strange rock outcrops and the Long Mountain. Both, in their entirely different ways, have the stimulating characteristics of the Frontier; both are interfaces between different outlooks, patterns of thought, and ways of life. While the "Middle West" is where the pragmatic Saxon meets the intuitive and emotional Celt and Iberian, Ironbridge Gorge is an outpost of a well-wooded and still deeply rural countryside in collision with Telford New Town, a western extension of the industrial Midlands. And, since challenge-and-response is one of the basic essentials of creativity, the psychological conflicts involved are, I believe, more conducive to new initiatives than more settled modes of thought and living.

The "Wild West" has a singularly archaic atmosphere. It contains Shropshire's version of Stonehenge, the stone circle called Mitchell's Fold, as well as a Bronze Age trackway called by the Welsh name Yr Hen Ffordd (the Old Road). Round a wooded eminence in the foothills of the Long Mountain are the remains of the dead town of Caus, which are little known even to Salopians. Named after Caux in Normandy, the ancestral home of the dominant medieval family of Corbet, the town was burnt to the ground during a Welsh rebellion in the fifteenth century and finally abandoned in the seventeenth century. A few remnants of the Corbet stronghold, including a gigantic well, can still be disentangled from the undergrowth.

In the south of this area, below the site of a stone-axe factory on the slopes of Corndon Hill, and right astride the English-Welsh boundary, live Rita and Robert Acton, expert craftspeople who, every January, used to cut down and take away the "wands" from my osier coppice— for basketry.

Basketry is believed to be the earliest of all crafts. The first human artifact may well have been a simple container, formed of plaited twigs, stems, creepers, or vines and used to carry berries, nuts, roots, and other edibles gathered by the forest wanderers. A later development would have been a primitive loom used to weave forest fibers into skirts and cloaks to protect naked bodies from the elements. Thus basketry is supposed to have led to the invention of weaving.

The use of baskets should be regarded as one of the hallmarks of responsible, eco-friendly living. A well-made basket is a strong, durable, long-lasting container that, in the past, was used for most of the purposes for which throwaway cardboard, plastic, and wood-strip containers are used today. Basket-making is a wholly nonpolluting manual skill; no basket-making machine has ever been devised. On the other hand, our present container industry involves the wholesale

Basket-making

destruction of trees, massive pollution, and a colossal waste-disposal problem. When, after years of use, baskets eventually rot, they do not harm the environment, as does plastic, but, like other forms of biomass, gently disintegrate to form life-giving compost. A single basket will outlive 1,000 cardboard boxes. Durability is one of the outstanding characteristics of good hand-craftsmanship.

Rita Acton, a large, robust countrywoman with a ruddy face beaming with health and good humor, is both a skilled basket-maker—as is her husband Robert—and also an expert in all branches of home textile production, from the cultivation of flax to spinning, weaving, and lacemaking. The creation of linen goods seems to call forth her keenest enthusiasm and brings out to the full her innate artistic talents. A linen smock that she had fashioned through every stage of growth, from the sowing of the flax seed through all the arduous and complex stages of processing the fibers, is the most exquisite garment of its kind I have ever seen. A garment, moreover, that could endure, literally, for centuries. In the old days, farm laborers' smocks would be handed down from father to son to grandson. Ancient smocks can still be seen in museums.

Rita gave me a graphic description of all the stages of flax processing, from pulling the plants—they should not be cut—to "retting" them, that is, allowing them to rot in water or dew; to "scutching," that is fracturing the woody core, and "heckling," that is, combing out the fibers until they become filaments as fine and soft as silk.

The retting process involves fermentation, and the plants, if placed in troughs of water, can become so explosive that they throw off heavy blocks of wood laid on top of them to keep them down. Flax has been described as an "aristocrat" among plants with an imperious will of its own, which influences both the way it is treated and its ultimate use and form. The earliest indications of its use for fabric-making come from the prehistoric Swiss lake villages.

H. J. Massingham was a passionate admirer of traditional craftsmanship, and much of his most inspired writing was devoted to vernacular architecture and the lives and work of country craftsmen and craftswomen who, with grit and determination, managed to maintain their chosen vocations despite the pressures of industrialism. Owing to the disruption of cotton imports during the Second World War, the British government encouraged a revival of flax-growing in the southern counties, and Massingham enthusiastically supported the flax campaign. His masterpiece, *This Plot of Earth,* contains a vivid and memorable description of a flax workshop in Wiltshire, presided over by a friend who shared his sympathetic understanding of craftsmanship and its wider and deeper implications.

In this workshop, with its happy, cooperative family atmosphere—it was mainly staffed by members of the local farming community—utility was integrated with beauty, manufacture with art, mechanical work with field work. Almost all the work relied on manual skills; a few small "Intermediate Technology" machines aided and supported the handwork, but did not supplant or dominate it. Massingham's account is so overwhelmingly attractive as a living preview of work as it should be in a decentralized, ruralize, postindustrial society, that I must quote from it at length.

It was certainly the oddest kind of factory; the people in it moved in a leisurely fashion; they conversed as at a social gathering; they remained individuals; there was nothing automatic in their actions; no hurry; no regimentation and no clock . . . The key to the whole was the Scutching Room . . . I saw the girls scutching (dressing) the flax . . . and noticed something which gave me the clue not only to what kind of factory this was but to the philosophy of life underlying its operations. This was nothing more than a peculiar swing and curve of the arm when the strick of flax was applied to the ends of the lathes attached to the wheels. Some of the girls were doing their scutching better than others and one was doing it superbly. I could not but link this in my mind's eye with two things I had already seen—the curve of the flax-heads in the field and a magnificent round stack in the factory yard. . . .

But the culmination of this strange and beautiful affinity between the way the flax grew in the fields and the way the girls were handling it was when I saw two girls dressing the flax. One of them was the champion at the hand-scutching. I do not pretend to be able to give an impression of this carding of the tresses of the flax between the fingers. The looser gossamer-like strands are teased out, and there is a peculiar turn of the wrist and toss of the arm when they rejoin the cascade of lustrous flax fiber from the other hand. The leveling and evening are done by a caressing motion of the fingers. All I can say is that the action or series of actions was like a figure on a Greek vase. *Noblesse oblige:* the flax itself ordained this art and the genius of the Director had transformed the factory to a gallery where girls made gestures as in a sculpture or painting and quality and skill were the final arbiters . . . The greater the skill, the finer the grace . . .

The wise Director, being a husbandman himself, is fully aware of the organic need for the correlation between field and workshop. He gets the workers out into the fields as often as he can, not only for their *health* but the *wholeness* of this essentially country industry. The steepled flax is set up in parallel lines of sheaves . . . But something more there is. That is the girls moving between the aisles in bright tops and dungarees and turning each steeple so that wind and sun can reach the straw. The action has all the elements of ritualism . . .

With the conviction that all genuine husbandry and craftsmanship are an art like any other, the Director is using . . . the machines to build up a hierarchy of function of which mechanical work shall be the basis and the hand-skills the ultimate purpose . . . This is surely the beginning of man's mastery over the machine without which no civilization can or deserves to survive.

At the northern edge of Wenlock Edge stands the small market town of Much Wenlock, which has been a center of regional culture for some 1,300 years, by virtue of its priory and two remarkable women who made their homes there: St. Milburga, who brought the civilizing influence of Celtic Christianity to much of West Mercia, and Mary Webb, the novelist and poet, whose writings unlocked the heart and springs of Shropshire's deep rurality for millions of people in Britain and abroad. Surviving lists of medieval and Tudor craftsmen and musicians underline the creative vitality of this small town in the past. They include masons, thatchers, dyers, embroiderers, goldsmiths, pewterers, glassmakers, potters, pipers, fiddlers, harpers, drummers, and organists. The wealth of skilled craftsmen in Much Wenlock and other towns and villages in the district was a major factor in the early success of the Industrial Revolution.

The New Town of Telford is being built on the site of the Shropshire coalfield. All the seams had been worked out, and many of the industries associated with it had closed down. The result was a landscape with large areas of derelict semiwilderness, spoil heaps covered with scrub, and extensive stretches of natural woodland. On the southern edge of this landscape, lining the River Severn, are the enormously impressive and multifarious remains of the world's first industrial area, which has been designed by UNESCO as a "World Heritage Site." At the western end of the Gorge, in the town of Coalbrookdale, is a new initiative, masterminded by a dynamic Welshman, Gerwyn Lewis, to manage and make the best possible use of the Telford woodlands. Called the Green Wood Trust, its headquarters occupy the Victorian buildings of Coalbrookdale railway station and an attractive half-timbered building called Rose Cottage. With the motto, "Our feet in the past but our sights on the future," Lewis is reviving a number of traditional woodland crafts, striving to improve their techniques and finding practical outlets for them in tune with the needs and fashions of the present age. In his opinion, the potentialities of the forest have been grossly undervalued. When a forest is felled large quantities of "LOP AND TOP" are simply wasted. These are among the raw materials of the many craft products that Lewis sponsors and whose construction techniques he teaches.

At the center of the station site is a small building that immediately struck me by its unusual beauty. It is a medieval-style "cruck-frame" barn with slatted walls, made from local oak, ash, and sweet chestnut. (In cruck construction the roof is supported, not by the walls, but by two large, curved timbers meeting at a point). Over the doorway is a characteristic piece of traditional Shropshire wood sculpture, showing the "Green Man," a Celtic woodland deity, surrounded by branches and leaves. The barn is used for courses and exhibitions. Among woodland crafts taught or demonstrated at the center are charcoal-burning, the making of chairs, hurdles, bowls, rakes, and spoons, wood sculpture, and the use of the pole-lathe, a very ancient implement powered, not by machinery, but by treadle. The center has also revived a craft going back to prehistoric times, which survived tenuously through the ages in Shropshire and Mid-Wales. This is the making of the coracle, a small, circular, portable boat. I suggested to Gerwyn that coracles might be useful for expeditions exploring forested areas with numerous rivers and streams, like Amazonia, as they could be carried on the back all day long, like rucksacks.

An important long-range aim of the Green Wood Trust is to market do-it-yourself timber-frame house-building kits, which could be assembled by semi-skilled labor, enabling people to build their own homes at a fraction of the cost charged by professional builders, and thus helping to solve the problem of the shortage of low-priced rural housing.

My own osier coppice is cut by the Green Wood Trust every January, and by September some of he new "wands" are fourteen feet high. In the case of other trees, harvesting intervals vary from three to sixty years. "Stools" spread as they grow older, and some in existence today are fifteen feet in diameter; one ash stool in East Anglia is known to be over 1,000 years old. What are believed to be the oldest living things are certain naturally formed stools of southern beech in Tasmania, the result of trees being constantly blown over in gales. Some are reckoned to be 30,000 years old.

Sustainable supplies of timber can also be obtained by the regular cutting of sukers, or root-shoots, from those trees, particularly elm and aspen, which produce them after felling, and by pollarding, which means cutting larger shoots and branches from tree trunks some six to fifteen feet above the ground. These ancient systems of sustained woodland management are far wiser, more economical, and kinder to the environment than the clear-cutting that is commonly practiced today.

At an early period our forebears learned to understand and appreciate the distinct properties and appropriate uses of different types of timber: oak, with its great strength and solidity, for the framework of houses and boats; ash, with its toughness combined with elasticity, for tool handles; sweet chestnut, with its strength and water-resistance, for fencing and gates; lime, with its soft, "cheeselike" texture, for ornamental carving; wild cherry and walnut, with their beautiful graining, for fine furniture; hazel, with its coppicing quality, for "underwood crafts" such as hurdle-making; maple and sycamore, with their relatively nonstaining surfaces, for kitchen utensils.

Birch and elder, scornfully dismissed by present-day foresters as "weed-trees," have in the past been highly regarded for their many uses. In the Scottish Highlands, with their paucity of broad-leaved trees, birch was used for everything, from houses to plows, from mill-wheels to ropes. Its thin, supple, springy twigs are still used for besoms and whisks, while its bark has been used as a substitute for parchment and, by North American Indians, for making canoes. As regards the elder, it has been said to have a wider range of uses than any other temperate plant. While its timber has been used for many small objects, from flutes to the cogs of mill-wheels, its every part is believed to have medicinal value. With typical Teutonic thoroughness, a seventeenth-century German physician devoted a 230-page book to the elder alone.

Knowledge of the properties and uses of woodland plants has not been confined to their potential as timber, fuel, food, or medicine. In the absence of factories and chemicals, our ancestors applied their ingenuity, inventiveness, and powers of observation to finding ways of satisfying all their physical needs from within the natural world. And today, with ever-rising prices and the urge of increasing numbers of people, such as devotees of Permaculture, to adopt ecological, sustainable, nonpolluting lifestyles, many ancient practices are being revived. One can gain a profound, atavistic satisfaction, which penetrates to the very core of one's instinctive being, from finding practical uses for the wild plants, with their fascinating forms and fragrances, which nature—Gaia—provides freely and in such profusion. My living room is adorned with herb rack hanging from the ceiling, and every autumn it is filled with aromatic herbs, which are left throughout the winter to dry, and which, in powdered form, can be added to salads and stews or laid among garments and bedding as moth deterrents. These drying herbs give a delicious and healthful atmosphere to the room.

Healing scents are emitted not only by herbs but also by balsam poplars, of which I have a magnificent specimen in the arboretum, and by the resins that are common to all conifers. Resins consist of two main elements: a volatile oil, turpentine, and a solid, rosin. The function of resins so to block wounds in the trees' bark and thus act as an antiseptic dressing against disease germs and fungi. Turpentine, rosin, and tar are among the products commercially known as "naval stores," a name that goes back to Elizabethan times, when they were used to waterproof wooden ships.

Among many plants much valued by housewives in the past are soapwort, the vegetable detergent, otherwise known as Bouncing Bet, whom Richard Mabey surmises may have been the "archetypal wash-erwoman," and horsetail, a living fossil whose ancestry goes back to the Carbonifeous period 200 million years ago, and which was once used for polishing pots, pans, milk pails—and even suits of armor. This function it was able to perform because the stems and leaves are densely covered with minute crystals of silica. I can testify that horse-tail is an effective substitute for a nylon scourer.

The most hated of "weeds," the stinging nettle, has long been, for countrypeople in the know, one of the most valued of wild plants. Not only is it one of the most nourishing of foods and potent of med-icines, but its fibers can be "retted" like flax and woven into garments and ropes. When Germany ran short of imported cotton during the First World War, enormous quantities of nettles were collected and used to manufacture military uniforms. Rita Acton possesses a piece of nettle lace.

During the Second World War, Sweden found itself largely isolated from external sources of supply, but managed to achieve almost com-plete self-sufficiency, while maintaining a high standard of living, by extremely intelligent and creative application of its forest resources. Factory complexes, powered by wood or wood products and centered on sawmills, turned out textiles, building materials, synthetic rubber, synthetic leather, paints, varnishes, soaps, adhesives, and other essen-tial industrial goods, while a fair proportion of the nation's protein re-quirements was met by torula yeasts nurtured on wood sugar. While millions of Britons subsisted largely on Spam, one of the standard del-icacies of the Swedes' wartime diet was "hamburgers" made of *Cellu-losa-biff*. Motor vehicles of all kinds were adapted to run on wood gen-erators. From the waste sulphite liquors of the pulp industry, twenty-five million gallons of ethyl alcohol were produced per year, most of which were used as motor fuel. The old art of wood distillation was revived to supply motor lubricants. Tar and pitch distilleries supplied a wide range of industrial and even edible oils. By 1944 Sweden's forests were producing practically everything the country had previously imported, except tea and coffee, and it was the only nation in Europe with higher food rations, warmer houses, and more hot baths than in 1941. This wonderful achievement in harnessing and releasing the underexploited resources of the cold northern forests owed much to the vigor, imagination, and tenacity of one man: Eric Lundh, Chief Forester of the Royal Fuel Commission.

*I*n many preindustrial societies craftwork was and is often accompanied, stimulated, and vitalized by work songs. Each craft has its own set of songs, attuned to its special rhythms and designed to alleviate the strain and tedium of labor. The songs, in fact, supply the equivalent of mechanical energy, with the difference that they uplift the singer, raising his or her consciousness above the mundane plane of work, while machinery is often deafening and depressing. The creation of a work song may be described as the transmutation of labor and the often painful forces of nature into a constructive entity on a higher plane, so that the toil and stress are transcended and thereby assuaged.

The region of Britain where work songs were most widely performed was the Outer Hebrides, and the most characteristic and numerous of Hebridean songs were those that accompanied the "waulking" or fulling of the tweed. A group of women would sit at a long table, passing a length of damp cloth from one to another, while tossing, stretching, and thumping it to cause it to shrink. they would perform this arduous task in unison, swinging their bodies to the pulse of an invigorating choral chant. The words were often improvised, bringing in local gossip and sometimes referring to the love affairs of some of the participating girls.

Kenneth Macleod, the well-known Gaelic poet and scholar who collaborated with Marjory Kennedy-Fraser in arranging many of the Songs of the Hebrides, wrote:

> It is hardly necessary to say that the measure and the time of the labor-songs are suited to the special type of work involved. In the spinning-song, for instance, the long-drawn-out and gradually accelerating phrase culminating in a long pause is evoked by the periodic rhythms of the spinning itself. The wool is carded into rolls or "rowans" . . . and the time of the song is determined by the spinner's manipulation of the roll . . . The wheel and the long chorus go merrily together, gradually getting quicker, till the spinner, prolonging a note, stretches out as far as her right hand can reach what remains of the roll, and then . . . runs it through the bobbin.

What, then is the place of hand-craftsmanship in the modern Western world? Why should men and women subject themselves to the mental and physical strain, the intricate discipline, of making homely objects by hand, when it is so easy to buy all that one needs—or that one thinks one needs—at the supermarket or hypermarket, the hardware store, the furniture store, or the "fashion shop?" The answer is twofold, and it goes very deep. Firstly, in our industrial society human beings are subjected to intense and continuous external pressures and above all pressures from the mass media, from advertising. To some people these pressures are almost suffocating and they feel that, at all costs, they must be themselves, they must discover and assert their own identity, they must "do their own thing." This deep biological and psychological urge leads to the road of holistic self-development: that is the development of all sides of one's being, physical, mental, emotional, and spiritual. This is true freedom, true health, true wholeness, but to achieve it considerable and continuous effort is required. As one explores the different sides of one's nature, so they make their different demands. The soul demands emotional fulfillment, the mind intellectual satisfaction, the spirit higher realms of experience, and the hands sensitive creativity. This is the basic reason why people take up crafts; they feel that within their hands are constructive potentialities, which must at all costs be realized, otherwise they will atrophy.

The second factor that leads people to take up crafts is care for the environment. They feel that the manufacture of industrial goods involves pollution and destructiveness, which become ever more intolerable. The answer must be to produce goods that do not involve harmful chemicals and effluents, even if one is obliged to make these goods oneself.

The rewards of creative activity, such as craftsmanship, however much anguish it may at times involve, are immeasurable. The objects that one produces are a source of endless satisfaction, which has nothing to do with mere conceit or self-congratulation.They are emanations from one's inmost being, extensions of oneself, almost like new faculties, new states of consciousness, new limbs. And their creation brings a sense of lasting inward security, of serenity. In his book, *The English Countryman,* H. J. Massingham cites this quality of serenity as a common characteristic of all the village craftsmen he had known. Writing of the period of the Second World War, he says, "They are survivors into an alien new world which takes no account of them at all, or, if it does, only as museum pieces" and he adds:

> To be men of inward peace and balance in such circumstances
> calls for a toughness of spiritual fiber capable of sustaining no
> small degree of stress and tribulation. This equanimity of temper,
> exceeding rare in an age of schizophrenia, is conferred upon them
> by the nature of their work and their intimate contact with Nature
> herself. It is not insensibility but poise and, if it owes something to
> inheritance, still more to lack of frustration, more yet to con-
> sciousness of service and even more to the small green world in
> which they live, it owes most of all to an attunement with the will
> of Creation itself.

A writer quoted by Massingham in *The Curious Traveler* says, "No higher wage, no income, will buy for men that satisfaction which of old—until machinery made drudges of them—streamed into their muscles all day long from close contact with iron, timber, clay, wind and wave, horse strength. It tingled up in the niceties of touch, sight, scent. The very ears unawares received it."

In the same book Massingham speaks with warmth and respect of a Cotswold couple who had achieved a full and rounded self-sufficient existence devoted to craftwork combined with organic horticulture. Both were spinners and weavers, while the man was also an expert wood-turner. His aim was for the whole craft of textile-making to be the work of a single individual. "Wholeness can only be accomplished by the worker controlling and literally having a hand in every process of his work, from the raw material to the finished article."

In this he was of one mind with Gandhi, who founded his system of Basic Education, "education for living," on practical experience of the making of cotton fabrics, from the sowing of the seed to the completion of a garment. To Gandhi the spinning-wheel was a symbol of self-sufficiency, of freedom from exploitation and oppression. Wilfred Wellock, in *Gandhi as a Social Revolutionary*, writes:

Basic Education is a process of learning through doing. It recognizes the organic connection between the fingers, the senses and the mind, and the greater vitality and retentiveness of knowledge that is gained by doing and making things than by merely reading books or listening to lectures.

In the exercise of all man's powers in purposive, social living, which is essentially cooperative living, Gandhi discovered a unifying principle by which the human person might become a whole person, who must be the foundation of integrated families, integrated communities, and of a peaceful world.

11

Agroforestry Against World Want

*Until very recently, archeologists considered the forest people of Amazo-
nia to be descendants of the Clovis culture, big-game hunters who, it was
assumed, had migrated south from the open lands of North America.
Now it appears that an independent culture developed in the Brazilian
Amazon around 11,000 years ago. At one site, Caverna da Pedra Pintada
(Cave of the Painted Rock), there is evidence that Paleoindian peoples
lived comfortably and harmoniously for at least 1,200 years—fishing,
hunting, and foraging for fruits and nuts in the rain forest.*

*Some 10,000 years later, we have forgotten the lessons these ancient hu-
mans knew so well. Managed intelligently, the forest can provide for many
of our needs. Today, the standard agribusiness scheme for feeding the
world's expanding population is to plow up more land, apply more chemicals, and introduce more super-hybrids and bioengineered crops. A wiser
course would be to look to Kerala, India's most densely populated state,
whose people have managed to feed and support themselves abundantly,
on marginal agricultural land, by cultivating 3.5 million forest gardens.*

*We should be concerned about overpopulation, of course, but not be-
cause the Earth is "played out" and can no longer support and sustain
us. We are clearly making use of nature's bounty in the wrong way—
using resources as if we were a much smaller race.*

The best answers to Third World problems can generally be found in
the Third World itself. Its people have vast reserves of skill, resourcefulness, creativity, inventiveness, energy, survival techniques, and will to

win, of which most Westerners seem largely unaware. But since many Western aid schemes, notably the "Green Revolution" and a number of big dams, have proved costly failures, an increasing number of relief workers and agronomists have, from the mid-1970s onwards, been taking a close scientific interest in indigenous methods. When asked to solve the problems of a particular valley, far-sighted administrators have learned to turn, not to Western mechanical and chemical know-how, but to systems practiced in the next valley.

Of course this does not mean that Western expertise in many fields has no role to play in tackling the Third World's colossal and multifarious problems. In the realm of forestry one name must stand out, that of a man of enormous energy and all-encompassing vision, who foreshadowed and inspired the present worldwide Green movement, and even shared Gandhi's convictions linking a postindustrial society with lasting peace. This man was Richard St. Barbe Baker, who, as a young forester in 1922, founded the Men of the Trees in Kenya, a country that is now playing a leading role in tree-planting and which holds the headquarters of the International Council for Research in Agroforestry.

In his book, *My Life My Trees,* St. Barbe describes the devastation of the forests in the Kenya highlands caused by nomadic herdsmen, land-hungry white farmers, and logging contractors. The young forester's response was to demarcate a wide area and get it designated as a forest reserve. With the cooperation of a man who was to be his lifelong friend and colleague, the Kikuyu chief Josiah Njonjo, St. Barbe had thousands of indigenous trees planted between rows of grain and yams—an agroforestry system. At the same time he started Kenya's first large tree nursery, planting olives in conjunction with Mutarakwa cedars, an association found in the natural forest. Thus, from the first, as he admitted, St. Barbe took advantage of the local tradition of mixed cropping.

Later St. Barbe became responsible for the sustainable development of mahogany rain forests in Nigeria, where he observed another example of plant symbiosis:

Each mahogany is surrounded by numerous trees belonging to other families, amongst which is that important family of Leguminosae—the soil improvers. These I have observed to be good nurse trees for the mahoganies. The more important species of mahogany require the services of a succession of nurse trees throughout their life to bring them to perfection. Some of these provide just sufficient competition to coax the young sapling upwards. Others do their work in secret under the surface of the soil, interlacing the roots, a sort of symbiosis, like the mycelium, which starts as an independent weblike growth, surrounds the sheath of plant rootlets and prepares food that can be assimilated by the growing trees.

In the 1950s and 1960s St. Barbe undertook two extensive expeditions through and around the Sahara, and put forward a breathtaking plan for the reclamation of the world's largest desert by progressive tree-planting.

In their foreword to St. Barbe's book, *Sahara Conquest,* John Hutchings and Knut H. Scharnhorst write:

This outstanding book introduces us—in a bold yet down-to-earth manner—to a new way of thinking. Against the somber background of a worldwide population explosion with its serious food problems the author calls for immediate, concerted efforts to restore to the world in general and to the Sahara in particular, the potential productiveness of abused and abandoned land. Man must stop defying the laws governing him in his relations to Nature, especially the basic law of balances. Instead, the nations must adopt and adapt the principles of ecology in dealing with human problems. This goes—in the author's opinion—not only for reforestation but, logically, also for reduction of animal husbandry to adequate proportions. Never has ecology had a more objective and articulate spokesman than in Richard St. Barbe Baker, who also more than any other Westerner loves Africa and her people.

. . .

Cooperation on a large, international scale, such as Mr. Baker invites in the case of the Sahara, would go far to change the political climate of the nations. Just as Mr. Baker's reclamation plan envisages the creation of microclimates in the Sahara, which will eventually coalesce into a beneficial climate over the whole area, so will the total African venture in itself act like a microclimate, which will gradually expand to the whole of our fractious and contending planet.

What is here presented is not just an abstract scheme proposed by a poet dreamer (though the author is indeed a poet). It is the plan of a practical forester, who has spent his life in the pursuit and study of his subject from every technical point of view, who has traveled the world over and who has seen for himself the cancerous condition in which the surface of our planet finds itself...

Mr. Baker is an acknowledged world authority, who can point to huge areas reclaimed or saved by his inspiration and who here assures us that with up-to-date knowledge and modern techniques a million square miles of the Sahara can now be reclaimed. In a sorely perplexed world, this book is a sweeping Charter of Sanity that points the way to sound prosperity, well-being and peace, not only for the Uniting States of the Sahara, but for all of us.

In fact St. Barbe did not put forward a detailed program but encouraged the Saharan states that he visited to proceed with schemes best suited to their individual talents, policies, and resources. He was particularly impressed by large-scale desert colonization schemes being pioneered by Egypt, one of which involved five-acre family orange groves with leguminous crops such as peanuts and cowpeas growing beneath the trees.

While water for some of the projects was provided by irrigation channels from the Nile, in other cases wells were sunk, some of depths as great as 3,600 feet. Ancient wells, some going back to Roman and pre-Roman times, were discovered and opened up. There is said to be an underground sea the size of France beneath the Sahara. This could doubtless be made available for irrigation by modern oil-drilling techniques.

The remains of ancient civilizations have been found near the center of the Sahara. Their water supplies must have been ensured by the presence of forests, but when these were cut down and regeneration made impossible by browsing animals, the water table, maintained by the trees' roots, would have sunk to great depths.

St. Barbe's vision of a Green Belt round the Sahara was revived at an exhibition in London in October 1989, sponsored by a number of relief agencies. The exhibition did not envisage an endeavor to plant a continuous shelterbelt round the desert's entire perimeter, but a mosaic of protective zones, comprising forests of drought-resistant trees and crops, which would eventually merge.

Innumerable forms of land use practiced in Africa, Asia, and Latin America, whether traditional or extemporized, have agroforestry characteristics. It is being increasingly recognized that symbiotic systems, involving the integration of trees with other crop plants, constitute a vast and complex subject of study, which contains the seeds of a comprehensive new-old technology for meeting all basic human physical needs.

Paul Harrison in *The Greening of Africa* praises "the resourcefulness and energy of Africa's farmers" and adds:

There is here a tremendous untapped potential for rapid innovation . . . Africa's peasants, in my experience, are among the most inventive and adaptable in the world. They have to be, because they are dealing with the most varied and unpredictable environment in the world. They are always open to new varieties, even new crops, that can make the best of their limited resources . . . British anthropologist Paul Richards has shown that traditional farmers, untouched by conventional development projects, select and breed their own improved varieties, carefully adapted to the needs of their location . . . In no other continent is there such a diversity of farming methods . . . They have developed dozens of ways of molding the soil, planting sometimes in ridges and mounds in wet areas to improve drainage, sometimes in furrows and hollows in dry areas, to collect scarce water.

Patterns of intercropping are even more diverse. In northern Nigeria as many as 156 separate crop combinations have been observed.

In southeastern Nigeria, to meet the challenge of one of Africa's most densely populated areas, a sophisticated system of forest gardening has been developed. "Compound farms," some very small, are established in the immediate vicinity of homesteads. A very wide diversity of trees, bushes, and other crop plants are grown, designed to meet all the basic needs of the farmers and their families: fruits; vegetables (including perennial tree vegetables); timber for building, staking, and fencing; fuel; fertilizers; leaf wrappers; medicines; fibers for ropes, stuffing mattresses, and thatching; calabashes for containers; charcoal; wood for tool handles; snake repellents; gums; dyes; kitchen utensils; spices; and water purifiers. Many of the trees are used for multiple purposes. So sophisticated and complex is the "architecture" of some of the gardens that as many as nine distinct "stories" have been counted: from high emergent coconut and oil palms to medium-sized trees such as breadfruit and pear and lower trees such as mango, orange, and lime. On a still lower level grow papaya and bananas, with pepper bushes occupying the shrub layer. Maize and vegetables constitute the herbaceous layer, while melons, peanuts, and other horizontally spreading plants cover the ground, and root vegetables occupy the rhizosphere. The vertical dimension is formed by yam vines trained up trees. The genetic diversity of the plants makes the gardens important as germplasm banks, supplying replacements for genes lost as a result of forest destruction. The system, which is believed to have originated 1,000 years ago, and so has been tried and tested over the centuries, could serve as a model for many other parts of Africa—and the world. People who have evolved and are prepared to maintain such a complicated system must be determined to survive at all costs!

Another forest garden system with more commercial implications has been developed by the Chagga people of Tanzania amid glorious scenery on the slopes of Mount Kilimanjaro. The special sophistication of this system lies in the network of skillfully aligned irrigation channels designed to make full use of the melting snows. The network, which is very complicated, is managed cooperatively by all the smallholders and is so arranged that each one gets his fair share.

The Chaggas were originally members of a number of different tribes who, over a century ago, moved into the dense montane rain forest on the lower slopes of the great mountain, which covers an area of more than 3,000 square kilometers (1,170 square miles), and rises to 5,895 meters (19,340 feet) above sea level. (When the first missionaries reported seeing a snow-capped mountain just south of the Equator, their superiors refused to believe them.) The pioneer Chagga settlers refrained from felling the larger and more valuable trees in the forest, but planted bananas and other fruit and vegetables in their shade. Now the individual plots, which average 0.68 hectares (1.7 acres) in size, each one maintaining a family of about ten people, generally have a seven-story structure. At the top are the tall timber trees, including teak, of the natural forest. In their shade grow shorter trees, providing fuel and fodder. Lower still is the fruit story, mainly comprising bananas but including other fruit and fodder trees as well. Next comes the coffee layer, which also includes some medicinal plants. The herbaceous layer comprises vegetables such as beans, cabbages, cowpeas, onions, and tomatoes, as well as maize, and also young saplings of native species that have been allowed to survive. The rhizosphere is occupied by potatoes, taro, and other root crops, while a vertical dimension is created by yams, which are trained up trees.

Over a hundred different species are grown, supplying most of the families' personal needs throughout the year, as well as bananas and coffee, which are sold as cash crops. The Chagga area contributes more than fifty percent of Tanzania's coffee output and therefore makes an important contribution to the country's GNP. The most valuable products are the choice timber trees.

An intensely interesting feature of the system, which deserves scientific research, is that a number of plants are grown for their symbiotic qualities, in repelling nematodes and other pests. Chemicals are seldom used.

Great expertise is shown in managing the system, as the smallholders have an intimate knowledge of all the plants and their ecological requirements. For example, when the time is ripe, the canopy is opened out to facilitate the fruiting of the coffee bushes, while each banana clump is pruned to ensure that it has three to five pseudostems of different ages, thus making for continuous harvesting. Young timber trees are grown in close proximity to other plants to encourage straight stems with few branches. The wide diversity of very carefully chosen plants is an insurance policy against both epidemics and crop failures. If one crop fails, another is likely to be a resounding success.

Tenure of each forest garden, or *vihamba*, is hereditary, and is based on a very strong conviction that a close link exists between a person's ancestors and the soil. Traditionally the land was divided only between the deceased owner's sons, but now the daughters are included. Each family, also has another plot, called a *kishamba*, held by annual tenancy, in the plains. These plots are mainly used for annual crops, though a few trees are grown in them, mainly for fuel.

This combination of upland and lowland husbandry reminds me of a system that I found operating in the Val d'Anniviers in Switzerland. There, dairy farming was the main occupation in the mountains, while each family also had a share in a vineyard in the Rhone Valley. At the beginning of spring all the men marched down to the valley to work in the vineyards, carrying their hoes and headed by a fife band, leaving the women to look after the cattle.

Another very interesting forest garden system in a mountainous rain forest area is that of Maninjau, an extinct volcano on the island of Sumatra. the setting is dramatic in the extreme: steep mountainsides clothed with remnants of primeval forest sloping down to a volcanic lake, subject to dangerous landslides and violent storms.

Just as the inhabitants of Saxon England left patches of virgin forest undisturbed close to their villages, to supply them with timber, herbs, and other necessities, so the inhabitants of Maninjau build their villages around tongues of natural rain forest. Above the 900-meter line is a large state-run forest reserve, from which the villagers are forbidden to collect wood and rattans (creepers). In the buffer zone between the forest and villages are the majority of the forest gardens, though smaller homegardens surround many of the houses. In these the villagers plant their most valued fruit trees, for security reasons. The villagers also cultivate rice in permanent irrigated fields at the bottom of the slopes and by the lakeside. The land in general is owned communally by the clan.

The forest gardens are densely planted with a wide diversity of trees and other deep-rooting perennials, to guard against landslides and erosion. Annual vegetables and maize are grown beneath the trees and also in the ricefields, between harvests. All the gardens are dominated by six specially favored trees and bushes: durian, cinnamon, nutmeg, coffee, *Pterospermum javanicum* (a large timber tree commonly grown in association with durian), and *Toona sinensis,* (a medium-sized timber tree regarded as particularly suitable as a shade tree for nutmeg and coffee). At the head of all these trees in local preference must come the durian, whose large, spiny fruits are loved by millions of people in Southeast Asia but detested by others for their sewage-like smell. Appropriately enough, durian rinds are used for manuring coffee bushes, which, together with nutmeg trees, are often grown beneath the shade of the durian trees. Among other fruit grown or collected from the wild are bananas, papayas, guavas, mulberries, mangoes, and mangosteens. Many bamboos are grown both for their edible shoots and for construction purposes. The peasants have an intimate knowledge of their plants' ecological and cultural requirements. Almost all the work is done using family labor; very little machinery and no chemical fertilizers are used. The whole system is highly stable and sustainable, and yet readily adaptable to changing needs and economic conditions. To counter the unreliability and fluctuations of market demands for the cash crops—coffee, cinnamon, and nutmeg—the peasants maintain a solid nucleus of subsistence crops, so they are never obliged to go short of necessities.

As in the case of other forest garden systems, the wide diversity of home-bred and semiwild species provides a gene bank which is potentially of great value for plant breeders in other parts of the world, who find many sources of supply dried up by the destruction of the natural forests.

That the rain forest peoples should be allowed to survive and develop in their own indigenous ways, aided and supported by legitimate, constructive types of Western technology, mostly in its "intermediate" or "alternative" forms, is of importance to us all. One American psychologist, Jean Liedloff, has even created a system of psychology and child care which she calls *The Continuum Concept,* based on several years' intimate contact with the Ye'cuana, a tribe of Amazonian Indians. Briefly, the Continuum Concept describes the security derived from the extension of maternal protectiveness and stimulus, which has been the main biological means responsible for the evolution of the higher animals and human beings, into the sphere of communal living. The autonomous village community, which is the highest unit of Ye'cuana society, is the solid, supportive matrix within which almost all activity takes place. In an emergency, any member of the community can rely on the wholehearted aid and support of the rest. Social responsibility rather than competitiveness characterizes the whole of Ye'cuana life, and, as everyone, from earliest childhood, is expected to act altruistically without compulsion, unbroken harmony is the general rule.

The forest community is so deeply embedded in its environment that it conforms to the laws of its ecosystem as implicitly as do the animals and plants. Peter Bunyard in *The Colombian Amazon* writes:

The dynamic of the forest and the interchange of matter between one species and another, including that of life-force, provides the Indians with a ready model of their own existence within the community of the *maloca* (communal house). Hence the local economy both within the community and with neighboring communities relies heavily on the principle of exchange and reciprocity both within themselves as human beings and with nature . . . Gerardo Reichel-Dolmatoff has good evidence that the rituals and beliefs of the Indians of the eastern part of the Colombian Amazon are based solidly on their conscious experience of how the ecosystem works and is an attempt to reflect that natural functioning within their own cosmologies.

A dominant feature of all true, unspoiled forest peoples is a respect for the environment, amounting sometimes to religious reverence, based on intimate, inherited understanding of its flora and fauna, its processes and rhythms. The Yanomani of the Amazon rain forest, the largest unacculturated tribe in the Americas, have an amazingly varied diet and pharmacopoeia derived from both wild and cultivated sources. While they collect more than 500 different wild plants, including many fruits, they also clear small areas in the forest, called *chagras,* in which they create temporary but highly diversified forest gardens. These, after a short time, they allow to become overgrown, in order to restore the fertility of the thin rain forest soils, while they move on to clear other patches. The forest gardens thus become constituents of the forest ecosystem, which is thereby enriched, becoming even more productive of economically valuable plants.

The Ye'cuana village community apportions its cultivating and foraging area into a number of distinct zones. Immediately around the village or *maloca* lies the forest garden, in which they plant their favorite fruit trees, such as peach palm, papaya, pear, mango, lemon, and *maraco,* a kind of cacao. Next comes the nearby forest, from which the people reckon to collect some 170 different species of wild plants, not only for food but also for timber, fuel, medicines, utensils, and dyes. In this and the more distant forested areas are found sites destined for *chagras* as well as *rastrojos*, abandoned forest gardens in various stages of regeneration, which are still visited for their surviving fruit trees. There are also various wetland areas, including *cananguchales*, permanently or seasonally flooded, which contain a tree called *canangucho*, which is much prized for its fruit.

The Baka of the Central African rain forest divide their lives into settled periods, when they do some cultivation, and a nomadic phase, which begins with the onset of the rainy season and the fruiting of the wild mango tree. Their camps comprise small igloo-shaped huts woven by the women from wild saplings and thatched with large leaves.

One of the supreme benefits that the human race could gain from the rain forest, which in many countries is being so ruthlessly destroyed, is an immense expansion and diversification of its diet. As present the vast majority of the world's population suffer from inadequate nutrition. There is the malnutrition of poverty and the malnutrition of affluence. While hundreds of millions of people eat too little, tens of millions eat too much of the wrong foods. Comparatively few people consume sufficient quantities of the two basic essentials for all-round, lasting, positive health: raw green leaves and fresh fruit. Moreover, if one is to be sure of obtaining all the desirable vitamins, enzymes, minerals, and other nutrients, a widely varied diet is needed. For this reason, a far-ranging program of nutritional research should be undertaken into the foods consumed by the Yanomani and other forest people who are experts on the environment. At the same time there are numerous neglected food plants in the comparatively species-poor temperate regions. Also, we should not forget that *every variety* of common fruits such as the apple, plum, pear, raspberry, and gooseberry has a different biochemical constitution, and therefore contains different trace elements. As a very limited number of varieties are obtainable in the shops, and most of these have been sprayed and grown with chemical fertilizers, everyone with a garden of any size should endeavor to grow a few of the noncommercial varieties, which are generally superior in flavor to shop fruit. This is why I grow a wide diversity of fruit and nut trees, including uncommon ones, such as *Sorbus* species and the azerole, an edible hawthorn.

Forest gardening, in the sense of finding uses for and attempting to control the growth of wild plants, is undoubtedly the oldest form of land use in the world. One of the newest is "alley-cropping," a form of agroforestry developed during the 1970s and 1980s by B. T. Kang, an Indonesian soil scientist, and his colleagues at the International Institute of Tropical Agriculture in Ibadan, Nigeria. It was an attempt to find answers to two problems: soil erosion on sloping ground, and the acidification and impoverishment of the soil, which are the long-range results of using chemical fertilizers. The system that Kang and his colleagues came up with involved the growing of cereals and vegetables crops in narrow strips between hedgerows of leguminous trees. The trees, with their deep roots, prevent erosion, and with their nitrogen-fixing ability fertilize the crops. They are regularly and heavily pruned to prevent them from shading the crops, the prunings being used as mulch to suppress weeds, as stakes or firewood, or as fodder to be fed to livestock. Hedgerows planted along the contours of sloping ground accumulate lose soil, and in time a series of terraces develops.

The trees must be fast-growing, and among those that have proved most satisfactory are *Leucaena leucocephala,* a native of southern Mexico, otherwise known as ipil-ipil or subabul; *Calliandra calothyrsus,* a small Central American tree with showy flowers resembling crimson powderpuffs; and *Sesbania grandiflora,* a very valuable multipurpose tree from Asia with large white or wine-red flowers that have been described as "vegetable hummingbirds!" Philistine though it may seem, these flowers, which are rich in sugar, are sold in many Asian markets for food—they are said to taste like mushrooms. Sesbania pods are eaten like runner beans and the seeds, among the richest in protein of all legumes, are dried and eaten like soybeans. The leaves, which are also rich in protein as well as vitamins and minerals, are eaten as spinach. In traditional agroforestry the tree is used as a support for pepper and vanilla vines.

Bill Mollison told me that sesbania roots are so powerful that he has seen the tree used for reclaiming rock-hard lateritic soils. Leucaena, another tree with an aggressive taproot that can shatter rocks, and which is also amazingly fast-growing, has, in numerous field trials, proved the most satisfactory hedgerow tree for alley-cropping. Crop yields are not reduced but increased in its neighborhood. It was a favorite tree of the Maya and Zapotec civilizations of Mexico and Central America, in whose area traditional forest gardens, which doubtless owe their origin to those civilizations, are still found.

Following the successful Nigerian field trials, alley-cropping has spread to other parts of Africa, Indonesia, the Philippines, India, and Sri Lanka.

Leguminous plants should be an essential constituent of all agroforestry/permaculture schemes in every habitable part of the world, because of their value as companion plants, giving fertility to their neighbors. The fruits and seeds of many leguminous plants are sources of the first-class protein in which many Third World diets are deficient. It is true that some pulses contain toxins, but reliable methods have been developed over the centuries of detoxifying them. These include boiling them and throwing away the water, and also various forms of fermentation practiced in the Far East, which have resulted in products well known in Western health-food stores, such as tofu, tamari, soymilk and soy cheese. In fact, soybeans have been among the main sources of protein for thousands of years in China, Japan, and Korea, areas where livestock farming is far less widespread than in the West.

As many leguminous plants are fast-growing, they can provide a regular source of fuel and biomass energy. One of the most heartrending human tragedies in many parts of the arid tropics is the long and grueling journeys that millions of women have to take, week in and week out, to fetch firewood from ever-receding and dwindling patches of woodland. In parts of the Himalayas women have been known to fall to their death out of sheer exhaustion. But leguminous trees exist that can flourish in the most arid and even heavily salinated soils, as well as in rock crevices on mountainsides with no visible soil. So there is no reason why leguminous trees should not be grown in abundance in all deprived areas, to provide fuel for cooking, lighting, and heating, thus releasing women from the chore of firewood-gathering and enabling them to use their talents and energies in more creative ways: bringing up their children and practicing the crafts in which many of them excel.

In order fully to understand agroforestry/permaculture at its best, as illustrated by the tropical forest garden systems I have described, it is essential to appreciate that it involves skilled craftsmanship—and more. The task of creating balanced relationships, rhythms, and patterns of growth demands intuitive, aesthetic qualities, comparable to those that lie behind the exquisite artifacts—textiles, pottery, metalwork, carvings—produced in many countries of the Third World.

A tropical rain forest is a supreme and infinitely varied work of art, but, with a touch of human genius, it can be converted into a forest garden system, even more beautiful and vastly more productive. That is why it is not enough merely to campaign for the preservation of the rain forest. It is a compound resource of potentially enormous value to humankind as a whole, if developed—not devastated—in a wise, constructive, sustainable way. Its vast diversity of vegetation, up to now so inadequately studied by science, could be used as a source of new and nourishing foods, of timber for building and crafts, of fibers and dyes for textiles, of medicines, of biomass for energy, of gums, resins, and plastics, to meet almost all human needs, above all the basic soul-need of beauty.

Wagner in his operas strove to achieve a *Gesamtkunstwerk*, a total work of art. A forest garden, replete with fruit and foliage, blooms, birds and insects, mammals and fungi, fascinating scents and sounds, can be a work of art comparable to any of humankind's highest cultural attainments.

The new but also age-old technology involved constitutes a safe, sustainable, nonpolluting and above all profoundly practical answer to the technology developed since the Industrial Revolution, which, despite the many benefits conferred, is now inflicting ever greater and more unacceptable damage on the environment. The new technology has very deep roots in the hereditary manual skills, which, above all in the Far East, have enabled workers to adapt to the stringent demands of the most advanced and intricate forms of "hi-tech." This new technology must be developed so that it can help to lead humankind into a safer, kinder, calmer, and more peaceful postindustrial age.

12

~

Green Is Real

In A Short History of the Printed Word, *Warren Chappell quotes the Spanish philosopher José Ortega y Gasset, who wrote in 1930 that "the mass-man took the civilization into which he was born as a matter of course, 'as spontaneous and self-producing as Nature'. This, claimed Ortega, made a primitive of him, with civilization his forest."*

In other words, we citizens of "developed" nations are not so very different from the world's "primitive" peoples, and we probably resemble our ancient ancestors much more than we usually recognize. This fact gives us an opportunity to celebrate our common humanity and attempt to strip away the outward distractions of civilization, to understand who we truly are and what we need to fulfill ourselves and strengthen our society.

From the example of the forest garden, it is only a short step to the forest village—which could serve as a model for the Green Age to come. This village may resemble an exemplary, self-reliant rural hamlet—and Robert Hart offers many examples in this chapter—but we can also think of transforming our cities into "villages." Cities of the future would produce most of their food locally, and neighborhoods would once again be socially cohesive, safe, and vital places, with jobs and homes and shops mixed together. This may sound like a dream, but it is a dream that is within our reach.

*I*n *The Great U-Turn,* Edward Goldsmith describes how the Industrial Revolution has transformed the "real" world of forests, fields, orchards, gardens, rocks, rivers, and lakes, which, until the last two centuries, satisfied almost all human physical needs and enabled human beings to attain the highest peaks of cultural achievement, into a "surrogate" or artificial world of cities, factories, motorways, and airports. He then goes on to suggest various steps by which this surrogate world could be "deindustrialized."

In putting forward a skeleton program of action, Goldsmith emphasizes that "it must be designed to reverse all the essential trends set in motion by the industrial process." The first stage, he maintains, must be to develop a new world-view to replace the "aberrant worldview of industrialism," in order to see how its basic principles may be "modified to give rise to an adaptive and hence stable social behavior pattern." After enumerating and refuting these principles as humanism, individualism, materialism, scientism, technologism, institutionalism, and economism, Goldsmith concludes: "For economism must be substituted ecologism, the notion that things must be done to satisfy not a single end but all the basic, and often competing requirements of the community and its natural environment."

Goldsmith's second stage is a shift from "capital intensive industry" to developing the "appropriate" technology for decentralized living. His third is "the transformation of society" so that it would once more be composed of people who are, above all, members of families, communities, and ecosystems, and whose behavior is basically that which satisfies the requirements of these systems and hence of "the larger system of which they are a part, the biosphere." His fourth is to "reverse the system of capital generation by means of the production-consumption process, until the need for capital is reduced. The fifth and sixth stages of his deindustrializing process are "reducing the scale of the production process and producing goods that are ever less destructive to the natural environment" and "reducing the scale of technological activities to permit the restoration of the self-regulating social systems which make up the real world."

Goldsmith also proposes the formation of a Restoration Corps, recruited from the ranks of the unemployed, to "clean up the mess left by a century and a half of industrialization—restore derelict land, replant hedgerows, restore forests, clean up tips where poisonous waste threatens groundwater reserves."

Some of these aims would be fulfilled by the implementation of a Community Forest program that has been put forward by Britain's Countryside Commission and Forestry Commission. In July 1989 these two national bodies launched a program to establish twelve new forests on the fringes of large urban areas in England and Wales. Also an extensive new forest is to be planted in the Midlands and another between Edinburgh and Glasgow. By the turn of the century it is hoped that every major city and town in Britain will have its own community forest. Many areas of industrial dereliction and abandoned farmland will be restored to something of their pristine beauty, with innumerable trees, flower-filled glades, lakes, clear streams, and abundant wildlife. While some commercial forestry will be undertaken, lessening Britain's present overwhelming dependence on imported timber, and some farming and market gardening will continue, the main aim of the new forests will be to provide leisure and recreation facilities for town-dwellers, such as open-air concerts, plays, art exhibitions, and sporting events.

Any initiative that involves large-scale tree-planting must be warmly welcomed, but to what extent will the new community forests further the aims of a Green Society? In their primary role as "amenity areas," the forests will be regarded as marginal to the "real" world of industry, commerce, and finance. But in the opinion of Edward Goldsmith and the vast majority of members of the Green-Alternative movement, that is not the real but the "surrogate" world. The real world is Green. But how real is real, and how Green must we be in order to be realistic?

To my mind, the basic criterion must be *responsibility*. The Green world is the responsible world. It recognizes that the basis of all life is the miracle of the green leaf. The green pigment, chlorophyll, is the only substance on earth that is capable of harnessing the energy of the sun to create living matter. Moreover, the green leaf absorbs carbon dioxide, the principal cause of the greenhouse effect, and exhales oxygen, without which no living organism can exist for more than a few minutes.Therefore our first duty to all life is to preserve as much greenness as possible and to promote an ever-increasing abundance of green growth. Industrial society, on the other hand, is essentially hostile to greenery. It kills it with its acid rain, it buries it beneath layers of concrete, it burns and bulldozes it out of existence. Therefore measures to ameliorate the colossal harm that it does are not enough. For the sake of all life, we must at all costs progress as speedily as possible towards a postindustrial society, which will meet the majority of its physical needs from the infinite and largely unexplored potentialities of the Green world.

In the Third World two prophet-pioneers, little known in the West, have, for many years, been waging a series of truly heroic struggles to build Green, just, and compassionate societies, dedicated to the development of whole human beings. They are Murlidhar Devidas Amte, known to millions of Indians as "Baba"—Father—and Ahangamage Tudor Ariyaratne, known to millions of Sri Lankans as "Ari." Both are disciples of Mahatma Gandhi, which means that they are totally and constructively nonviolent in their methods, though both have frequently been obliged to confront conflict situations. Amte's greatest achievement so far has been Anandwan, a large ad mainly self-supporting community in Central India, comprising sufferers from leprosy and other severe handicaps, most of whom have attained a surprising degree of self-fulfillment by acquiring manual and intellectual skills.

Anandwan started in a forest and is now restoring its tree cover in the form of a large and thriving agroforestry research project and what must be the largest forest garden in the world—comprising 25,000 trees!

The foundations of Anandwan were laid in 1950 when Amte applied to his state government for a grant of land to start a leprosy rehabilitation center, and was allocated fifty acres of stony jungle infested with tigers, wild boars, poisonous snakes, and giant scorpions. With a mixture of indomitable courage and cynical humor he named it

Anandwan—"Garden of Bliss!" With his young wife Sadhana, two baby sons, six leprosy victims, and a lame cow, he set to work to convert this forbidding area into a model farm. And, astonishingly, within two years he succeeded. The little colony was self-sufficient in food except for sugar, salt, and oil. Crop yields were three times the local average. From then on progress was rapid. The state government gave Amte another 200 acres, patients flocked in and helped to build workshops, homes, a dairy, and a flour mill. In 1964 patients and cured leprosy sufferers demonstrated the effectiveness of their acquired skills by building a college for 1,400 students from the local town.

Over the years Anandwan has thrown out a number of offshoots, all in difficult areas and all demanding the highest human qualities from the handicapped people who participated in their reclamation. Most difficult of all was a remote expanse of rain forest inhabited by a "Stone Age" aboriginal tribe, the Madia-Gonds. It is a country of wide, crocodile-infested rivers, cut off from the rest of India for seven months of the year by flooding. Amte had first visited the area on a lone trek at the age of fourteen, and he had fallen in love with its high-spirited, fun-loving, generous, honest people. Forty-five years later he returned with his elder son Vikas, a trained doctor, and was appalled to find how their condition had deteriorated. Following contacts with "civilization," malnutrition, malaria, tuberculosis, and leprosy were rife. Baba and Vikas established a small clinic and traveled round the area, treating the sick. The following year their work was taken over by Amte's younger son Prakash, a surgeon who shares his father's adventurous and dedicated spirit, as does his wife Mandakini, an anesthetist. After twelve years, with the aid of volunteers, the young couple have set up a hospital, several health centers, a project for training aborigines as "barefoot doctors" on the Chinese model—and a zoo for orphan animals!

But in the early 1980s a new threat to the tribal people's very existence appeared in the form of proposals to build a series of giant dams that would submerge large areas of the forest, which is their main life-support system. Mainly involved is the Narmada, one of India's sacred rivers. After campaigning, so far in vain, to halt the proposals, Amte decided to devote himself entirely to putting forward constructive counterproposals to develop the area primarily in the interests of the local inhabitants. In a booklet entitled *Cry the Beloved Narmanda*, he outlined a strategy for replacing the proposed irrigation and power-generating schemes with alternative systems more beneficial to the environment, the local people, and India as a whole. Among his suggestions are: agroforestry; improved dry farming methods, including strip-cropping and intercropping; erosion-control measures; water-harvesting techniques; and numerous small hydroelectric stations.

Having left his beloved Anandwan to dedicate himself wholly to this new venture, the running of the community remains in the capable hands of Sadhana and Vikas, who are developing a number of projects, especially involving renewable energy and agroforestry, which they hope will make the whole vast enterprise into a model for the new India. In 1990 Vikas traveled to London to accept, on his father's behalf, a prize for religious achievement. In his address of thanks, Baba wrote:

At Anandwan we, outcasts living with outcasts, have built a world which embraces all who wish to come and join. A world where you do not stand alone, where you belong to others who belong to you . . . Where those rejected by an unconcerned and uncomprehending world realize their own worth with their own hands . . . These rivers, these forests, these forms of life—we have not inherited them from our forefathers, we have borrowed them from our children yet to be born. Their preservation, their enrichment is the solemn responsibility we bear.

Today I have become part of the battle to save the Narmada . . . there is a plan to build thirty massive damns on the river, which will destroy an entire civilization that has grown in the Narmada valley . . . The battle is not to save the Narmada alone. The larger goal is to bring the message of Mother Earth to the whole world.

To stop the process of destructive development and to ring in this new vision—of a new way of being in the world.

A similar all-embracing vision inspires Dr. Ariyaratne (Ari) of Sri Lanka, founder of Sarvodaya Shramadana, which must be the biggest community development movement in the world, involving six million people in 8,000 villages. Sarvodaya is a Sanskrit word meaning "welfare of all," and it was coined by Gandhi to define his politico-economic system after reading Ruskin's *Unto This Last*. Shramadana is a Singhalese word that means "sharing of human energy." The movement was started eight years after Amte laid the foundations of Anandwan, when Ari, then a science teacher at a leading Colombo college, organized a fortnight's "work camp" for a group of his senior pupils outside a remote village of destitute, outcast people.

In Ari's own words, he wanted his students to "understand and experience the true state of affairs that prevailed in the rural and poor urban areas . . . to develop a love for their people and utilize the education they received, to find ways of building a more just and happier life for them." Instead of imposing their ideas on the villagers, the students asked them what were their principal needs, while experiencing their living conditions by sharing their homes, food, and work. They had long discussions at village "family gatherings." The "work-camp" concept caught on, and soon similar camps were organized in many parts of the island. In these camps well-balanced teams of heath, agricultural, and educational specialists worked side by side with unskilled laborers to restore the villages' traditional self-sustaining lifestyle, while introducing modern "alternative technology" mechanisms where these were appropriate. Once the development work had been set in motion, it was largely placed under the control of the villagers themselves, some of whom were trained as cadres to maintain the momentum of reconstruction.

Ari, in an article in *Ceres*, the organ of the United Nations Food and Agriculture Organization, wrote:

Shramadana camps are the places where the young and old, the educated and illiterate, the privileged and the forgotten, all meet and serve one another as equals. The Shramadana volunteers . . . identify themselves with the traditional culture of the community and . . . do not impose their will on the people nor adopt a patronizing attitude towards them . . . In the camp each person according to his or her capacity shares energy and skills with others . . . The camp with its songs and dances, work and study, truly becomes the ideal human family in microcosm where self-fulfillment and joy of living become a reality . . . This type of experience, sometimes knee-deep in mud, brings about a new awareness.

Awareness—awakening—this, in Ari's view, is the indispensable psychological foundation of the Shramadana process. Joanna Macy, in *Dharma and Development*, writes:

The Sarvodaya Movement sees any development program as unrealistic which does not recognize and alleviate the psychological impotence gripping the rural poor. Sarvodaya believes that by tapping their innermost beliefs and values, one can awaken people to their *swashakti* (personal power) and *janashakti* (collective or people's power).

It sees this awakening as taking place not in monastic solitude, but in social, economic and political interaction . . . Sarvodaya's goal and process of awakening pulls one headlong into the "real" world.

Basic to the Shramadana process is the identification of *real* human needs—common to all—as opposed to the factitious "needs" inculcated in Western society by the power of advertising. These real needs, in Ari's words, are:

1 A clean and beautiful environment
2 A clean and adequate supply of water

3 Minimum clothing requirements

4 A balanced diet

5 A simple house to live in

6 Basic health care

7 Simple communication facilities

8 Minimum energy requirements

9 Total education

10 Cultural and spiritual needs

In Australia, one of the leading philosopher-pioneers of the alternative movement is Ted Trainer, an educationist at the University of New South Wales. While writing in cogent terms about the dangers and potentialities of this most critical period in world history, Trainer is building his personal development model in the form of a "Mini-Machynlleth" (referring to the Centre for Alternative Technology in Wales) at a place with the delightful name of Pigface Point.

In a paper entitled *The Conserver Society,* Trainer writes:

It must be a *far less affluent* way of life. We must aim at just producing and consuming as much as we need for comfortable and convenient living standards. We must cut right back on unnecessary consumption and we must recycle, design things to last and to be repaired. We must phase out entire industries, such as sports cars.

This is not primarily a matter of reducing unnecessary personal consumption, although that is important. The main changes that are needed here are in our social system and procedures. For example our food-producing system involves much transport, meaning that we must change to having much more food produced where people live, which in turn means we must redesign suburbs and cities to have market gardens within them.

We must develop as much self-sufficiency as we reasonably can at the national level (meaning less trade), at the household level, and especially at the neighborhood or local regional level. We need to convert our presently barren suburbs into thriving regional economies which produce most of what they need from local resources.

Market gardens could be located throughout suburbs and even cities, e.g., on derelict factory sites and beside railway lines. This would reduce the cost of food by seventy percent, especially by cutting its transport costs. More importantly, having food produced close to where people live would enable nutrients to be recycled back to the soil through garbage gas units. Two of the most unsustainable aspects of our present agriculture are its heavy dependence on energy inputs and the fact that it takes nutrients from the soil and throws them all away.

We should convert one house on each block to become a neighborhood workshop, recycling store, meeting place, barter exchange and library. We could dig up many roads, thereby increasing land area by one-third or more because we will not need the car very much when we reduce production and decentralize what's left. When we have dug up those roads we will have much communal property so we can plant community orchards and forests. Most of your neighborhood could become a Permaculture jungle, and "edible landscape" crammed with long-lived, largely self-maintaining productive plants such as nut trees.

As a living, practical example of the kind of society that he has in mind, Trainer described in a newspaper article a farm community that he visited near Lismore, New South Wales, on the edge of "the Big Scrub," which was once Australia's largest rain forest. The community occupies a farmhouse and a number of smaller houses, all built by community members from local materials and dotted round a very beautiful valley. They produce most of their food, including tropical and subtropical fruits and vegetables, and one of their main aims is to restore the forest; they are planting eroded slopes with native rain forest trees. All decision-making is by consensus and all members have a strong sense of mutual responsibility. Most have part-time jobs outside the farm, though, owing to their high degree of self-sufficiency, there is not much pressure to make money. In Trainer's opinion: "Without doubt they have a far higher quality of life than the average Australian—achieved on an outlay around one-tenth the national average income!"

From Lismore to Lightmoor is to cross from the other side of the world—from "Down Under" almost to my own doorstep—for the Lightmoor community has been established in a wooded area on the western fringe of Telford New Town. Both communities have much in common, above all the practical, no-nonsense, down-to-earth, pioneering spirit of the participants.

Lightmoor community comprises fourteen houses, all individually designed and built by their owners and all with passive solar heating features, surrounding an embryonic village green. On three sides is woodland, fourteen acres of which is a conservation area to be managed by the villagers, who also share an acre of communal growing land and a wet meadow. Each family has a half-acre plot, and I was told that six families thought of starting forest gardens. The community, which constituted itself a limited company, acquired the land—twenty-three acres in all—at a knock-down price from Telford Development Corporation, on condition that they built the road and drains themselves. That meant hard manual labor every weekend for three years before work on the houses could begin. But there is nothing like digging at the bottom of a three-foot trench on a cold winter's day to foster a community spirit. Among Lightmoorians one senses a pride and comradeship born of common achievement in the course of seven years' hard slog. This has been a great help when conflicts and personality clashes have occurred, and when it has been necessary to make hard decisions. The whole project has been an excellent training ground in grassroots democracy, and mutual assistance is the keynote in many ways, small and large. While most residents have "away" jobs, possibilities are brewing for partnership enterprises in the village. Residents share a sense of far-reaching potentialities and also of security in the face of an uncertain future, derived from built-in alternative strategies.

A sense of deep emotional and spiritual unity, rooted in common ethnic-ecological traditions, is the cement that maintains the structure of a very different community in New York State: Crows Hill Farm, the home of the Indigenous Permaculture Network of Native Americans. KatsiCook, a Mohawk, who founded the community with her husband Jose Barreiro in 1986, describes the well-wooded landscape as "just the place for developing an old-style Indian homestead, a place for Indians to gather and for our young people to experience something of their ancient culture." Among the community's main aims is to restore traditional Indian farming systems, including the companion planting of maize, beans, and squash. These crops, known to the Iroquois as the "three sisters," are mutually compatible: the squash vines act as a living mulch, suppressing weeds, while the maize stalks support the beans, which fertilize both themselves and their companions with airborne nitrogen. This interaction is typical of the ecological concepts employed in permaculture/agroforestry. Stephen C. Fadden, another Mohawk, has written: "Permacultural concepts are not foreign to people who come from a Native American tradition. The idea of land sustaining the people and the people holding the land in deep respect and care, underlies the basic world perspective of most Native American communities and philosophies." As another member of the Crows Hill community puts it, "Living in harmony with nature, living gently on the earth, by taking only what is necessary for life and giving in return, is the underlying philosophy of both permaculture and traditional Native American peoples."

A similar understanding and respect for the products of Mother Earth, of Gaia, in all their complexity, is typical of many of the people of southeast Asia, especially the inhabitants of the forest villages of Java.

Forest villages have existed for over 1,000 years in Java, where they ensure that one of the most densely populated rural areas in the world is also a landscape of great beauty. A forest village in the Javanese sense is a village built out of local materials, screened and protected by a ring of forest gardens, which supply many of the inhabitants' basic needs. The forest gardens, like others in the region, are multilayered structures supplying a wide range of products. As many as 250 different species of crop plants have been found growing in and around a single village. The Javanese enjoy an extremely varied diet, including more than 500 different plant foods.

In recent years forest villages have been established in Thailand, in an effort to bring stability to the lives of shifting cultivators and limit the damage they have done to the environment. Families who agree to give up shifting cultivation are allotted plots on which to build houses and establish homegardens, and are also allowed to grow crops within new forest plantations. They also receive free electricity, drinking water, medicines, transport, and education, as well as payment for plantation work.

This forest village system has proved successful, not only in Thailand, but also in Cambodia, India, Kenya, Gabon, Uganda, and Nigeria.

Advocates of a postindustrial world order (one that is geared to the satisfaction of human needs and the development of whole human beings), from Gandhi to the Greens, have postulated that the basic unit of such an order should be the decentralized, democratic, self-sufficient rural community. Surely the most attractive as well as the most effective setting for such a community would be the forest village, encircled by forest gardens. These would not only provide food, timber, fuel, energy, and craft materials for the villagers, but also beneficent microclimates, shelter from wind and storm, pure air, and reasonably assured supplies of pure water. Many rural areas in every country, not least Britain, are little better than featureless wildernesses, bereft of trees by sheep and shipbuilders, mineral workings and motorways, muirburn and prairie farming. Far too often human activities have brought ugliness, desolation, and pollution to the countryside.

But this has not always been so. There is no reason why human activities should not make the countryside more beautiful than ever before, with new forms, new colors, new rhythms, and a vastly increased diversity of plant life, which would, in turn, attract an increased diversity of animal life. This would be a real countryside, designed to satisfy the real needs—rather than artificially stimulated "wants"—of human beings; not only physical needs, but also emotional and spiritual needs. The fortunate dwellers in such a countryside would not want to indulge in war and other antisocial activities, but would, as parts of the ecosystem, automatically conform to its law of cohesiveness. And such a countryside would also create its own culture: new colors and sounds, new sights and insights, new senses and sensitivities, new challenges, new chords and discords, new conflicts resolved. Walter and Dorothy Schwarz in *Breaking Through* write:

When the shift to a more holistic style of life becomes more widespread, one of the most exhilarating developments will be the part that art will play in everyone's life. By art we mean, not a narrow interpretation of pictures seen in a gallery, programs watched on television or costly performances of nineteenth-century operas. We mean all the performing and creative arts and the artifacts, pots, chairs, rugs that people create for themselves.

Art can be used as a metaphor for society. Our arts reflect our involvement with, or our alienation from the world around us . . . In primitive societies art, everyday life and religion are so intertwined that there is little separation. Music, dance, pottery, carving and weaving are accessible to and created by everyone.

Progress is a spiral; the pendulum swings back as well as forward. The new postindustrial world, for which many of us are striving, will see an ecological renaissance, a rebirth of all that was best in "primitive" life and outlook, blended with new potentialities at which we can only guess.

13

~

Where Do We Go From Here?

~~~~~~

As Robert Hart writes in this chapter, "Western agronomists have until recently dismissed the arrangement of tropical forest gardens as 'haphazard' or 'chaotic'; now they seem to regard them, with a mixture of cynicism and awe, as 'mysterious', like the orthodox reaction to organic growing as 'all muck and magic'."

Clearly, we in the industrialized nations still have much to learn from the forest gardeners of the world, people who in general live closer to the Earth and its resources. These are people who lead lives that, while not necessarily "happier" or more idyllic than ours, are at least free from what John Steinbeck described as the burden of all "northern peoples": the "masses of wants growing out of inner insecurity."

The good news for temperate-zone gardeners is that degrees in horticulture or botany are not required to make one's own discoveries. A forest garden, as Robert Hart states, is not a static entity but a complex living organism that changes from year to year, and even from day to day. By observing and experimenting with plants, how they grow and relate and respond to one another, we can begin to regain a kind of intuitive plant knowledge that is common among forest peoples, but that most Westerners (even gardeners) have lost through disuse.

~~~~~~

The Wenlock Edge Project was born of a desire to achieve the highest possible degree of self-sufficiency throughout the year in a limited space with minimum labor. For the benefit of any who might wish to start a similar venture, this short chapter provides a summary of the necessary steps, based on many years' experience, many trials and some errors.

It must be emphasized at once that, in temperate zones, little or no fresh produce can be gathered from the forest garden during the winter months, as the trees and bushes cease fruiting and herbs and perennial vegetables die down. Hence the need for a winter garden of hardy annuals to supplement the forest garden. In my own case, this is one of the functions of the Ante (Anti) Forest Garden. Another function is to grow plants that are antagonistic to forest garden conditions: sun-loving herbs and *Vaccinium* species that require lime-free soils.

The primary *raison d'être* of the whole venture, as far as I am concerned, has been health. Having made a very deep study of natural health and healing, I have long been convinced that the most effective diet for all-round positive health is one containing a preponderance of fresh or naturally dried fruit, vegetables, nuts, and herbs. I also believe that a *wide* diversity of such foods is desirable, The human system, like other living organisms, is immensely complex, and, for optimum efficiency, clearly demands an extensive range of nutrients. Nutritional science has, in recent years, discovered a number of trace elements that go far beyond the generally recognized requirements of proteins, carbohydrates, vitamins, and minerals. There can be little doubt that other factors remain to be uncovered, factors that may well be the key to the prevention and cure of serious illness. A vast amount of research remains to be done into the full potentialities of plant life. Only about one percent of known plant species have been subjected to exhaustive scientific scrutiny. Little is known even about the nutritional and medicinal contents of some of our most common "weeds," plants that in less sophisticated and affluent times and societies have been major constituents of diet and medical care.

Every species of plant, even every variety of every species, has a different biochemical makeup, and therefore probably has a different contribution to make to the holistic health of the human system. For this reason, I am firmly convinced that the boundaries of diet should be extended far beyond the range of products available in the shops.

Hence, in my case, the Wenlock Edge Project; though I must emphasize that the products of a single-home self-sufficiency project, however diverse, are not likely to be fully adequate for optimum human nutrition. Also, one should not underestimate the legitimate pleasures of gastronomy, which in some countries, such as France, Italy, and China, attains the status of a fine art. Food that tastes good tends to be good for you. I well remember the spirit of reverence with which my mother's singing master, Ernesto Baraldi, savored the dishes that my mother had carefully prepared for his enjoyment at our Kensington dinner parties—another world from Wenlock Edge!

Those in temperate countries who enjoy gastronomic exploration naturally find themselves drawn to the delicious and exotic dishes of the Mediterranean and the Far East. But it is more exciting still, and even more healthful, to devise one's own recipes consisting of unusual fruits, vegetables, and herbs grown by oneself—and/or one's neighbors. For this reason, members of health clubs and other concerned people might care to establish forest gardens and winter gardens of complementary plants, so that they can exchange surpluses. Some adventurous souls might even consider embarking on joint projects like the Lightmoor Community, described in Chapter 12, for the supremely important goal of attaining the rare treasure of positive, lasting health. For such people a considerable amount of help and guidance is now available in Britain.

The Neighborhood Initiatives Foundation (NIF) was set up in 1988 by the Town and Country Planning Association and the Housing Association Charitable Trust to "work with communities that have set out to help themselves." Basing itself on the achievements of the Lightmoor Community, it aims "to improve housing, local environment, livelihoods and community facilities." Following seven years of field research at Nottingham University, the NIF has issued more than forty "Education for Neighborhood Change Packs", containing three-dimensional models that can be switched around, so as to enable people to visualize the kind of environment and facilities they would like, such as communal gardens and cooperative enterprises. For full information, NIF can be contacted at Chapel House, 7 Gravel Lea-sowes, Lightmoor, Telford, Shropshire TF43QL. Similar packs have been issued by government-sponsored organizations in Holland, Germany, and Australia.

Self-sufficiency projects, of course, need not be restricted to food and healing herbs. Among other products of a forest garden system can be fuel for wood-burning stoves; timber for fencing, stakes, carving, and turnery; fibers for spinning, weaving, matting, and basketry; and aromatic herbs for moth-proofing. In addition to my osier coppice, cut for basketry, Garnet coppices other willows in the arboretum and passes them, together with hedge clippings, through the "Viking" shredder to produce material for mulching, composting, and fuel. Coppicing is an excellent and well-established form of sustainable woodland management. The stumps of appropriate trees do not die when the trees are felled; instead, dormant or adventitious buds regenerate new shoots. This allows repeated harvests without the trouble of replanting. Meanwhile the ever-growing root network maintains soil structure and ensures that resprouts grow far more vigorously than rootless cuttings or seedlings or saplings with merely embryonic roots.

My whole project area, except the arboretum, is kept permanently mulched throughout the year. This not only suppresses weeds but also fertilizes the land as the mulch rots down and maintains near-ideal conditions for both plants and soil organisms. Of special importance at times of drought is that a mulch of straw remains surprisingly moist for weeks on end. Wood shreddings are a good substitute for peat, which we in Britain are being urged by conservationists not to buy, as peat bogs are a valuable but dwindling habitat for many forms of wildlife.

The permanent mulch cover makes it unnecessary to disturb the soil by digging or hoeing, except, of course, when planting and in the initial preparation of the ground. This is the only time when really hard work is necessary. If the site is, say, old pasture, as mine was, then it has to be thoroughly dug over and the soil thoroughly worked before planting. This can also be done with a mechanical cultivator, which can be rented, as no such machinery will be required after the initial phase. Before planting, it is a good idea to sow a green manure crop such as mustard or tares, which will be killed off by the first frosts and thus leave the soil in a rich, friable condition for the fruit or nut trees or bushes.

The trees in the arboretum were planted in holes dug and filled with compost in the old pasture. This area is mowed every two or three weeks throughout the spring, summer, and autumn, which has had a remarkable effect in improving the quality of the sward. As a result of regular cutting, the most obstinate weeds, such as docks, with which the pasture was infested, have simply disappeared, to be replaced by tender grasses and clovers.

An old orchard makes a very good nucleus for a forest garden, unless the trees are severely diseased. My forest garden was planted in a twenty-five-year-old small orchard of apples and pears, some of which were in a pretty poor condition. But the abundant aromatic herbs that have been planted beneath them seem to have rejuvenated them; a decrepit-looking 'Red Ellison' apple was given a new lease of life when Garnet grafted three young 'King of the Pippins' shoots onto it—a trick that was known to the ancient Romans. These old trees constitute the "canopy" of the forest architecture. If one is starting a forest garden from scratch, the best way to form a canopy is by planting standard apples, plums, or pears at the recommended spacing: twenty feet each way. Then fruit or nut trees on dwarfing rootstocks can be planted halfway between the standards, to form the "low-tree layer," and fruit bushes between all the trees to form the "shrub layer." Herbs and perennial vegetables will constitute the "herbaceous layer," and horizontally spreading plants like dewberries and other *Rubus* species, as well as creeping herbs such as buckler-leaved sorrel *(Rumex scutatus)* and lady's-mantle, will form the "ground-cover layer." For the root vegetables, mainly radishes and Hamburg parsley, occupying the "rhizosphere," a low mound can be raised, so that they will not be swamped by the herbs. As for the climbers that constitute the "vertical layer": grapevines, nasturtiums, and runner beans can be trained up the trees, while raspberries and hybrid berries, such as boysenberries and tayberries, can be trained over a trellis fence, forming a boundary to the garden.

Other possible boundaries to a forest garden are: a trellis fence adorned with espalier, cordon, or fan-trained fruit-trees; a 'Bouché-Thomas' apple hedge (see page 55), with the trees planted diagonally so that they grow into each other; a hedge of dwarf apples and pears planted at five-foot intervals, or an old-fashioned English multispecies hedgerow, comprising elders, crabs, damsons, and hazels, with blackberries, honeysuckle and sweet briar rose or eglantine *(Rosa eglanterra)* sprawling over them.

If rabbits are rife in the neighborhood, it is a good idea to encase the more valuable and delicate saplings in plastic tree guards, though a hedge of perennial onions is said to be an effective rabbit deterrent. To provide shelter for young trees against the prevailing winds, it may be necessary to erect a strong fence or a row of hurdles, or plant a windbreak of fast-growing Leyland cypresses *(Cupressocyparis leylandii)*.

The layout of the forest garden should preferably not be a regular square or rectangle but should adopt an interesting, rhythmical form in tune with the environment. When we come to questions of "significant form" and the precise placing of plants in relation to each other, we enter an intuitive, aesthetic realm which, to the down-to-earth horticulturalist or agricultural scientist, may savor of mystreism.

Western agronomists have until recently dismissed the arrangement of tropical forest gardens as "haphazard" or "chaotic"; now they seem to regard them, with a mixture of cynicism and awe, as "mysterious", like the orthodox reaction to organic growing as "all muck and magic." John B. Raintree, a Western scientist working at the International Council for Research in Agroforestry (ICRAF), asked in a conference paper: "Is it that ... seemingly haphazard combinations of such diverse components in the tropical homegarden or other 'forest-like' associations in traditional agroforestry lacks rational order, or is it that the traditional farmer in the tropics responds to different canons of rationality?" Then he went on to answer his own question by quoting from another Westerner's treatise on African agriculture, and saying: "De Schlippe's genius was to recognize that far from being devoid of order and rationality, the hidden order behind the seeming chaos of traditional agriculture in the tropics is the order imposed by nature itself. Does anyone . . . really question the rationality of nature?" Quoting de Schlippe again: "It can be seen now that the seeming disorder of Zande fields and courtyards (forest gardens) is due to the fact that the Zande embroiders his agricultural activity on a canvas and pattern provided for him by nature." Later the scientist commented: "If the patterns that result resemble the complexity of nature itself, that may be, not an accident of culture, but a deliberate strategy for achieving a sustainable or even a 'regenerative' agroforestry."

All this amounts to an admission that a forest garden is not an "unscientific" or "antiscientific" structure, but that it obeys an order decreed by ecological laws, which Western science has not yet fully identified. The tropical gardener, by a combination of intuition, insight, and observation, in the course of intimate caring for his plants, has learned many facts about their nature, requirements, interrelationships, and laws of growth—facts which escape the scientist with his microscope and test tubes. The same, of course, applies to temperate forest gardens. If they are productive, it means that they are activated by energies and conform to symbiotic relationships which await scientific confirmation. Like the tropical gardener, we who create our own forest gardens must not be afraid to trust our intuitions when deciding on the placement of different plants. If we envisage the vast complexity of the root network, while also observing the channels by which air and sunlight penetrate the canopy, we are likely to be led to select the right position for our introductions.

The whole question of symbiotic relationships, not only between plants, but also between plants and animals, is a vast and complicated subject which needs years of scientific research. As far as the plant-insect relationship is concerned, it is important to ensure that all the fruit trees in a forest garden, if not self-fertile, are compatible for pollination purposes. This means that each tree must have a nearby neighbor that blossoms at approximately the same time. When buying fruit trees it is most desirable to ask the nurseryman if they are compatible or self-fertile, or carefully to scrutinize the catalog which should give this information. Most ornamental crabapples, while being very attractive in their shapes and colors, make excellent pollinators for their common apple cousins. 'Golden Hornet' above all, which, as its name implies, gives a glorious display of gleaming fruit throughout the autumn, is said to be an effective pollinator for almost all common apple varieties.

When buying plants it is best, if possible, to go to a local, family-run nursery, where you can be reasonably sure of finding reliable stock suited to your own climatic conditions. That way, you can buy what really appeals to you; buying by mail order can sometimes result in disappointments. Most mail-order suppliers, however are very reputable, and you may want to order from them to obtain rare or unusual plant varieties not available at your local nursery. For a list of recommended mail-order nurseries in North America, see p. 215ff.

It always pays to go for quality, even if that means paying higher prices. A really strong, healthy, robust, and interesting plant will be a good friend for years, constantly rewarding you with fascinating and unexpected developments. Plants of rare species or those trained in special shapes, such as cordons, espaliers, and fans, tend to be much more expensive than the more ordinary plants, which can be just as interesting in their own way, and often more healthy and productive. However, if space is very limited it is worthwhile investing in one or two "family trees" or "Ballerinas," expensive as they are. A family tree comprises anything from three to six different varieties of fruit on a single rootstock. A Ballerina is a newly introduced form of apple or crab, in which the fruits grow very close to the stem, so that the tree, which may grow to a height of eight feet, occupies a minimum of lateral space.

When I learned that Permaculture expert Bill Mollison intended to visit me in October 1990 with an Australian TV team, I launched out into buying all the most interesting and showy trees, shrubs, and herbs that I could lay hands on in the neighborhood. Among them was a glorious 'Golden Hornet' and a Ballerina crab called 'Maypole'. A few bright, colorful ornamentals greatly enhance the appeal of a forest garden layout. Ornamentals tend to be more expensive than fruit trees and bushes, though cheap bedding plants, scattered here and there, can also add gay patches of color. I usually plant *Tagetes*—French or African marigolds—throughout the garden at the beginning of the season, not only for their brightness, but also because they are believed to be good companions to other plants, deterring aphids and nematodes. For winter or early spring color, nothing can equal pansies, which are now available in a fascinating range of colors and patterns. They are believed to have medicinal virtues and may have been used in love potions in the past, to judge by some of their attractive Elizabethan names: "Heartsease," "Johnny-jump-up-and-kiss-me," "Kitty-run-the-streets," and—most elaborate of all—"Call-me-to-you-Jack-behind-the-garden-gate"!

A good excuse for planting ornamentals is that they attract beneficial insects, which are important components of the forest garden system. One of the basic aims of agroforestry is to integrate conservation with the growing of food and other useful products. Agroforestry/permaculture is a holistic concept designed to serve whole human beings —in fact, the whole of life. The beauty of birds and butterflies, moths and dragonflies feeds the human soul as much as fruit, nuts, and herbs feed the human body. I shall never forget the sudden revelation, in the summer of 1989, of coming upon the deep purple buddleia on the rose mound in the arboretum, teeming with a multitude of many-colored butterflies. No scene in a tropical forest could have been more beautiful. It was an experience of a lifetime, a reward for years of hard labor.

A forest garden is not a static thing, it is a complex *living* organism, which means a developing organism; it changes from year to year, even from day to day. I would urge anyone who starts a forest garden to adopt a creative attitude towards it; to learn and observe, to study and do research. Humankind has an enormous amount to learn about plants, above all about their relationships between each other, and the amateur can make as important discoveries by observation and experimentation as can the trained scientist with his disciplines and instruments. In fact the work of the two bodies can be complementary. The peasants who have founded and fostered the centuries-old forest gardens of the tropics have an intimate knowledge of their soils and plants, reinforced by traditional lore inherited from their ancestors, which is beyond the conception of most Western gardeners. Their plant knowledge is based on empathy; they *feel* the characteristics, needs, and aspirations of each individual plant: "That young tree wants a bit more light; I must cut a gap in the canopy to let some more sunshine through." And this intimate knowledge, combined with loving care for the plant's welfare—and also, in many cases, with the bitter realization that the very survival of the peasant and his family depends on that welfare—leads to insights, intuitions, and "hunches," the truth of which only science can confirm. For instance, I recently noticed that a clump of raspberry canes growing out of a bed of nettles seemed to be particularly thriving; they were more vividly green than their neighbors, they radiated health and vigor. Was that a confirmation of the traditional lore that nettles, under conditions of controlled growth, can be good companions? Only science can give a definite answer. Root secretions and gaseous aromas can be analyzed, to ascertain whether nettles do in fact emit substances that fertilize and stimulate their neighbors and possibly ward off pests and disease germs. A partnership needs to be built up between gardeners, peasants, and scientists, to find out answers to many questions like these, on which the very future of large sections of humankind may depend. At this time of ecological crisis, of man-induced erosion, of wholesale environmental destruction caused by burning and bulldozing, flooding, chemicals, and industrialization, salvation for millions of people must lie in the recreation of intensive systems of horticulture to meet their essential needs.

Many of us, however small our gardens and however limited our qualifications, can participate in this vital movement. After all, the largely self-taught African-American scientist George Washington Carver developed more than 300 products from one humble plant, the peanut. Following his example, we can all experiment with new recipes, new salad combinations, and possibly new craft uses for plants, such as the extraction of dyes by boiling. We can allow annual vegetables to fulfill their life cycles and test the palatability of their flowers, fruit, and seeds. We can propagate fruit trees from seed, and, with patience, may develop new, more delicious, more nutritious varieties, since apples, in particular, never breed "true to type" from their seeds or "pips." In fact, some of the best-known apple varieties have been pippins," including the famous 'Cox's Orange Pippin' itself, bred by amateur gardeners.

A forest garden, whether in a London suburb or on a tropical hillside, can be a matrix of creative living, of holistic development; a place where women, men, and children can imbibe health through every sense, and engage in vital, constructive activities as parts of a wider ecosystem. Dare one say that it can be a microcosm of a new, postindustrial world order?

It is less than 150 years since the Industrial Revolution began to spread its blight across Europe and America. Before that time, humankind had satisfied almost all its basic needs direct from Mother Earth: from the fields and forests, orchards, market gardens, vineyards, quarries, and unpolluted waterways. The lack of manmade technology had not prevented humanity from reaching the highest peaks of culture. So there is no need to feel anxiety or regret about the imminent decline and fall of the Industrial Age, however many discomforts and dislocations it may involve. We can look forward to a new twist in the spiral of world progress, when much that is best in the past, such as many forms of traditional agroforestry, are rediscovered and find new applications in the light of modern science, while being combined with what is best in modern technology, mainly in its "appropriate" or "intermediate" forms.

For those with eyes to see, this Ecological Renaissance is already in progress. In moving away from the machine and all it stands for, human beings must come to realize that the "miracles" achieved by physical scientists and engineers can be dwarfed when more attention is focused on the infinite potentialities of Life.

Since the publication of the first edition of this book, forest gardens have been springing up in many parts of Britain and other countries. Of special significance for the future pattern of world development in this millennial era have been the efforts of some town-dwellers to reverse the urban invasion of the countryside by creating green oases in inner city areas.

London's first communal forest garden was started by a cosmopolitan group called Naturewise in Crouch Hill, near the home of my Spanish Basque grandfather, Nicasio Emigdio Jauralde, who served as a financial representative of the Spanish government in London for the astonishing period of seventy-two years.

The group, led by a Turkish Cypriot, Alpai Torgut, acquired from the local council a steep, south-facing bank, created out of rubble when some houses were demolished after the Second World War. It was covered with grass, with a few old trees, and daffodils grew there in the spring. The group, together with local helpers, dug out three terraces, supported with wattle fencing, and with two "swales" to each terrace for irrigation. These were mulched with compost and leftover fruit and vegetables supplied by the local greengrocer, and planted with a wide variety of fruit trees and bushes, with fragrant herbs as ground cover. By the first summer, wildlife was seen, in the form of nesting blue-tits, butterflies, and bees.

By then, local residents were beginning to take an interest, especially when they learned that the forest garden was for all. "We felt that they were rediscovering their own connection with nature," Alpai remarked. Though there was some vandalism, the group maintained a non-confrontational, *ahimsa* attitude towards everyone and gradually a community spirit has emerged. There have been encouraging signs of negative factors, such as destructiveness and depression caused by unemployment and poverty, being transmuted into collective creativity, as more and more local people have become involved with nature in building a local resource of value to them all. In time the forest garden will provide an abundance of fruit, vegetables, and herbs as well as the soul-food of beauty.

In particular, the project has brought happiness to many children, and in 1995 the group was asked to make a second forest garden on the grounds of a daycare nursery named after Margaret McMillan, who believed that children achieve a far higher degree of self-fulfillment if they have constant contact with nature.

Other forest gardens have been created or planned in or near the cities of Manchester, Middlesbrough, and Coventry.

A particularly impressive forest garden is being created by Martin Crawford of the Agroforestry Research Trust on the Dartington estate in south Devon. A very wide diversity of fruit and other economic trees, bushes, and herbs is being planted in carefully worked-out layers or "stories." Martin intends to make the project self-fertilizing by planting a large number of nitrogen-fixing trees and shrubs, as well as "dynamic accumulators"—deep-rooting perennials such as sorrel, comfrey, and coltsfoot, which draw up phosphates and potassium from the subsoil and make them available to other plants. Ultimately, Martin hopes that the garden will contain 35,000 plants!

"Centuries were needed to know a part of the laws of nature. A day is enough for the wise man to know the duties of man."

VOLTAIRE
Philosophical Dictionary

Epilogue

~

A New Twist in the Evolutionary Spiral

Over the years, people from many countries have come to visit the forest garden on Wenlock Edge. A number have spoken of making forest gardens of their own. Speaking to such people gives me great hope for the future of the world. I can detect signs of the evolution of a new breed of human being. *Homo sapiens* is developing into *Homo altruisticus.*

A spiral combines an upward thrust with a pendulum swing. The next development in humanity does not only involve new technologies, new outlooks, new modes of thought. It must also entail a readiness to look very far "back"—to tribespeople whom Western "civilization" dismisses as "primitive," and even to our nearest relatives in the animal world, the anthropoid apes and the woolly monkeys of the Amazon rain forest.

Among enterprises, families, and communities that have recently embarked on the adventure of forest gardening is the Monkey Sanctuary near Looe in Cornwall. Founded by the musician and philosopher Leonard Williams, the sanctuary expresses the one supremely important quality which must characterize the woman and man of the New Age: *compassion*. Most of the vast toll of suffering, which is one of the dominant features of today's world, could be avoided and healed if more people learned to *care* about their fellow beings, animal and human.

In the 1950s and 1960s, the woolly monkey *(Lagoethrix lagotricha)* was regarded as a particularly attractive pet, and thousands were taken from their homes in the rain forests of South America and brought to

Britain to be kept as pets or in zoos. Denied the communal life that is essential to their well-being, those intelligent and sensitive animals developed psychic disorders and lived tragically short lives.

Leonard Williams, who lived with his wife June at Chislehurst near London, was one of the many people who kept woolly monkeys as pets. With the hypersensitivity of the musician, Len realized intuitively that his pets would never really thrive unless they were given the space and freedom to develop their natural social instincts. In 1964, with his family and his monkeys' keeper, Sue Rickard, Len established the sanctuary in Cornwall, which is designed in every possible way to enable the animals to lead natural lives. He also appealed to pet owners and zoos to let him have their monkeys, so that they could be properly looked after and, when possible, returned to their jungle homes.

Now the sanctuary comprises a colony of happy, healthy, animals living in an environment carefully designed to fulfill their every need and looked after by a cooperative human community. Recently the community decided to start a forest garden, comprising a wide diversity of fruit trees and other edible plants for the consumption of both animals and humans.

Another, quite different cooperative community, which is also engaged in forest gardening activities, is the Centre for Alternative Technology near Machynlleth in Wales. Situated in a disused slate quarry, this fascinating establishment has been developed by people who care—about the fate of human beings and the environment. This has led them to produce and display a large variety of devices carefully designed for sustainable and nonpollutive living. The Centre's history, as related in *Crazy Idealists* (C.A.T., Machynlleth, 1995) is an inspiring tale of vision, courage, and devotion, of hardship, heartbreaking struggle, comradeship—and enormous fun—played out in the beautiful, well-wooded surroundings of a Welsh valley.

Quite different again is the achievement of a young couple, Pam and Peter, who have created a highly productive garden, partly designed on forest garden lines, on an almost precipitous hillside on the outskirts of the North Lancashire mill town of Todmorden, close to

the Brontë country of the Yorkshire Moors. Pam Colbran is an attractive, talented Lancashire lass, a schoolteacher, and Peter Two Bulls is of
Native American heritage, an initiated member of the Oglala Lakota
tribe. In the heavy clay soils of that cold northern hillside, which they
have terraced for ease of working, Pam and Peter have planted an amazing selection of fruits, vegetables, herbs, and flowers—some choice,
some very rare. They include greengage, cherry, medlar, Japanese
wineberry, boysenberry, tayberry, Cape gooseberry, huckleberry, wild
service tree, liquidamber, gingko, *Gaultheria procumbens*, asparagus,
cardoon, Chinese cabbage, papillon lavender, and—rarest of all—
Hopi blue corn, Hopi pinto beans, and "mummy" peas. The latter,
which are descended from seed found in an Egyptian tomb of 4,000
years ago, make tall, vigorous plants. In all, the garden contains more
than 200 plants. From Pam's observation, she finds that an apple tree
surrounded with tansy plants—a traditional association—thrives better than an apple with no tansy nearby. She uses some of the herbs for
medicinal purposes. Trees are grown to stabilize the very steep slopes.

William James, the famous American philosopher and pioneer of
the science of psychology, in an essay entitled *A Moral Equivalent of
War*, pointed out that the instinct for violence and the joy of conflict
were deeply ingrained in the masculine psyche; but that they could be
transmuted into a wholly positive and peaceful dynamic. This book
contains many examples of men—and women—who have successfully achieved this drastic internal revolution. Such people are the men
and women of the New Age.

Vast tasks, calling for all the courage, discipline, dedication, and
ingenuity commonly associated with war, will have to be carried out if
the majority of humankind are to survive and enjoy a tolerable future.
These tasks include the reclamation of deserts and desolated areas,
such as mining slag heaps, by agroforestry means. The techniques are
well known. First the ground is prepared by the planting of hardy,
drought and pollution-resistant "nurse-trees." These then act as protective screens for more tender but more valuable economic plants.
Even in grossly degraded former rainforest areas in Amazonia, coura-

geous colonists, some of Japanese origin, have successfully created forest gardens and other agroforestry plantations. Richard St. Barbe Baker, the original "Man of the Trees," had a stunning vision of a reclaimed Sahara, capable of providing homes, gardens, and livelihoods for three and a half *billion* people.

The new settlers could include many of today's tragic refugees—men, women, and children uprooted by war, natural disaster, or flooding caused by the building of big dams. In his autobiography, *My Life My Trees*, Richard wrote: "Is it too much to hope . . . that the Iron Curtain of the world will give place to the Green Front and the scars in the earth as well as the scars in people's hearts may be healed by tree-planting?"

Appendix 1

~

Temperate species and varieties recommended for a
Wenlock-Edge-type self-sufficiency project: Forest Garden,
Winter Garden, and Wetland Garden

Fruit & Nuts

Note: Fruit trees marked with an asterisk (*) are currently available from North American mail-order nurseries. For a list of recommended suppliers, see p. 214ff.

APPLES *(Malus domestica)*

Late Summer Dessert Apples
Ripening in July, August, or early September. Do not keep for more than ten days after picking.

'Devonshire Quarrendon'—Historical fruit recorded before 1650. Dark crimson with green patches. Crisp with distinctive flavor.

'Discovery'—Successful modern variety bred by amateur. Bright scarlet, juicy, and resistant to scab. Reliably cold-hardy to USDA Plant Hardiness Zone 4.

'George Cave'—Earliest of all. Mine cropped so heavily in summer drought of 1990 that branches had to be supported by scaffolding to prevent them from breaking.

Early Autumn Dessert Apples
Ripening in September, some keeping till October.

'Ellison's Orange'—Of Cox parentage. Taste described as "aromatic aniseed." Does well on light, sandy soil. Resistant to scab.

'James Grieve'—Of Scottish origin, so does well in the North. Taste described as "brisk." Juicy and handsomely striped.

'Katja'—A Swedish cross between 'James Grieve' and 'Worcester

Pearmain', so very hardy. Bright crimson and prolific cropper. Sold in shops as 'Katy'.

* *'Laxton's Fortune'*—A cross between 'Cox's Orange Pippin' and 'Wealthy'. Crispy, juicy, and sweet. Resistant to frost and scab.

Late Autumn Dessert Apples
Ripening in October, keeping till November and December.

'Allington Pippin'—Vigorous and self-fertile. Rather sharp-flavored. Used for my Bouché-Thomas hedge.

'Charles Ross'—Big and juicy. Does well on chalky soils and in coastal areas. Resists scab.

* *'Egremont Russet'*—Most popular of the russets, with characteristic musky flavor. Self-fertile and disease-resistant. A good keeper. Hardy to Zone 3.

* *'Greensleeves'*—'New James Grieve' x 'Golden Delicious' cross. Crisp and sweet.

* *'King of the Pippins'*—Also known as 'Shropshire Pippin'. Said to have a "highly aromatic almond flavor."

'Sunset'—My favorite and many other people's. Crisp, hardy member of the Cox stable. Has characteristic "setting sun" marking on tip.

* *'Tom Putt'*—Bred by Dorset parson of same name around 1700. Described as a large, crisp, acid, with vivid red stripes." Ripens earlier in US. Good cooking and cider apple.

Midwinter Dessert Apples
Ripening in November, keeping till January or February. Best picked in October.

* *'Kidd's Orange'*—Cox seedling from New Zealand. Less delicate and more disease-resistant than its parent. Ripens midseason in US.

* *'Pitmaston Pine Apple'*—Eighteenth century, believed to be descendant of 'Golden Pippin', which was the most favored apple in Elizabethan days. Small, crisp, and amber, with distinct pineapple flavor. Ripens in US mid-September.

'Ribston Pippin'—An old Yorkshire variety, circa 1700. Strong and vigorous, one of the most richly flavored, aromatic apples. A parent of Cox. Ripens in US mid-September.

'Spartan'—'McIntosh' x 'Newtown Pippin' cross. Of Canadian origin, therefore very hardy. Deep purple, almost black. Garden-grown Spartans are crisp with a rich port-wine flavor, streets ahead of flabby, tasteless shop products. Ripens mid-October in US.

New Year Dessert Apples

Ripening in December or early January, keeping till February or March. Should be picked before hard frosts.

'Ashmead's Kernel'—First raised by Dr. Ashmead of Gloucester before 1720. Russet type, voted as best-flavored of all apples. Ripens late October in US; hardy to Zone 3.

'Jupiter'—A recent release from East Malling. According to Deacon's catalog: "Aptly named Jupiter as fiery red with gold stripes."

'Suntan'—One of the newest of apples with one of the most ancient as its parent: cross between 'Cox's Orange Pippin' and 'Court Pendu Plat'.

'Winston'—An improvement on the popular 'Laxton's Superb'. Described as more "briskly" flavored.

Spring Dessert Apples

Ripening in December and January, and keeping till spring.

'Court Pendu Plat'—Possibly the oldest of all cultivated apples, going back to Roman times. Known as the "wise apple" as it blossoms after the last frosts. Scab-resistant. Ripens November through December in US.

'Sturmer Pippin'—Essex apple widely grown in Tasmania and New Zealand, with unique sweetness of flavor.

'Tydeman's Late Orange'—Yet another Cox offspring with true Cox flavor but exceptionally crisp. Ripens November through December in US.

Late Keeping "Cooking" Apples

'Annie Elizabeth'—Longest keeping of all English apples: can last till July.

*'*Bramley's Seedling*'—As good eaten raw in salads as in Mum's apple tarts. Trees are vigorous, spreading; scab- and mildew-resistant. Good cider apple; very high vitamin C content. Ripens early October to early November in US.

'Flower of Kent'—Specimen was in Sir Isaac Newton's garden at Woolsthorpe, Lincs, in 1660; it is believed that this tree inspired the Theory of Gravity!

*'*Howgate Wonder*'—Probably the largest of all apples. Sweet, crisp, and worth eating raw. Ripens September in US.

CRABAPPLES *(Malus baccata* and other spp.)

The flowering crabs are short, neat trees which are very suitable for the low tree layer of a forest garden, where they are first-class pollinators of the ordinary apples that are their neighbors. Many of them produce prolific crops of fruit, some of which are surprisingly palatable and, I am sure, rich in minerals and vitamins. One of the main aims of the forest garden project is to enable families greatly to extend their diets, by including wholesome, natural foods that are not available in the shops.

'Crittenden'—Notable for its heavy crops of bright scarlet fruit, which persist throughout much of the winter. Fruit just right for eating off the leafless tree after heavy frost.

*'*Dolgo*'—A Siberian crab popular in North America; dolgo means "long" in Russian, referring to the olive-like shape of the red fruit. Vigorous, upright tree; heavy cropper. Disease-resistant and hardy to Zone 2.

'Golden Hornet'—As its name implies, gives prolific crops of gleaming gold fruit. Said to be the best pollinator of ordinary apples.

'John Downie'—Exceptionally attractive, comparatively large, egg-shaped fruit, golden with orange-scarlet cheeks, and with a most intriguing flavor.

'*Red Glow*'—A splendid little tree with leaves that turn red in the spring and green in the autumn! Crimson blossoms followed by crimson fruit.

*'*Royalty Crab*'—Highly ornamental tree with deep red leaves, blossoms, and fruit. Resistant to fire blight. From Canada; hardy to Zone 2.

PEARS *(Pyrus communis)*

Can be divided into down-to-earth English varieties and highly scented epicurean fruit bred by wealthy amateurs in France and Belgium in the eighteenth and nineteenth centuries.

*'*Beurre Hardi*'—Reddish fruit of interesting subacid flavor but rather harsh texture. Very vigorous grower and scab-resistant. Hardy to Zone 4.

*'*Conference*'—Reliable but tasteless.

'*Doyenne du Comice*'—Large, juicy fruit generally acknowledged to be the queen of pears.

'*Glow Red William*'—Bright red fruit whose coloring is claimed to make it resistant to weather and fungus diseases.

'*Hessle*'—Tree with small russet fruit named after the Yorkshire village where it was bred. A "no-nonsense" fruit like the people of its native county.

'*Improved Fertility*'—In my experience the most reliable cropper of all pears. The centerpiece of my first experiment in agroforestry. Seems to have thoroughly enjoyed the companionship of the red, white, and black currants, raspberries, and herbs that have surrounded it. Fruit is small, russeted, sweet, and none the worse for being rather rough.

'*Jargonelle*'—An ancient pear of high quality first recorded about 1600. As hardy as 'Hessle' and will succeed in the same bleak, northern environment.

*'*Kieffer*'—P. cammunis* x *P. pyrifolia* hybrid. Golden fruit; crisp texture. Excellent blight resistance. Zones 4–9.

*'*Seckel*'—Also known as 'Honey Pear' or 'Sugar Pear'. Small, yellowish brown fruit with a russeted red check. Spicy, aromatic flavor; an out-

standing dessert pear. Naturally semidwarf trees are somewhat blight-resistant. Hardy to Zone 5.

'William's Bon Chretien'—Best known pear in England and, to my mind, overrated.

*'*Winter Nelis*'—A very late pear, greenish yellow and heavily russeted. Flavor, to my mind, is underrated. Blight-resistant. Ripens October to November in US.

PRUNUS SPECIES

A large and valuable genus that includes plums, peaches, apricots, and cherries. I have had little experience of any of them except plums, which include damsons and gages.

PLUMS *(Prunus domestica)*

'Coe's Golden Drop'—Golden fruit with reddish-brown spots and apricot flavor. "Melts in your mouth," said the nurseryman, but I wouldn't know: my tree has never fruited.

'Czar'—Reliable, early, heavy-cropping, black fruit said to be good only for cooking, but I disagree.

'Kirke's Blue'—An epicurean fruit, large, sweet, and violet-red, but a poor cropper.

'Marjorie's Seedling'—The latest of all plums. Stays on the tree till December unless there are frosts. Another underrated fruit. Vigorous and self-fertile.

*'*Opal*'—A newish early variety raised in Sweden. Self-fertile; good cropper. Good dessert quality.

'Purple Pershore'—Yet another underrated variety. Firm, meaty, enjoyable fruit, too good for jam.

'Rivers' Early Prolific'—Small violet-purple fruit. A hardy little tree.

*'*Victoria*'—Large pink to rose fruit with red dots and blue bloom; sweet golden yellow, freestone flesh.

DAMSONS *(Prunus institia)*

'Farleigh Damson'—Prolific and dense in growth, so used as windbreak in windy Yorkshire and Kent.

*'*Shropshire Prune Damson*'—Egg-shaped fruit, deep purple with dense bloom; richly flavored. A vigorous, hardy tree; self-fruitful.

GAGES *(Prunus institia* var. *italica)*

*'*Count Althann's Gage*'*—Originated in Hungary. Purple fruit with golden spots but without the fragrance of the green gages.

'Denniston's Superb'—"Superb" is the word. A yellowish green gage-plum sweet as honey. Of American origin, though not currently offered under this name in North America.

'Early Transparent Gage'—Described as "epicurean fruit of highest quality." Pale apricot yellow with white bloom and crimson dots.

'Oullin's Golden Gage'—Excellent flavor. Late blossoming helps frost-resistance. Ripens mid-August in US.

ACTINIDIA SPECIES

Fruiting climbers from China and elsewhere in the Far East, the best known of which is the "Chinese gooseberry," which produces the small sausage-shaped mini-melons now familiar in the shops as "kiwi-fruits." Extremely vigorous and said to be hardy. Bill Mollison told me he had seen Chinese gooseberries climbing to the tops of tall trees in chilly parts of Tasmania. Dioecious, so male and female plants needed for fruiting. In China, actinidia species are regarded as multipurpose plants. Oil can be extracted from the seeds; the leaves are rich in starch, protein, and vitamin C; the roots are used medicinally; the fibers are used in paper-making; and the abundant resin is used for dyes and plastics.

CRATAEGUS SPECIES

The hawthorns are among the hardiest and most adaptable of all small trees and shrubs. The fruits, or "haws," are regarded as valuable heart tonics, and those of some of the many species that are found in many countries are commonly eaten. The best edible hawthorn, which I grow, is the azarole *(C. azerolus)*, a Mediterranean species, hardy to Zone 7, with comparatively large yellow or pinkish fruits shaped exactly like miniature apples. This little tree fascinates visitors, who also enjoy the fruit.

ELAEAGNUS SPECIES

A genus of wind-hardy silvery shrubs or small trees related to the olives.

E. angustifolia—The Russian olive, wild olive or oleaster, has edible fruits. Cuttings were grafted by the Romans onto old olive trees to rejuvenate them, a practice that is mentioned in the Bible. Very hardy; to Zone 3.

E. multiflora—The cherry elaeagnus, or gumi. Has oblong, oxblood-red fruits, which are said to have a pleasant acid flavor. Hardy to Zone 5.

E. umbellata—Has very fragrant flowers followed by small red or orange berries, which are said to taste like red currants. Should be of particular value in a forest garden as it is shade-tolerant and is one of the few non-leguminous plants that fix nitrogen.

FICUS SPECIES

A vast genus of more than 600 species, of great nutritional importance in many countries.

*'Brown Turkey' Fig (Ficus carica)—The hardiest variety, which has been successfully grown in England since the early Tudor period. Best against a southern wall; a suitable subject for a patio garden. Hardy to Zone 8 (or to Zone 5 with winter protection).

GRAPES *(Vitis vinifera* and other spp.)

For forest garden purposes, grapes are best treated as climbers, occupying the "vertical story."

Brant Vine—A very hardy Canadian variety, which produces small, aromatic, dark-purple fruit and whose foliage has good autumn coloring. I have Brant vines trained over the 'Boney Higgins' damson and the old privy opposite.

Crimson Glory Vine (Vitis coignetiae)—Shows the most gorgeous autumn colouring when its large leaves turn brilliant scarlet and crimson. A very vigorous species that can climb to the top of the highest trees. Fruits black with purple bloom; described as "scarcely edible." Hardy to Zone 5.

Strawberry Grape (Vitus vinifera 'Fragoia')—I have one growing in the greenhouse, which produces small bunches of strawberry-jam–flavored fruit. But the type can also be grown out-of-doors.

JUNIPER *(Juniperus communis)*

One of the three British native conifers, the others being Scots pine and yew. Grown primarily for its berries, which have an essential oil of medicinal value. Many varieties available, both erect and prostrate forms; most hardy to Zone 3.

MEDLAR *(Mespilus germanica)*

An old-fashioned tree, to twenty feet tall, with remarkable, exotic-looking brown fruit. The catalogs say that, while this fruit ripens on the tree in the Mediterranean, in Britain it only becomes edible when "bletted," that is, half-rotten. But a member of the Hereford and Worcester Permaculture Group tells me he has an old medlar in his garden which gives prolific crops of ripe fruit. Hardy to Zone 6.

MULBERRY *(Morus nigra* and *M. alba)*

Another old-fashioned tree, long cultivated in England, which, after some years, gives prolific crops of luscious fruit like large raspberries. Hardy to Zone 5.

QUINCE *(Cydonia oblonga)*

A tree with fruit like hard, yellow pears, which acquire a delicious fragrance when cooked with apples. The Spaniards make a tasty "cheese" sold in flat slabs called *Dulce de Membrillo*, quince jam.

The Japanese flowering quince (*Chaenomeles japonica*) is a climbing plant with showy orange-flame blossoms, which produces fruit like small quinces. Many cultivars are available, with different colors and flower forms. Both quince and Japanese flowering quince are hardy to Zone 5.

RIBES SPECIES

This genus, which comprises gooseberries and black, white, and red currants, is an essential constituent of any temperate forest garden, where it forms the backbone of the shrub layer. The bushes are woodland plants in their native state.

Gooseberries and some currants can act as alternate hosts for the white pine blister rust, and are still restricted by law in some areas of the Northeast US. Check with your county Agricultural Extension Service for restrictions.

GOOSEBERRIES *(Ribes uva-crispa)*

A traditional form of agroforestry practiced in the Fen area of Eastern England has been the growing of gooseberries in orchards. A feature of Lancashire life used to be giant gooseberry competitions and Roger's Nursery, Pickering, Yorkshire, still stocks many of the old Lancashire varieties. One with large, red, hairy fruit is called 'Dan's Mistake'. It recalls the *Schadenfreude* felt towards a fellow competitor by a grower, who won a prize with a bush which he had cultivated from a seedling that his friend had thrown away. Another generally available gooseberry with pink-purple hairy fruit, 'Whinhan's Industry', is particularly appropriate for the forest garden, as it is an especially shade-tolerant, productive variety with very sweet fruit.

BLACK CURRANTS *(Ribes nigrum)*

Some of the best modern black currants have been bred in Scotland. Outstanding is 'Ben Sarek', which produces fruit as large and sweet as grapes. I have a 'Ben Sarek' hedge along the western edge of the forest garden. Black currants also feature in traditional agroforestry systems in the West Country, being interplanted with plums.

In general, European black currants are most susceptible to white pine blister rust in the Northeast US and Canada. In restricted areas, try growing 'Consort' or another resistant cultivar.

JOSTABERRY *(Ribes nidigrolaria)*

A black currant-gooseberry cross of Dutch origin. Resistant to white pine blister rust. Hardy to Zone 4.

WORCESTERBERRY *(Ribes divaricatum)*
Once believed to be a hybrid, but is now known to be a wild American gooseberry, and one of the parents of jostaberry. It has small, deep-purple fruit which are very sweet.

CLOVE CURRANT *(Ribes odoratum)*
Also called "buffalo currant", this is a native American species with fragrant yellow flowers and edible fruit. 'Crandall' is one excellent variety. Hardy to Zone 5.

ROSES *(Rosa* spp.*)*

The Rosaceae is among the most important of all plant families. It includes most temperate fruits: apples, pears, plums, cherries, raspberries, blackberries, among others. The roses themselves have exceptional medicinal value. They are regarded as a tonic for the whole system and especially for the heart. The hips are one of the richest sources of vitamin C, beneficial for female ailments, and make a delicious tea. Wild and traditional varieties of rose are more medically potent and often more fragrant than the sophisticated modern types featured at flower shows and dedicated to ladies of fashion and film stars. What could be more refreshing than the scent of the humble sweetbriar of the hedgerows *(R. eglanteria)*? The dog rose *(R. canina)* is said to derive its name from the fact that the ancient Celts used it as a remedy for infected dog bites and wolf bites. The Bulgarians and Turks grow vast acreages of roses interplanted with garlic, which is said to enhance the fragrance required for the concentrated essence, known as "attar of roses." Roses make delightful spots of color in the forest garden. Of special interest are a number of historic roses, several of which are featured on my Rose Mound.

Apothecary Rose (Rosa gallica var. *officinalis)*—Said to have been first bred 3,000 years ago in Persia. Much used by medieval herbalists. Hardy to Zone 6.

Rosa mundi—A sport from *Rosa gallica*, striped red and white. Cultivated since at least 1310.

White Rose of York (Rosa x alba)—Said to have been cultivated by the ancient Greeks and Romans. Used symbolically in the Wars of the Roses. Hardy to Zone 5.

Provence Rose (Rosa centifolia)—Known as *rose des peintres,* as it was a favorite of the seventeenth-century Dutch artists. Hardy to Zone 6.

Damask Rose (Rosa damascena)—Introduced into Europe from Asia Minor in the sixteenth century. Hardy to Zone 5.

Rosa rugosa—Of Japanese origin. Has large, meaty, tomato-shaped hips that are very rich in vitamin C and can be eaten raw. Often used for hedging. Extremely hardy; to Zone 2.

RUBUS SPECIES

This genus, which includes raspberries, blackberries, and many well-known hybrid berries, is another that is essential to the forest garden. They include climbers, groundcover plants, and shrubs.

BLACKBERRIES *(Rubus ulmifolius)*

The most picturesque of the cultivated varieties is the parsley-leaved blackberry, *(R. laciniatus),* hardy to Zone 5.

JAPANESE WINEBERRIES *(Rubus phoenicolasius)*

With red, hairy stems. Hardy to Zone 6.

BLACKBERRY-RASPBERRY HYBRIDS

These include the well-known loganberry *(Rubus ursinus* var. *loganobaccus);* the tayberry, a recent Scottish introduction with long, tapering fruits; and the boysenberry. (A visitor once thought I said "poisonberry." She exclaimed: "Can you really eat them?") All hardy in Zones 5–8.

RASPBERRIES *(Rubus idaeus)*

A Scottish specialty. An excellent variety that I grow in 'Glen Clova'. A very late variety that I also grow is 'Autumn Bliss', which can fruit as late as December.

GROUNDCOVER PLANTS

Among *Rubus* species that spread horizontally are the dewberry *(R. caesuis),* the Japanese strawberry-raspberry *(R. illecebrosus), Rubus tricolor,* and *Rubus nutans.*

Thimbleberry *(Rubus parviflorus)*
A vigorous shrub whose fruit, like large raspberries, is relished by the Indians of America's Northwest. Reliably hardy to at least Zone 4.

Salmonberry *(Rubus spectabilis)*
Another shrub from the American Northwest, whose magenta blossoms appear as early as February, to be followed by large orange berries. It is sometimes called "cloudberry," but that name strictly belongs to a low shrub that grows in the heathlands of the Far North and is much appreciated for its berries in Scandinavia and Finland. Reliably hardy to Zone 6.

SORBUS SPECIES

A number of attractive small trees bearing currantlike fruits, which should be explored by those who are interested in extending the boundaries of their normal diet. Several have fruit that are acknowledged to be edible. Others have fruit that *may* be edible—brave pioneers might like to experiment! They include two of the rarest of all Britain's wild plants: *Sorbus arranensis,* which only grows wild in two glens on the Isle of Arran (of which I have a specimen), and *Sorbus birstoliensis,* which is only found in its wild state in the Avon Gorge.

Rowan *(Sorbus aucuparia)*
The familiar European mountain ash, whose bitter but fascinating fruits are made into jelly by the Scots and are juiced by the Swiss. I have a variety officially pronounced to be edible—*Sorbus aucuparia edulis*—but its fruits are only a shade less bitter than those of the wild tree. However they are very rich in vitamin C, and, mixed with sweet fruit and a bit of honey, they make an intriguingly original fruit salad. Hardy in Zones 4–6. *S. americana* is the American mountain ash, hardy in Zones 3–7.

Whitebeam *(Sorbus aria)*
Another native British tree. It s fruits are faintly reminiscent of old-fashioned fruit drops, without a trace of bitterness. Hardy to Zone 6.

Wild Service Tree *(Sorbus torminalis)*
Another rare British native, whose fruits used to be sold in markets

in the Kent and Sussex Weald under the name of "chequerberries"; they have been described as "the most delectable of all England's wild fruit." The Prime Minister's country residence is named for the wild service trees that grow on its grounds. Hardy to Zone 6.

STRAWBERRIES *(Fragaria* spp.*)*

In their native state strawberries are woodland plants, and the Victorians used to take a delight in growing them in old, disused coppices. They are said to benefit from a mulch of pine needles; pine branches passed through a shredder should be equally beneficial. Wild strawberries make an ideal constituent of the forest garden's groundcover layer; they should be surrounded by a barricade of mulch to prevent them from being overwhelmed by invasive herbs or *Rubus* plants. F.C. King, the veteran Westmoreland gardener who pioneered the no-digging system and was an advocate of companion planting, claimed to have restored a clump of heavily diseased strawberry plants to perfect health by allowing them—temporarily—to become infested with weeds.

The American wild strawberry *(Fragaria virginiana)* is common in fields and meadows. Its tiny berries are time-consuming to pick in quantity, but their flavor is unmatched. Other "wild" strawberries that have been somewhat developed for cultivation include the alpine strawberry *(Fragaria vesca)*, which is hardy in Zones 3–10, and the musk strawberry *(Fragaria moschata)*, which is rare in Europe and almost unknown in America. The musk strawberry has self-pollinating flowers, larger fruit than the alpine strawberry, and is hardy in Zone 5.

SUMAC

The staghorn sumac *(Rhus typhina)*, with its hairy reddish branches and hairy crimson fruit, makes a striking feature on the edge of the forest garden. In America the fruits are soaked in water to produce a beverage similar to lemonade. The sumac belongs to the *Rhus* genus, which also includes the Japanese wax tree *(R. succedanea)* and the Japanese varnish tree *(R. verniciflua)*, which is poisonous to the touch. Among its more distant relatives are the pistachio and mango.

NUTS

The only nuts that are grown commercially in Britain are cobs or hazelnuts *(Corylus avellana)* and filberts *(C. maxima)*, but there is little doubt that other nuts could be grown with equal success if more trouble were taken to breed or import improved varieties.

SWEET CHESTNUT *(Castanea sativa)*

'*Marron de Lyon*'—Fruits at an earlier age and produces larger nuts than the "Spanish" sweet chestnut commonly grown in Britain. After only two years my tree gave a fair crop of the characteristically spiny fruits—like small green hedgehogs. The large nuts sold in the shops are the result of intensive French breeding programs to develop improved clones. The chestnut is a highly prized food in France, where it is made into the expensive delicacy, *marron-glacé*, and ground into flour to make bread and cakes. Chestnut trees have enormous potential value in agroforestry schemes as perennial "tree cereals," like the mesquite trees *(Prosopis* spp.*)*, whose beans are ground into flour by the Indians of the Southwest United States. The sight of chestnut forests on Corsican mountainsides inspired J. Russell Smith to write his classic *Tree Crops: A Permanent Agriculture*, the pioneer work that led to the development of agroforestry in Japan and the West.

WALNUTS *(Juglans regia)*

The common walnut is a slow-growing tree which takes up to fifteen years to come into bearing. It has been grown in England for many centuries, more for its highly prized timber than for its nuts. However, new clones have been developed, especially in Germany, for earlier fruiting and better quality nuts. I have one of these, called 'Buccaneer'.

Butternuts *(Juglans cinerea)*

An American member of the *Juglans* genus, to which walnuts belong. A fast-growing tree with large, hairy leaves and exceptionally
large nuts, of which I have a young specimen. Hardy to Zone 3.

Shagbark Hickory *(Carya ovata)*

An American member of the *Carya* genus, allied to the walnuts,
which is regarded as the most valuable nut that America produces.
Difficult to establish and slow to grow, as it spends the first years of
its life doing nothing but driving an enormously tough taproot deep
into the soil. Once in full growth, its immensely strong timber, used
for axe-handles, can resist almost anything that nature throws at it,
including the ravages of the grey squirrel, which tears the bark (hence
the name "shagbark"). Hardy to Zone 5.

American Oaks *(Quercus* spp.*)*

A number of these trees have sweet acorns, which can be eaten by
human beings without boiling to eliminate the bitter tannins. The
famous Scottish naturalist John Muir once said that an acorn cheese
which he had been given by some Indians was the most sustaining
and palatable survival food he had ever tasted.

Nut-Bearing Conifers

The Romans introduced nut pines to Britain to provide rations for
their troops. The umbrella-shaped form of the stone pine *(Pinus
pinea)* is one of the characteristic features of the landscape of Italy,
from which large quantities of *pignolia* pine nuts are exported. There
is little doubt that homegrown nuts could be a regular part of the
British diet, if we took the same trouble to breed suitable varieties as
we do to breed apples. The stone pine is well-suited to British conditions, especially in sandy and seaside districts. Among other nut pines
that are suited to our climate are the Swiss arolla pine *(P. cembra)*, of
which I have a specimen, the Mexican nut pine *(P. cembroides)*, Ger-
ard's pine *(P. gerardiana)*, and the digger pine *(P. sabiniana)*. I also
have specimens of two other nut-bearing conifers: the ginkgo or mar-
denhair tree *(Ginkgo biloba)*, a "living fossil," which survived only as a
temple tree in China; and the "monkey-puzzle" tree *(Araucaria arau-*

cana), whose nuts are part of the staple diet of the Indians of Southern Chile. A native American species, the piñon pine *(P. edulis)*, is hardy to Zone 3.

Vegetables

As I explained in Chapter 13, very little fresh food can be expected from a temperate forest garden during the winter months, as most trees and bushes are bare, and herbs and perennial vegetables die down. The only exceptions are the hardy crabs, 'Golden Hornet' and 'Crittenden', which retain their fruit till the new year, root vegetables, and a few lingering herbs and weeds. Therefore forest gardeners who want regular supplies of fresh vegetables throughout the year must make a winter garden outside the forest garden precincts, which can also, incidentally, be the home of some sun-loving herbs.

PERENNIAL VEGETABLES

ARTICHOKE, GLOBE *(Cynara scolymus)*
These giant thistles or their cousins, the cardoons *(C. cardunculus)*, make a striking architectural feature growing at the edge of the forest garden.

ASPARAGUS *(Asparagus officinalis)*
A neighbor of mine grows asparagus in his herbaceous border, but it would be a mistake to allow this fussy and luxurious vegetable to disappear, even temporarily, amid the ordered chaos that is the forest garden in summer. It is best to plant the octopus-like roots, or "crowns," in their own exclusive mound.

BAMBOO SHOOTS
A small clump of bamboos makes an excellent forest garden feature, where it is useful for supplying canes to support young trees. A number of temperate bamboos, which are members of the Grass Family (Poaceae), produce edible shoots. These include *Arundinaria simonii*, the "bottle-brush" (*Chusquea couleou*), *Phyllostachys bambu-*

soides, P. flexuosa, P. nigra, and *P. mitis,* the most favored source of
the bamboo shoots served in Chinese restaurants.

BROCCOLI *(Brassica oleracea)*
'Nine Star Perennial'—I tried growing this variety from seed in the
forest garden but, one snowy night, it was eaten to the ground by pigeons. However, three plants appeared out of the blue in the AFG,
possibly sowed with a useful accompaniment of manure by the very
same pigeons. I was not sorry to see its departure from the forest
garden as, like other brassicas, it is too greedy and demanding to
find a fit place in a cooperative community.

CHICORY *(Cichorium intybus)*
Useful, hardy, nourishing, mineral-rich, varied, and visually attractive. The wild chicory, or succory, is a pasture herb with beautiful
sky-blue flowers but otherwise similar in form and bitter flavor to
the dandelion, which has long been used as a digestive tonic. Evelyn
described it succinctly as "more grateful to the Stomach and to the
Palate." But in recent years there have appeared in British shops and
seed catalogs some of the many varieties of chicory that have been
cultivated in Italy since Roman times. These, generally known as
radicchio, are named after the towns and districts where they have
been bred ('Treviso', 'Verona', etc.). Some are like compact lettuces
and acquire beautiful shades of maroon and white in the autumn.
Some even change shape; all are far less bitter than the wild succory.
Many of them put out fresh leaves throughout the winter months,
and are ideally suited to the cut-and-come-again system.

CHIVES *(Allium schoenoprasum)*
A cut-and-come-again onion, grown for its leaves. A variety recently
introduced from the Far East is the Chinese garlic chive.

DANDELION, CULTIVATED *(Taraxacum officinale)*
Described as "probably the most nutritious green there is. Very rich
in minerals and vitamins." Like chicory, its root can be roasted and
ground for use as a caffeine-free coffee substitute.

GARLIC, WILD, OR RAMSONS *(Allium ursinum)*
One of the first leaves to appear in the forest garden in early spring.

With its mild, sweet garlic flavor, it is, to my mind, the most delicious of salad ingredients.

GOOD KING HENRY *(Chenopodium bonus-henricus)*
A wild vegetable that has long been appreciated for its leaves, which are cooked like spinach, and for its asparagus-like shoots.

HORSERADISH *(Armoracia rusticana)*
The young leaves have a taste similar to that of the well-known shredded roots, but far milder.

LOVAGE *(Levisticum officinale)*
In summer this pungent member of the Celery Family makes an impressive feature rising to a height of nine feet in the middle of the forest garden. Its leaves and stems give an original flavor to soups, stews, and salads, but must be used with discretion.

LUCERNE, or ALFALFA *(Medicago sativa)*
This deep-rooted leguminous plant makes a very useful contribution of nitrogen to the forest garden. Its leaves can be served in salads and its seeds can be sprouted.

MITSUBA *(Cryptotaenia japonica)*
A hardy Japanese form of parsley, served raw in salads.

NETTLES *(Urtica dioica)*
No need to cultivate these! The job is to keep them under control, but the best way to do this is by eating the young leaves as soon as they appear. These are very rich in minerals and are surprisingly palatable if cooked briefly with potatoes or cereals such as sesame, quinoa, or buckwheat. Nettles contribute to the forest garden's wildlife population by acting as food plants for the larvae of several butterflies.

ONIONS, EGYPTIAN, TREE, or "WALKING" *(Allium cepa var. proliferum)*
Grotesque plants with small bulbs at the tip of their stems.

ONIONS, WELSH or BUNCHING *(Allium fistulosum)*
Like large chives, but come from Siberia, not Wales. Extremely hardy.

SAMPHIRE *(Salicornia europaea)*
An intriguing fleshy plant that must have been regarded as a great delicacy in Shakespeare's day as people risked their lives to pick it (see *King Lear*). Evelyn says of it "That growing on the Sea-Cliffs (as

about Dover etc.) not only pickl'd, but crude and cold, when young and tender . . . is in my Opinion, for its Aromatic, and other excellent Vertues and Effects against the Spleen, Cleaning the Passages, sharpening Appetite etc., so far preferable to most of our hotter Herbs and Sallet-ingredients that I have long wonder'd, it has not long since been propagated in the potagene." Plants now available should be grown in a light, well-drained soil.

SORREL *(Rumex acetosa)*

A garden green useful for soups or salads with a delightful, mild lemon flavor. 'Belleville' is one common cultivar. French sorrel *(R. scutatus)* is the largest-leaved garden strain, and the leaves are said to taste milder and less acidic than other wild and garden sorrels.

SEA-KALE *(Crambe maritima)*

A form of cabbage that must be one of the toughest plants in the world, as its natural habitat is shingle beaches, where it pushes down deep roots to reach the underlying soil. A favorite vegetable among the Victorians, who blanched the young shoots to produce a very tender asparagus equivalent. Hardy to Zone 6.

WATERCRESS *(Nasturtium officinale)*

It used to be thought that this popular vegetable could only be grown in running water, but now seeds are available that can be sown in moist soil.

ROOT VEGETABLES

Those most suited to the forest garden mound are either shade-tolerant plants such as Hamburg parsley *(Petroselinum crispum)* and some radishes, or winter roots that come into their own when the perennial herbage has died down. I can particularly recommend the 'Black Spanish' radish *(Raphanus sativus)*, the purple French radish 'Violet de Gournay' and salsify *(Tragopogon porrifolius)*, the "vegetable oyster."

WINTER VEGETABLES

Among the many hardy annuals suitable for the Winter Garden which

I have grown and can recommend are some less common vegetables:

CHARD, RUBY, or LEAF-BEET *(Beta vulgaris* var. *cicla)*
  Possibly the most beautiful of all vegetables, with its large, glossy scarlet-ribbed leaves.

ENDIVE *(Cichorium endivia)*
  'En Cornet de Bordeaux'—An old French variety which provides constant cut-and-come-again harvesting throughout the winter.

KALE, or BORECOLE, 'PENTLAND BRIG' *(Brassica oleracea,* var. *acephala)*
  An old broccoli-like vegetable from Northeast Scotland, where it was called "The Green Doctor," as those who consumed it through the winter were believed to avoid illness.

LEEK *(Allium ampeloprasum* var. *porrum)*
  'St. Victor'—An old French variety with deep purple leaves.

LETTUCE *(Lactuca sativa)*
  'Parella'—One of the hardiest of all lettuces, from the mountains of northern Italy.
  'Rouge d'Hiver'—A decorative small French lettuce with reddish leaves.

MUSTARD *(Brassica juncea)*
  'Green-in-the-Snow'—A piquant and super-hardy vegetable from China.

SPINACH *(Spinacia oleracea)*
  'Medania'—An outstanding vegetable which, it is claimed, will stand the hardest winters.

Herbs

"The deft use of herbs transforms an ordinary salad into something rich, memorable and unique." So writes Joy Larkcom in her inspiring book, *The Salad Garden.* Herbs play many roles in the forest garden: as good companions for other plants, as attractants for beneficial insects, as medicaments, as flavorings, and as foods in their own right. In that capacity we are returning to the practices of our forefathers, whose "sallets" comprised a wide variety of herbs as well as vegetables and fruit. Herbs can be divided into those that in their natural state are woodland plants, and are therefore suitable for the forest garden, and those that naturally inhabit grasslands, sandy heathlands, or rocky hillsides and therefore demand full sunlight. These can be planted in the "Winter Garden."

Shade-Tolerant Herbs

BALM or LEMON BALM *(Melissa officinalis)*

A small, hardy shrub with the delicious scent and flavor of lemon, which is said to "radiate a beneficial influence all round." John Evelyn described it as "Cordial and exhilarating, sovereign for the Brain, strengthening the Memory and powerfully chasing away Melancholy." Adds a stimulating nip to fruit salads.

BARBERRY *(Berberis vulgaris)*

One of the best liver tonics, because its bitter principle is more closely related to human bile than any other natural substance. This small shrub at one time was cultivated for its edible berries. I have the cultivated form *Berberis thunbergii* (Japanese barberry) with pink-purple leaves, which makes an attractive patch of color in the forest garden. In North America, the cultivation of barberry is prohibited by federal law in wheat-growing regions, because barberry is a host for wheat rust. Hardy in Zones 4–8.

BORAGE *(Borago officinalis)*

Once you've had it, you've had it. Though an annual, there is no need to sow it more than once. A prolific self-seeder, it will crop up all over the place year after year. With its gay, sky-blue flowers it is always welcome. The bees love it too. Hairy leaves are reputed to "taste like cucumber," but I can never see it. Another traditional antidote to melancholy.

BROOM, SCOTCH *(Cytisus scoparius)*

Leguminous shrub that adds valuable nitrogen to the forest garden, where it thrives, even though its natural habitat is open ground. Flower buds are used as a caper substitute. Yields a yellow and green dye. Tonic and internal cleanser. Hardy to Zone 6.

BUCKWHEAT *(Fagopyrum esculentum)*
Contains rutin, an antidote to hardening of the arteries. Attracts bees and other beneficial insects. Excellent soil improver. Cultivated in northern countries for its very nourishing grain.

COMFREY, RUSSIAN *(Symphytum x uplandicum)*
One of the most valuable and vigorous of herbs. Strengthens muscles and even helps to knit broken bones (its old country name is "knit-bone"). Contains mucilage used in lung disorders. Wonderful soil fertilizer. Should be eaten daily for positive health; its leaves lose their roughness if lightly cooked.

Recent studies suggest that large doses of comfrey when taken internally may be harmful to human health. Many people dispute the finding, but, fortunately, comfrey is excellent as well used externally, as an ingredient in salves and soothing foot-soak preparations.

JACK-BY-THE-HEDGE *(Alliaria petiolara)*
Also called garlic mustard, which perfectly describes its flavor. Valuable wild herb with antiseptic leaves, which can be used in salads. Food plant of the orange-tip butterfly.

LADY'S-MANTLE *(Alchemilla vulgaris)*
Useful for the forest garden ground layer. Traditional wound herb and treatment for feminine ailments.

MARIGOLD, FRENCH and MEXICAN *(Tagetes spp.)*
Among the most important of companion plants, used for deterring nematodes and aphids.

MINT *(Mentha spp.)*
My Forest Garden is fragrant with the scents of the eight varieties of aromatic mint that thrive there: apple mint, curly mint, eau-de-cologne mint, ginger mint, peppermint, pineapple mint, spearmint, and water mint. I also grow a nonaromatic mint, gipsywort, which shares the medicinal qualities of the others. The mints are both soothing and stimulating as well as good for the digestion. In Arab countries, where alcohol is banned, mint tea is the regular social drink.

NASTURTIUM *(Tropaeolum majus)*

Useful for the forest garden vertical layer; trained up apple trees, it is said to deter woolly aphids. Peppery leaves are rich in vitamin C, and add zest to salads. Antiseptic.

POT-MARIGOLD or CALENDULA *(Calendula officinalis)*
Another wound herb still important today (calendula ointment). Flowers used in salads.

SAGE *(Salvia officinalis)*
One of the most potent of herbs, especially effective in nervous complaints. As the Arabs drink mint tea, the Greeks drink sage tea. Dried sage leaves are delicious in stews.

SOAPWORT *(Saponaria officinalis)*
Known in America as "Bouncing Bet." Rich in saponin, a substance with valuable healing, cleansing, and soil-conditioning qualities. If steeped in water, the plant acts as a natural detergent with none of the harmful qualities of manufactured detergents. As such it is still used for cleaning valuable fabrics, such as old tapestries. Decoction used for treating skin troubles.

SWEET CICELY *(Myrrhis odorata)*
The lacy, aniseed-flavored foliage of this plant is used as a general tonic. Removes some of the bitterness if cooked with sour fruit like rhubarb.

TANSY *(Tanacetum vulgare)*
Harshly aromatic herb that is said to be good companion for fruit trees, as it deters harmful insects.

WOUNDWORT *(Stachys* spp.*)*
The name refers to several members of the Lamiaceae (Mint Family), with attractive purple blooms and soft, downy leaves, which were used to dress wounds in the Middle Ages.

Sun-Loving Herbs

CATNIP *(Nepeta cataria)*
Intoxicates cats but deters rats. Traditional baby remedy for expelling wind and curing hiccups.

CENTAURY or KNAPWEED *(Centaurea* spp.*)*
Pasture herb with lovely star-shaped pink flowers arranged in

rosettes. Bitter tonic for blood and liver. Anglo-Saxons prescribed it for snake bites.

FENNEL *(Foeniculum vulgare)*
Feathery leaves used for treatment of gastric ailments, cramps, and rheumatism. Lotion used for eye troubles.

FEVERFEW *(Chrysanthemum parthenium)*
Tall white member of the Daisy Family (Asteraceae), used to treat migraine headaches and feminine ailments.

GOAT'S-RUE *(Galega officinalis)*
Tall, showy member of Bean Family (Fabaceae) said to promote milk-yield in goats and other mammals.

HOREHOUND *(Marrubium vulgare)*
Plant contains a powerful substance called marrubium, which makes it a valued remedy for throat and lung troubles. I was told of a beekeeper who kept his hives in a clump of horehound and removed the supers as soon as the plants had ceased flowering. He kept the honey as a cough mixture.

HYSSOP *(Hyssopus officinalis)*
A decorative small shrub that is also a superb bee plant. Leaves contain sulphur, which makes them an excellent body cleanser. Also nerve and eye remedy.

LAVENDER *(Lavandula angustifolia)*
Yet another bee herb—bees are especially attracted to blue or bluish flowers. Deters harmful insects. Lavender tea is a nerve tonic. Hardy to Zone 5. Mulch plants heavily with straw to protect over winter, except in warm climate zones.

MARJORAM *(Origanum spp.)*
Name means "joy of the mountain," owing to its handsome pink-purple flowers. Much used as seasoning in Mediterranean cooking (oregano). Contains an aromatic oil that aids digestion and expels impurities.

ROSEMARY *(Rosmarinus officinalis)*
Another characteristic Mediterranean herb that is hardy to Zone 6 if given winter protection. Said to be good companion to vegetables, as

it deters harmful insects. Yields a camphorated type of dark green oil that has many medicinal uses, including treatment of high blood pressure and heart troubles. A former gypsy specialty was "Queen of Hungary's Water," made from rosemary flowers and reputed to be a general tonic and beautifier.

RUE *(Ruta graveolens)*

Acrid-scented plant with vivid blue-green leaves, especially appreciated in many parts of the Islamic world. Like buckwheat it contains rutin, which has been proved effective in strengthening blood vessels, nerves, and glands and in hardening teeth and nails. Also used for treatment of nerves and female ailments. John Evelyn writes that Pliny "reports it to be of such effect for the Preservation of Sight; that the Painters of his Time us'd to devour a great quantity of it."

SOUTHERNWOOD, or LAD'S-LOVE *(Artemisia abrotanum)*

Subshrub with apple-scented leaves. Like other members of the *Artemisia* genus, it contains a bitter principle called absinthol, which is highly antiseptic. Hardy in Zones 4–8.

TEASEL *(Dipsacus fullonum* or *D. sativus)*

"You must grow teasels in your wildlife garden. The pollen from their tall elegant flowers turns the bumble bees pink and in the autumn swarms of gold-finches will feed on the seeds." So wrote Chris Baynes, the wildlife gardening expert. The teasel is a curious plant whose flowers are encased in a unique thorny receptacle, which has been used from time immemorial for dressing cloth, as it has been found impossible to reproduce it artificially. Another peculiarity of the plant is that it stores water in its leaves, which the gypsies believe has medicinal properties.

THYME *(Thymus* spp.*)*

This well-known aromatic shrub contains the antiseptic oil thymol, which is used in many disinfectants, toothpastes, and hair lotions. The plant provides safe remedies for many ills involving the nerves.

WORMWOOD *(Artemisia absinthium)*

A plant with grey leaves, an indication that it is relatively drought-tolerant. In fact it is found in rocky and desert places. Like southernwood, another *Artemisia,* it contains absinthol, which should be used with discretion as a digestive tonic. It is a powerful repellent of harmful insects.

YARROW *(Achillea millefolium)*

This pasture herb owes its Latin name *Achillea* to the fact that its potency as a wound-healer is said to have been discovered by the Greek warrior Achilles. It is still used as the main ingredient of a healing salve.

Wetlands Plants

No garden is complete without a pond, and a forest garden is no exception. If possible, room should be found for a pond to accommodate reeds, rushes, and other useful water plants, with an adjacent bog for fruits of *Vaccinium* species, which require moist conditions. My reedbed contains the following plants:

ARROWHEAD *(Sagittaria sagittifolia)*

Plant with arrow-shaped leaves and edible tubers, for which it is commonly cultivated in China.

BULRUSH *(Scirpus lacustris)*

The young shoots are edible, and the leaves can be used for making mats and baskets.

FLOWERING-RUSH *(Butomus umbellatus)*

A plant with bold, attractive pink flowers and edible seeds. For mild climates; hardy to only Zone 9.

GALINGALE *(Cyperus alternifolius)*

A decorative rush with umbrella-like leaves, whose roots were esteemed as a spice in the Middle Ages.

PICKEREL-WEED *(Pontederia cordata)*

A plant with upstanding heart-shaped leaves and fleshy spikes of blue flowers. The leaf stalks are edible, and the seeds can be eaten raw or ground, as a flour substitute. Hardy to Zone 3.

REEDMACE or COMMON CATTAIL *(Typha latifolia)*

The familiar "bulrush," with long brown flowering spikes on tall stalks.

The flowers, young shoots, and seeds are edible. The leaves can be used for making hats and mats and the stems for papermaking.

My bog gardens have also been planted with cranberries *(Vaccinium macrocarpon)*, swamp blueberries *(V. corymbosum)*, cowberries *(V. vitis-idaea)*, bog whortleberries *(V. uliginosum)*, and *Vaccinium cylindraceum,* a rare shrub with cylindrical flowers and blue-black edible berries from the Azores.

Appendix 2

∼

*Select list of plants suitable for tropical
and subtropical Forest Gardens*

𝑇his list should give some idea of the enormous variety of delicious and nutritious fruit, nuts, vegetables, herbs, spices, and cereals, as well as other useful plants, that can be grown under tropical and subtropical conditions. If the forest gardens and other agroforestry systems that are now thriving in many tropical areas were widely extended, shortages and famines could be a thing of the past. By using such systems, many deserts and other deprived areas could be reclaimed and revived. Not only could the indigenous inhabitants be adequately fed, clothed, warmed, and housed, but large surpluses could become available for export, so that more people on low incomes in the West could enjoy tropical products. There should be a greatly increased exchange of foods between the tropical and temperate zones, so that people throughout the world can enjoy the diversified diets that are essential for positive health.

The tropical rain forest has a far greater diversity of plants than any other ecosystem on earth—many of them not yet identified by science—and, if developed in a wise, sustainable way on forest-garden lines, it can provide an equally wide diversity of foods and other useful products for the benefit of mankind. At the opposite extreme are the deserts, some almost completely devoid of vegetation, which cover about one-third of the world's land surface and many of which are rapidly spreading, in most cases owing to removal of tree cover for firewood or to overgrazing. But these too can be reclaimed by agroforestry and other tree-planting methods, as has been proved by a number of countries, above all China. The first stage is to plant hardy, drought-tolerant, deep-rooting plants that can tap any groundwater resources that may be available. Once these are established, they can be used to "nurse" more tender crops, including fruit and nut trees.

The following lists include many plants that can flourish in sustainably developed rainforest areas, as has been proved by many successful forest garden schemes in India, Sri Lanka, Indonesia, and East and West Africa. It also lists some valuable drought-tolerant plants which can help to cause the deserts to "bloom and blossom as the rose."

Fruit

AVOCADO *(Persea americana)*

This vegetable-fruit, native to Central America but now grown in many other tropical and subtropical countries, plays an important part in the diets of many people of those areas because of its exceptionally high content of protein, fat, vitamin A, and vitamin B. Its flesh, which can be spread on bread like butter, is a valuable digestive tonic, tissue builder, and glandular food. It is the fruit of a small to medium-sized tree that is particularly resistant to pests and diseases. An ideal forest garden constituent, it is one of twenty-five species featured in a diagram of a Guatemalan garden illustrated in Bill Mollison's *Permaculture One.*

BANANA *(Musa* spp.)

One of the principal components of the Chagga gardens of Tanzania, where cooked unripe bananas are a staple "vegetable" and dried bananas, ground into flour, are sometimes used as cereal substitutes. Some bananas are also grown for their fibers, and the leaves are used for thatching. So the banana is one of many examples of the ingenuity shown by indigenous peoples in finding multiple uses for staple plants. It is one of the most valuable of all foods, rich in minerals and vitamins as well as carbohydrates.

BREADFRUIT *(Artocarpus altilis)*

Another vegetable-fruit, usually eaten roasted in the Pacific zone, where it is native and where it is often consumed as a staple food. The fruit, like large melons with a thick, warty rind, grow on tall trees that may reach ninety feet. They have now become established in most parts of the tropics.

CARAMBOLA *(Averrhoa carambola)*

The ribbed, golden, juicy fruit of a small tree which originated in Indonesia and has spread to other parts of Southeast Asia. It is used to prepare a refreshing drink.

CERIMAN *(Monstera deliciosa)*

Green, cone-shaped fruit of a Central American creeper, having incised leaves, which are unique in the plant world, and long aerial roots. The pineapple-flavored juice makes a delicious drink.

CHERIMOYA *(Annona cherimola)*

Another pineapple-flavored fruit from the American tropics, which is also widely grown in Asia. The fruit, which has a thick scaly skin, is very popular in the areas where it is grown.

CUSTARD APPLE *(Annona squamosa)*

A closely related fruit with a custard-like consistency, also known as "sweet sop," which is very popular in the West Indies.

DATE *(Phoenix dactylifera)*

One of the most nourishing of foods, and believed to be the oldest of all cultivated plants. A single tree, during its lifetime of 200 to 300 years, can produce up to 600 pounds of fruit a year. A component of agroforestry schemes in desert oases and of forest gardens in Bangladesh, it is one of the supreme multipurpose trees, every part being utilized. It has been estimated that over 800 articles can be made from the date palm tree. The sugary sap has valuable medicinal qualities; dried dates are ground into a cereal-equivalent flour; the stones are roasted and ground to make date coffee; young leaves are eaten as vegetables; older leaves are woven into mats and baskets; the fibers are made into ropes and brushes; the timber is used for building houses and dhows; the stalks are used as fuel.

DATTOCK *(Detarium senegalense)*

A fruit consisting of a pod with a sweet, farinaceous pulp, which is common in parts of tropical Africa. An edible oil can be extracted from the seeds. The tree furnishes a valuable timber, sometimes called "African mahogany."

DURIAN *(Durio zibethinus)*

A fruit whose taste and smell have been the subject of some extremely uncomplimentary descriptions including "custard passed through a sewer" and "old cheese and onions flavored with turpentine." However, an odorless variety is said to have been discovered, and it has been suggested that this might be the subject of a breeding program to produce a fruit acceptable to world commerce. The tree, which can reach a height of 100 feet, is the main component of the canopy of the Maninjau forest gardens of Sumatra, where it is grown in association with cinnamon.

EUGENIA *(Eugenia* spp.)

A large genus of tropical and subtropical fruits, with glamorous names such as rose-apple, Java jambosa, rumberry, arrayan, maigang, pitanga tuba, surinam cherry, and uvalha.

FIG *(Ficus* spp.)

An enormous number of species of fig, cultivated and wild, grow in the tropics. Figs are rich in energizing fruit sugars as well as vitamins and minerals, including iron, which means that they are especially beneficial for the blood. A combination of calcium, potassium, and sodium, which figs contain, is said to make them a valuable aid to normal heart action and the efficient functioning of the nervous system, as well as preventing lung and chest complaints.

GRAPEFRUIT *(Citrus* x *paradisi)*

Appeared "out of the blue" in the eighteenth-century West Indies, apparently as a result of cross-pollination between oranges and pomelos, the largest of all citrus fruits, which are native to Southeast Asia and pips of which were deposited in Barbados by an English sea captain named Shaddock in 1696. The grapefruit contains two particularly valuable substances, a form of quinine, which is helpful in the treatment of malaria and feverish colds, and biotin, which is a useful slimming agent.

GUAVA *(Psidium guajava)*
Has spread from the American tropics to become one of the most
commonly planted tropical fruits. An occupant of the low-tree layer
of forest gardens in Kerala, India. Valued for its particularly high
content of vitamin C.

INDIAN GOOSEBERRY *(Emblica officinalis)*
Another component of the Kerala forest gardens. One of the most
widely appreciated fruits in tropical Asia, both for its nutritional
and medical uses. One of the richest sources of vitamin C. When
virgin land is cleared wild Indian gooseberry trees are always left
standing. In Thailand buses stop in the countryside to allow passen-
gers to pick the fruit to quench their thirst.

JACKFRUIT *(Artocarpus heterophyllus)*
Probably the largest of all fruit, weighing up to seventy pounds. Re-
lated to breadfruit; despite its strong odor it is relished cooked or raw.
Component of forest gardens in Nigeria and Kerala.

JAMBOLIN *(Syzygium cumini)*
Somewhat acid, plumlike fruit of one of the most popular of tropical
ornamental trees. Especially favored as avenue tree in India. Flowers,
rich in nectar, yield high-quality honey. Hardy; tolerates both drought
and flooding.

JUJUBE *(Ziziphus jujuba)*
Prolifically produced farinaceous fruit of one of the world's hardiest
trees, one that can withstand severe heat, frost, and drought. Another "tree cereal," which can also be made into a butter or a cheese.
Wood used for making sandals. One of the few trees that is host to
the lac insect, resinous encrustations from which are used to produce shellac and lacquer.

KUMQUAT *(Fortunella* spp.)
Like a small orange; not a true citrus but closely related. Specially
prized in China because it can stand cold better than oranges.

LEMON *(Citrus limon)*
Excellent source of phosphorus, the mineral that is essential for the
healthy functioning of the nervous system, and one of the few fruits

that is a good source of calcium, necessary for sound teeth and bones.

LITCHI or LYCHEE *(Litchi chinensis)*

Mainly grown in tropical and subtropical parts of China, where it is much esteemed as the last course of the traditional Chinese dinner. Like a small plum with a pinkish crimson warty rind, enclosing a translucent jellylike substance that has a "sweet-and-sour" flavor.

LOQUAT *(Eriobotrya japonica)*

Another Chinese native; one of the few subtropical members of the Rosaceae (Rose Family), which includes many of the most important temperate fruits, such as apples and pears. The loquat is like a small golden pear, about the size of and similar in flavor to a 'John Downie' crab.

MANGO *(Mangifera indica)*

The best-known fruit grown in India, where enormous quantities are produced—for export. An Indian friend tells me that the ordinary Indian seldom sees one. However the forest gardeners of Kerala and Bangladesh are careful to include mangoes in their planting schemes. One of the most prolific of fruit trees; a single big old tree is said to be capable of producing a bumper crop of 35,000 mangoes—enough to feed a whole town! Like many other tropical and subtropical trees, it can function as a tree cereal, the large kernels being dried and ground into flour. "Mango butter" is made from half-ripe fruit.

MANGOSTEEN *(Garcinia mangostana)*

Sometimes described as the most delicious of all tropical fruits, with a plumlike texture surrounded by a thick purple rind. Not as widespread as it could be, largely because the small tree is slow to grow and fruit. Research has been suggested into the possibilities of improving its performance.

NARANJILLA *(Solanum quitoense)*

"The golden fruit of the Andes," related to but wholly unlike the tomato. The juice is said to taste like a mixture of strawberries and pineapple. Much like an orange in appearance, the fruit grows on a large, robust, hairy shrub and is produced throughout the year.

OLIVE *(Olea europaea)*
Fruit of a small, slow-growing tree that often lives to a great age in fairly arid areas. Olive oil is used medicinally, both internally and externally, as well as for cooking, lighting, lubrication, and soap.

PAPAYA *(Carica papaya)*
Oval, melonlike fruit of one of the world's fastest-growing plants. Looking like a small palm, it is in fact a woody, herbaceous plant with a crown of large leaves on top of a straight, unbranched trunk. It can bear quite a heavy crop of fruit within a year of seeding. The fruit has a delicate aroma and a taste that contains elements of strawberry, peach, and Galia melon. It is particularly appropriate for use in a forest garden context, because its unripe fruits may be eaten as a perennial green vegetable, thus reducing the need for annual vegetables that require constant cultivation of the soil. An enzyme called papain that is present in latex extracted from the unripe fruits has important medicinal and industrial applications. One use of it is as an anti-shrinking agent for textiles. From the leaves a medicinal alkaloid called carpaine is extracted and the seeds yield a useful oil. The plant will not tolerate chemical fertilizers, so it has to be grown organically.

PASSIONFRUIT *(Passiflora edulis)*
One of the most delicious of all fruits, and one of the most beautiful of all flowers; as a perennial climber it is one of the components of the vertical layer in the Kerala forest gardens. The fruit has a purple skin enclosing a sweet fragrant pulp, from which a popular beverage is extracted.

PINEAPPLE *(Ananas comosus)*
The fruit, which is fact a fusion of 100 or more small fruits, has important nutritional and medicinal virtues owing to its content of magnesium and manganese, both of which benefit the nervous system. It is also a good source of vitamins A and C, which work together to build up the body's protective system. The juice contains a digestive enzyme similar to papain and can be applied externally to treat skin complaints. The juice is also a useful remedy for sore

throats. From the sharp, sword-shaped leaves a strong fiber can be extracted, which can be woven into hardwearing cloth.

POMEGRANATE *(Punica granatum)*

The fruit of a small tree or shrub notable for its vivid, flame colored blossoms, which yield a red dye. The most useful part of the fruit is the sweet but astringent juice extracted from the translucent, pink pulp, which has many medical applications. A jet-black ink can be madae from the leathery rind.

POMELO *(Citrus maxima)*

This largest of the *Citrus* genus thrives in the lowland tropical zone, unlike other members of the group, which require subtropical climates. Another peculiarity of the species is its high tolerance of salinity, which makes it a plant with great potentialities for exploiting barren seacoasts. In Thailand, its main center of cultivation, it is grown around river deltas and in brackish marshes. The Thais claim that the salt in the soil and atmosphere enhance the flavor of the fruit.

RAMBUTAN *(Nephelium lappaceum)*

Another product of the tropical lowlands, where its "sweet-and-sour" taste is very popular. Related to the litchi, the fruit is similar in size and color, but strikingly adorned with soft spines.

TAMARIND *(Tamarindus indica)*

A bean with an acid-sweet pulp that is borne by a long-lived leguminous tree, which thrives in tropical coastal regions where it is known for its resistance to hurricanes. It is used as an ingredient of sauces, chutneys, and beverages. The pods, when immature, as well as the young leaves and flowers, are consumed as perennial vegetables. Another valued component of Kerala forest gardens.

UVILLA *(Pourouma cecropiaefolia)*

A wild grapelike fruit of the Amazon rain forest, borne in abundance during the wet season and much appreciated by the Indians. A publication of the National Academy of Sciences in Washington, D.C., suggested that it should be the subject of research, to see if it is suitable for a "homegarden" (or forest garden) crop throughout the humid tropics.

Nuts & Oilseeds

BABASSU PALM *(Osbignya phalerata oleifera)*
Another of the many wild trees of the Amazon rain forest, which has been largely neglected by science but which is potentially of enormous value to mankind. A tall, majestic, fan-shaped palm with large, elegant, curved leaves, it is widespread in many parts of the Amazon basin. It bears huge crops of nuts very similar to coconuts, which are extremely rich in an oil that is both edible and has industrial uses, especially in the manufacture of soap. The only disadvantage is that the shells are very tough, but a machine has been built that can crack them. Babassu palms are sometimes grown as components of forest garden projects in northern Brazil.

BAMBARA GROUNDNUT *(Voandzeia subterranea)*
Named after a district near Timbuktu in the Sahara, this is an extremely nourishing protein food that will grow in some of the harshest deserts, where few other plants will survive, but also in the African rain forests. Like the peanut, the plant buries its fruits in the ground, where they are safe from flying insects such as locusts. The seeds are eaten raw when immature or boiled or roasted when fully ripe. Roasted seeds are often ground into a flour that is considered to be as energizing as most grains. Bambara groundnut is thus one of many tropical plants that are cereal equivalents, whose cultivation avoids the complications involved in growing conventional cereal grains and which lack the gluten that is a cholesterol-forming agent in wheat, oats, barley, and rye. Bambara groundnut has proved to be suitable for mixed cropping in West African forest gardens.

DIKANUT *(Irvingia gabonensis)*
The edible fruit of a multipurpose tree grown on the "compound farms" of Southeast Nigeria. Oil is extracted from the kernel, which is also valued as a soup condiment, as are the fermented seeds. The leaves, roots, and bark have medicinal properties. The hard timber is used for making tool handles and for carving.

JEHEB Nut *(Cordeauxia edulis)*
One of the few food plants able to survive in the arid wastes of the African Sahel. It has a very deep taproot able to search out any ground-water that may be available and which enables the plant to remain green throughout the year. A dwarf, many-stemmed shrub, the jeheb grows slowly, especially in the seedling stage while it is establishing its massive root system. But after three to four years, under favorable conditions, it will yield abundant harvests of pods containing seeds of rich and well-balanced nutritive value. The leaves contain a vivid red dye. The jeheb is ideally suited for establishing pioneering out-posts for agroforestry schemes designed to reclaim the Sahara and other deserts.

OIL PALM *(Elaeis guineensis)*
An important constituent of the Nigerian "compound farms"; also widely grown in other parts of West Africa. The orange-red nuts form tightly compacted bunches shaped something like pineapples. Harvesting of mature trees, which may reach fifty feet, is usually by climbers supported by ropes wound round the trunks. The oil is very nutritious, being especially rich in carotene, the precursor of vitamin A. It is also used for soap-making. A sugary sap is extracted from the trunk and flowers, and the fronds are used for thatching.

PEACH PALM *(Bactris gasipaes)*
A tropical American species that produces extremely nourishing nuts similar to chestnuts. A multistemmed tree, it is considered es-pecially suited for the production of "hearts of palm" or "palm cab-bage," a vegetable delicacy.

Vegetables

The most important vegetable grown in many parts of the tropics are beans and other pulses, because they tend to be the principal sources of protein.

LABLAB or HYACINTH BEANS *(Dolichos lablab)*
Among the most ubiquitous and adaptable of tropical legumes, and also among those best suited for agroforestry schemes, as they are already widely used as cover crops in rubber, coconut, and oil-palm plantations. Not only are the dried seeds eaten as pulses, but the young pods and leaves are eaten as green vegetables.

MARAMA BEANS *(Tylosema esculentum* or *Bauhinia esculenta)*
Natives of the Kalahari Desert and adjacent regions of southern Africa, these beans rival soybeans and peanuts in protein and oil content. The fruits of long, prostrate vines, they are eaten roasted or ground into flour. A golden oil similar to almond oil is extracted from the seeds. The plants also have enormous red-brown succulent tubers that are particularly appreciated, not only for their food value but also as emergency sources of water.

MOTH BEANS *(Vigna aconitifolia)*
Believed to be the most drought-tolerant pulse crop grown in India, these beans are extensively cultivated in the Rajasthan Desert area. Thriving in periods of minimal rainfall, the plants form dense mats that create a living mulch, shielding the soil from the sun and conserving moisture. As such they would be good companions for other plants in agroforestry desert reclamation schemes. The seeds make a nutritious pulse and the young pods are eaten as chlorophyll-rich vegetables.

TEPARY BEANS *(Phaseolus acutifolius)*
Another drought-tolerant crop, these beans have been cultivated in arid regions of North America for more than 5,000 years. Today they are among the staple foods of the Hopi and Papago Indians. In their wild state they are tall vines which often climb up desert shrubs, but under cultivation they tend to form self-standing shrubs. Rich in protein, the beans are either treated as pulses or ground into meal.

WINGED BEANS (Goa Bean, Asparagus Pea) *(Psophocarpus tetragonolobus)*
Native to New Guinea and Southeast Asia, these are multipurpose

plants, every part of which—seeds, pods, leaves, and tubers—is edible. Exceptionally rich in protein, the seeds also yield an edible oil. They also contain tocopherol, an antioxidant that increases the viability of vitamin A in the human body (vitamin A deficiency is common in many tropical regions). Fast-growing perennial vines, the plants are exceptionally resistant to pests and diseases.

Among tropical root and tuber crops, taros *(Colocassia antiquorum)* and yams *(Dioscorea* spp.) have been found to be more suitable for forest garden conditions than the ubiquitous cassava *(Manihot utilissima)*, because they are more shade-tolerant. Farmers in the Kenya Highlands train their yams up strong and hardy mururi trees, which they plant as living stakes. Another valuable climber is the Central American chayote *(Sechium edule)*, a vigorous perennial vine with curious ribbed, pear-shaped fruits, every part of which, like the winged bean, is edible. Another perennial Central American vegetable is the similarly named *chaya*, which, for years on end, produces prodigious quantities of greenery that is consumed like spinach.

Waxes, Gums, & Fibers

Though the industrial world produces a large number of synthetics from petrochemicals and other sources, natural substances are preferable. Not only are they often more efficient, containing elements that cannot be reproduced artificially, but—important in this age of ecological crisis—their production and processing do not pollute the environment, and they are derived from resources that are readily and easily renewable. A few examples follow.

CANDELILLA *(Euphorbia antisyphilitica)*
A leafless shrub that grows abundantly in the deserts of Mexico and the southern United States, whose stems exude a wax that is used as a substitute for beeswax. When refined, it is used in the manufacture of

candles, polishes, varnishes, dental molds, and electrical insulating materials. The wax is removed from the plants by boiling or the use of solvents. In Mexico the candelilla industry is subsidized by the government, as a way of supporting inhabitants of remote desert regions.

CAUASSÚ *(Calathea lutea)*

A tall herb, having large wax-coated leaves, that grows in dense clumps along the banks of the Amazon and other rivers in South and Central America, as well as in upland areas. The wax, for which there is considerable industrial demand, can be removed easily, without mechanical aids; so wax production would be a good subject for small communal enterprises associated with forest gardens, such as those of Kerala.

GUAR or CLUSTER BEAN *(Cyamopsis tetragonolobus)*

A leguminous bush with gum-bearing seeds, related to the soybean, which grows in tropical Asia. There is a constantly rising demand for the gum from papermaking, food-processing, pharmaceutical, mining, and oil industries. A robust plant that thrives in semiarid areas and tolerates saline soils, guar has been cultivated in India for centuries as a food crop. The seeds are rich in protein, while the young pods are eaten like French beans or dried and salted.

JUTE *(Corchorus capsularis)*

A perennial fiber plant that thrives in low-lying tropical areas such as Bangladesh. An extremely versatile fiber, it can be processed into many different types of thread, including one resembling wool. With sponsorship from Oxfam and other relief agencies, a large network of cooperatives has been set up to help Bangladeshi women to make knitwear and other jute-based articles of many kinds. Jute leaves can be eaten like spinach.

RAMIE *(Boehmeria nivea)*

Formerly called "Chinese grass," this is a tall, slender, perennial fiber plant that thrives in humid tropical and subtropical regions of East Asia. Harvested from two to five times a year, it can continue to yield good fibers for 100 years. Its use in China goes back to Neolithic times. The fibers are long, strong, durable, and almost as lustrous as silk. With tensile strength seven times that of cotton, they can be used for parachute cords, fire hoses, transmission belts, and other products where strength is essential. Blended with terylene, they form a permeable fabric that is ideal for tropical clothing.

Fuel Crops

Wood is the main fuel used throughout most of the Third World, and it is regaining popularity in the West as concern is rising over the environmental pollution caused by fossil fuels. Trees most likely to prove useful for energy plantations are those of "pioneer" species, which, under natural conditions, colonize deforested areas. Such trees are hardy, aggressive, adaptable, and able to withstand degraded soils, drought, and strong winds. In tropical areas many of the best firewood trees are fast-growing members of leguminous species, able to fertilize themselves with atmospheric nitrogen. Ability to coppice or regrow from root suckers are other useful characteristics. Attention should also be given to the calorific value of different woods. In general, heavy woods give off more heat than softwoods, though the resins in conifers enhance heat when burning, as do the oils and gums sometimes found in hardwoods.

CASUARINA, or HORSETAIL TREE *(Casuarina equisetifolia)*
A native of the Southern Hemisphere, this hardy, fast-growing, salt-tolerant tree produces wood that has been described as "the best firewood in the world." In India it has even been used to fuel railway engines. Equally at home in the humid tropics or in semiarid regions, on high mountain slopes or coastal sand dunes, it is commonly used for erosion control. Having an abundance of switchy twigs, it makes an excellent windbreak. Though not leguminous, it has the ability to fix atmospheric nitrogen.

GLIRICIDIA, or MADRE *(Gliricidia sepium)*
A fast-growing, coppicing leguminous tree from tropical America, it

is planted not only for fuel but to shade plantation crops such as cacao, as it has an abundance of foliage. As such it is well suited for agroforestry projects. A notable feature of the tree is that, though its wood is used for fuel, the living tree is relatively fireproof. As such it is commonly used in Java for fire-belts around forests.

GMELINA *(Gmelina arborea)*

A native of the rain forests of Southeast Asia, this high-yielding, adaptable coppicing tree has been planted for fuel in many tropical countries, including Brazil and parts of Africa. It has been used as the main tree constituent of *taungya* systems, in which short-lived horticultural crops, such as cashews, peanuts, corn, and beans, are planted in the neighborhood of saplings during their period of establishment. Its pulp is used to make a high-quality paper.

LEUCAENA *(Leucaena leucocephala)*

Probably the most popular "pioneer" tree planted in the tropics in recent decades. Amazingly fast-growing, it can reach heights exceeding twenty feet in its first year. Especially high-yielding varieties have been planted in the Philippines to supply fuel for power stations. With an aggressive root system that can split rocks and an ability to thrive on steep, barren slopes, it has been used to restore forest cover to denuded watersheds. A legume originally from southern Mexico, it has become a truly pantropical tree.

PONGAM *(Derris indica)*

Another leguminous tree, originating from the Indian subcontinent, pongam is planted to provide not only fuel, but also lighting oil. Being shade-tolerant, it could be a constituent of the low-tree layer in a forest garden. The dried leaves are ground into derris powder, which is used as an insect and nematode deterrent.

Wetland Plants

A number of useful plants grow on lakes, in rivers, or in marshes, and many such areas, at present totally neglected, could be made the sites of interesting and exciting agroforestry/permaculture projects.

BURITA PALM *(Mauritia flexuosa)*

Growing by the millions in swampy areas throughout Amazonia, this valuable tree was described by the famous naturalist Alexander von Humboldt as "the tree of life," because it supplied all the basic needs of several Indian tribes. It has bunches of sweet, tangy fruit, which are reported to contain as much vitamin C as citrus, and an oil containing even more vitamin A than carrots or spinach. The kernel contains another oil, which is reported to be similar in quality to that of the oil palm. From the pith of the trunk is obtained a starch similar to sago, which is roasted by the Indians to make bread. The trunk also contains a sweet sap, and the unopened flower clusters are eaten like vegetables. The bark is a light wood like balsa, which the Indians use to make rafts. A corklike material obtained from the leaf stalks has been used to make sandals, and the leaves contain a fiber that has been used for hammocks, mats, and baskets.

EELGRASS *(Zostera marina)*

An amazing flowering cereal that grows in shallow seawater, and which has been harvested for centuries by the Seri Indians of the west coast of Mexico. The plant grows fully submerged, but when the grain is ripe it floats to the surface and drifts to shore. An important mud-flat stabilizer, eelgrass is considered to have great potentialities as a food crop for tropical estuaries.

LOTUS *(Nelumbo nucifera)*

This water plant, which grows wild in many parts of Asia, is the sacred lotus of Indian and Chinese mythology. The rhizomes are roasted or steamed and are said to taste like Jerusalem artichokes. In China a kind of arrowroot powder is sometimes prepared from them. The seeds are usually boiled or roasted, the fruit can be eaten after the removal of the seeds, and the stems and bell-shaped leaves can be eaten as green vegetables in salads.

PAPYRUS *(Cyperus papyrus)*

Another water plant, now scorned in Africa as a pernicious weed, which once played a key role in the civilizations of Egypt, Greece, and Rome. In order to make the writing material used for the masterpieces of classical literature, the ancients stripped the fibrous covering off the stems and slit the pith into strips. Laid side by side, with other strips placed crosswise on top, the strips were dampened and pressed, so that the gluelike sap cemented them together; they were then dried into sheets. From the outer fibers of the stems, the Egyptians made ropes, baskets, mats, and sails; the roots were used as fuel and the pith was eaten. The papyrus reed could be used for all these purposes today, and yet it is regarded as a scourge that should be destroyed. It forms floating islands in lakes that obstruct navigation, and a large area of Uganda is papyrus swamp that is considered a useless wilderness. All this vast quantity of papyrus could be used to make paper, hardboard, and rayon and so save thousands of square miles of forest from destruction.

Spirulina *(Spirulina platensis* or *S. maximus)*

Another lake plant: a blue-green alga that forms vast sheets on the surface of lakes in Mexico and Chad in Africa, where for centuries it has been dried and consumed as a high-protein food additive. It is now being produced on a small scale commercially. Spirulina was the marching ration of Aztec warriors.

Water-Chestnut *(Trapa natans)*

An attractive aquatic plant that produces large, curiously shaped nuts like buffalo's horns, which are eaten raw, boiled, or roasted like ordinary chestnuts. The Chinese water-chestnut is an entirely different plant, cultivated for its round, edible corms.

Water-Spinach *(Ipomoea aquatica)*

A tropical, trailing herb that grows in lakes and marshes in India, Southeast Asia, Taiwan, and southern China, where it is widely cultivated for its edible leaves and stems. A quick-growing plant, it may be harvested more than ten times in a season. Relatively high in protein for a green vegetable, it has been estimated that a single hectare (2.5 acres) could produce 770 kilograms (1,700 pounds) of protein per year—a simple answer to the protein-deficiency problem that dogs the people of many tropical regions with vast unused wetlands.

Drought-Resistant Plants

Deserts are already estimated to cover an area the size of North and South America, and they are rapidly expanding. Yet large areas of these deserts could be reclaimed by agroforestry techniques, using some of the many plants that have developed remarkable mechanisms, enabling them to survive in areas of minimum moisture. Kew Gardens has a database that lists 500 species having "green glue" attributes. The common characteristic of such plants is an extensive and quick-growing root system that can enable the plant to become rapidly established, stabilize shifting sands, and extract any water that may be available. Extensive surface growth is also desirable to halt sheet and wind erosion as well as to shade the soil and other less heat-tolerant plants. Several such plants have already been mentioned; others include the following.

ACACIA SENEGAL

One of the hardiest trees in the world, found throughout the Sahel, in many parts of which it is the only woody species able to survive. A small thorny tree or bush, it can thrive in the poorest rocky or sandy soils and face up to hot, dry winds and sandstorms. Stated to be "highly suitable for agroforestry systems," it is already widely grown in association with crop plants including watermelon and millet, the principal dryland cereal. Its principal product is gum arabic, a multipurpose adhesive, for which it has been cultivated for at least 4,000 years.

LEBBEK TREE *(Albizia Lebbeck)*

Another tropical leguminous tree with an open, spreading canopy that is already used extensively in agroforestry schemes: as a shade and nurse tree in cocoa and timber plantations; as the top story in forest gardens devoted mainly to pineapples, bananas, other fruit trees, and bamboos; and as a living stake for pepper vines. A native of tropical Asia, Africa, South America, and northern Australia, it is sometimes known as "woman's-tongue tree."

CAROB *(Ceratonia siliqua)*

A subtropical leguminous fruit-cereal that can thrive on rocky slopes with no visible soil. It is commonly planted on hillsides above orange groves. Originally a native of the Near East, the beanlike fruit is believed to have been the "locusts," which, with wild honey, sustained John the Baptist in the wilderness. The mucilaginous pulp is a particularly sustaining food, as it is almost fifty percent sugar. A confection made from it is sold as "St. John's bread." An industrially valuable gum is extracted from it. A single large tree can produce a ton of pods and remain productive for 100 years.

CHRIST THORN *(Ziziphus spina-christi)*

A long-lived bush or small tree that flourishes in the Sahel-Sahara area of Africa and the Arabian Desert, and is notable for its exceptional regenerative powers. It owes its name to the fact that it is believed to have supplied Christ's crown of thorns. Because it develops an extremely deep taproot and wide-spreading lateral roots, it is used for stabilizing sand dunes. It is also used for windbreaks and shelterbelts. The foliage is eaten by camels. The wood, said to be termite-proof, is used for cabinetmaking and household utensils and burns with an intense heat.

MESQUITE *(Prosopis juliflora)*

A tree-cereal native to Central America, which produces long, straw-colored pods that, when ground into flour, are a palatable substitute for cornmeal. A thorny, deep-rooted, leguminous bush or tree, it has been planted in many arid or semiarid tropical zones.

MOPANE *(Copaifera mopane)*

A characteristic tree of many arid parts of Africa, where it sometimes forms pure stands called "Mopane woodland." The scented, butterfly-shaped leaves are rich in protein. The wood is exceptionally hard, being used for bridge piles and railway sleepers. It burns very slowly, giving off intense heat.

NEEM *(Azadirachta indica)*

A multipurpose tree native to the dry forest areas of the Indian subcontinent and Southeast Asia, neem is one of the most valuable of all arid-zone trees. It produces high-quality timber similar to mahogany and tougher than teak. The seeds are up to forty percent oil, which is used both for burning and for lubrication. Extracts from the seeds, leaves, bark, and roots have medicinal and toiletry application. The seeds and leaves also contain an insect repellent called azadirachtin. In northern Nigeria, neem has been the subject of a successful taungya experiment: after being interplanted with groundnuts, beans, and millet, the trees showed markedly superior growth.

PIGEON PEA *(Cajanus cajan)*

A leguminous woody shrub grown in many parts of the tropics that has great importance as a producer of perennial vegetables in arid areas. As a pulse, the dried seeds are rich in protein, while the immature pods are often eaten as a green vegetable.

RED RIVER GUM *(Eucalyptus camaldulensis)*

One of two eucalyptus that are most widely planted throughout the tropical and subtropical world. Extremely adaptable, it will flourish in areas of both low and high rainfall. In the Sudan it is planted to protect crops from blowing sand. With its wide-spreading crown, it makes a valuable shade tree.

TAMARUGO *(Prosopis tamarugo)*

A leguminous evergreen tree related to the mesquite, this is the most remarkable arid-zone tree in the world. It grows in the Atacama desert of northern Chile, where the soil is covered by a salt crust several meters thick. Rain is sometimes absent from the area for seven years, but the tree is able to extract moisture from the atmosphere through its leaves by a process called "reverse transpiration." The leaves, pods, and seeds are nutritious and palatable.

References

AMTE, M. D. *Cry the Beloved Narmada* (privately published).

BAKER, R. St. B. *My Life My Trees*. London: Lutterworth, 1970.

___. *Sahara Conquest*, London: Lutterworth, 1970.

BUNYARD, PETER. *The Columbian Amazon*. Cornwall: Ecological Press, Withiel, 1989.

DOUGLAS, J.S., and HART, R.A de J. *Forest Farming*. London: Intermediate Technology Publications, 1984.

FORSELL, M. *The Berry Garden*. London: Macdonald Orbis, 1989.

GIRARDET, H. *Earthrise*. London: Paladin, 1992.

GOLDSMITH, E. *The Great U-Turn*. Hartland: Green Books, 1988.

JUNG, C.G. *The Secret of the Golden Flower*. English translation by Cary F. Baynes. London: Kegan Paul, 1945.

LARKCOM, JOY. *The Salad Garden*. Leicester: Winward, 1984.

___. *Oriental Vegetables*. London: Murray, 1991.

___. *Salads for Small Gardens*. London: Hamlyn, 1995.

LEVY, J de B. *Herbal Handbook for Everyone*. London: Faber, 1966.

LIEDLOFF, JEAN. *The Continuum Concept*. London: Duckworth, 1975.

MABEY, R. *Food for Free*. London: Collins, 1974.

___. *Plants with a Purpose*. London: Collins, 1977.

MACY, JOANNA. *Dharma and Development*. W. Hartford, Conn.: Kumarian Press, 1985.

MASSINGHAM, H.J. *The Curious Traveller*. London: Collins, 1948.

___. *The English Countryman*. London: Batsford, 1942.

___. *This Plot of Earth*. London: Collins, 1944.

MOLLISON, B. and HOLMGREN, D. *Permaculture One*. Melbourne: Transworld, 1978.

___. *Permaculture Two*. Tasmania: Tagari, 1979.

___. *Permaculture: A Designer's Manual*. Tyalgum, Australia: Tagari, 1988.

NATIONAL ACADEMY of SCIENCES (NAS), *Energy for Rural Development.* Washington, D.C. 1976.

___. *Making Aquatic Weeds Useful.* Washington, D.C.,1979.

NEARING, HELEN and SCOTT. *Living the Good Life.* New York: Schocken Books, 1964.

SCHWARZ, W. and D. *Breaking Through.* Hartland: Green Books, 1987.

SHEWELL-COOPER, W.E. *The Compost Fruit Grower.* London: Pelham, 1975.

STEPPLER and NAIR. *Agroforestry: A Decade of Development.* Nairobi: ICRAF, 1987.

TURNER, NEWMAN. *Fertility Farming.* London: Faber, 1951.

___. *Herdsmanship,* London: Faber, 1952.

WALLACE, ALFRED RUSSEL, *The Malay Archipelago.* New York: Dover Publications, 1964.

WELLOCK, WILFRED, *Gandhi as a Social Revolutionary.* Tiripur, India: Sarvodaya, 1953.

Suggested Further Reading

ADAMS, WILLIAM D., and THOMAS R. LEROY. *Growing Fruits and Nuts in the South.* Dallas: Taylor, 1992.

BAINES, C. *Wildlife Garden Notebook.* Sparkford: Oxford Illustrated Press, 1984.

BELL, GRAHAM. *The Permaculture Garden.* London: Thorsons, 1994. A comprehensive guide to the subject.

___. *The Permaculture Way.* London: Thorsons, 1992.

BENNETT, JENNIFER. *The Harrowsmith Book of Fruit Trees.* Camden East, Ont.: Camden House, 1991. Excellent reference for North American varieties.

BOOKIRD, S.A., et al. *Forest Villages: An Agroforestry Approach.* Nairobi: ICRAF, 1985.

CREASY, ROSALIND. *The Complete Book of Edible Landscaping.* San Francisco: Sierra Club Books, 1982.

DOUGLAS, J.S. *Alternative Foods.* London: Pelham, 1978.

ELLIOTT, D.B. *Roots: An Underground Botany.* Old Greenwich, CT: Chatham Press, 1979.

EVELYN, JOHN. *Acetaria: A Discourse of Sallets.* London: Tooke, 1699 (facsimile ed. pub. by Prospect Books, London, 1982).

FERNANDES, E.C.M., and P.K.R. NAIR. *Structure and Function of Tropical Homegardens.* Nairobi: ICRAF, 1986.

FITTER, A. *Wild Flowers of Britain and Northern Europe.* London: Collins, 1987.

FLOOD, M. *Solar Prospects.* London: Wildwood, 1983.

Forest Gardening with Robert Hart (videotape). Dartington, Totnes: Green Earth Books, 1996. Order from Chelsea Green Publishing Company, PO Box 428, White River Junction, VT 05001; (800) 639-4099.

FORSYTH, TURID, and MERILYN SIMONDS MOHR. *The Harrowsmith Salad Garden.* Camden East, Ont.: Camden House, 1992.

FRANCK, GERTRUD. *Companion Planting.* London: Thorsons, 1983.

FUKUOKA, MASANOBU. *The One-Straw Revolution.* Emmaus, PA: Rodale, 1978.

GARDNER, JO ANN. *The Heirloom Garden.* Pownal, VT: Storey, 1992.

___. *Living with Herbs.* Woodstock, VT: Countryman Press, 1996.

___. *The Old-Fashioned Fruit Garden.* Halifax, N.S.: Nimbus, 1989.

GIONO, JEAN. *The Man Who Planted Trees.* Chelsea, VT.: Chelsea Green, 1985.

HARPER, PETER. *The Natural Garden Book.* New York: Simon & Schuster, 1994.

___. *Crazy Idealists.* Machynlleth, Wales: Centre for Alternative Technology, 1995.

HARRISON, PAUL. *The Greening of Africa.* London: Paladin, 1987.

HARRISON, S.G., et al. *The Oxford Book of Food Plants.* London: Oxford University Press, 1982.

HART, ROBERT. *Beyond the Forest Garden.* London: Gaia Books, 1996.

HILL, LEWIS. *Fruits & Berries for the Home Garden.* Pownal, VT: Storey, 1977.

___. *Pruning Simplified.* Pownal, VT: Storey, 1986.

___. *Secrets of Plant Propagation.* Pownal, VT: Storey, 1985.

Hilliers' Manual of Trees and Shrubs. Newton Abbot: David and Charles, 1977.

HOLMES, ROGER (ed.). *Taylor's Guide to Fruits and Berries.* Boston: Houghton Mifflin, 1996.

JACOB, V.G., and W.S. ALLES. *Kandyan Gardens of Sri Lanka.* Nairobi: ICRAF, 1987.

JEANS, HELEN. *About Tropical Fruits.* London: Thorsons, 1972.

KENTON, L., and K. KENTON. *Raw Energy.* London: Century, 1984.

KOCH, M. *Whole Health Handbook.* London: Sidgwick and Jackson, 1984.

KOURIK, ROBERT. *Designing and Maintaining Your Edible Landscape Naturally.* Santa Rosa, CA: Metamorphic Press, 1986.

LARKCOM, JOY. *The Salad Garden.* New York: Penguin Books, 1996.

LEVY, J. DE. B. *Herbal Handbook for Everyone.* London: Faber, 1966.

MAY, P.H., et al. *Babassu Palm in the Agroforestry Systems of Brazil's Mid-North Region.* Nairobi: ICRAF, 1985.

METCALF, J. *Herbs and Aromatherapy.* London: Bloomsbury Books, 1993.

MICNON, G., et al. *Multistoried Agroforestry Garden System in Western Sumatra.* Nairobi: ICRAF, 1987.

MOLLISON, Bill, and Reny M. Slay. *Introduction to Permaculture.* Tyalgum, NSW: Tagari, 1994.

NAIR, M.A., and C. SREEDHARAN. *Agroforestry Farming Systems in Kerala, Southern India.* Nairobi: ICRAF, 1987.

NATIONAL ACADEMY OF SCIENCES (NAS). *Firewood Crops,* 1980.

___. *Tropical Legumes,* 1979.

___. *Underexploited Tropical Plants,* 1979.

OKAFOR, J., and E.C.M. FERNANDES. *Compound Farms of Southeastern Nigeria.* Nairobi: ICRAF, 1987.

ONSTAD, Dianne. *The Whole Foods Companion.* White River Jct., VT: Chelsea Green, 1996.

OTTO, STELLA. *The Backyard Berry Book.* Maple City, MI: Otto-Graphics, 1995.

___. *The Backyard Orchardist.* Maple City, MI: OttoGraphics, 1993.

PAGE, STEPHEN, and JOE SMILLIE. *The Orchard Almanac: A Seasonal Guide to Healthy Fruit Trees.* 3rd Edition. Davis, CA: agAccess, 1994.

Permaculture Activist (journal), P.O. Box 1209, Black Mountain, NC 28711; (704) 683-4946. Valuable publication covering permaculture in the United States; $16 per year for three issues and three newsletters.

Permaculture International (journal), P.O. Box 6039, S. Lismore, NSW 2480, Australia. Published quarterly; distributed in the UK by Permanent Publications (see below). Highly recommended.

Permaculture Magazine, Permanent Publications, Clanfield, Hants. Gives regular information about developments in permaculture and forest gardening. Published quarterly.

PHILBRICK, H., and R. GREGG. *Companion Plants.* London: Robinson and Watkins, 1967.

PRATT, SIMON (ed.). *The Permaculture Plot.* Clanfield, Hants.: Permanent Publications, 1994. A guide to 52 sites throughout the British Isles that can be visited by the public.

REED, MARY. *Fruits and Nuts in Symbolism and Celebration.* San Jose: Resource Publications, 1992.

REICH, LEE. *Uncommon Fruits Worthy of Attention.* Reading, MA: Addison-Wesley, 1991.

RIOTTE, LOUISE. *The Complete Guide to Growing Nuts.* Dallas: Taylor, 1993.

SEYMOUR, J., and H. GIRARDET. *Far from Paradise.* Basingstoke: Green Print, 1986.

SILCOCK, L. (ed.). *The Rainforest: A Celebration.* London: Barrie and Jenkins, 1989.

STEIN, SARA. *Noah's Garden: Restoring the Ecology of Our Own Back Yards.* Boston: Houghton Mifflin, 1993.

TOKE, D. *Green Energy.* London: Green Print, 1990.

TURNER, NEWMAN. *Fertility Pastures.* London: Faber, 1955.

VERGARA, N.T., and P.K.R. NAIR. *Agroforestry in the South Pacific Region.* Nairobi: ICRAF, 1987.

WATKINS, DAVID. *Urban Permaculture.* Clanfield, Hants.: Permanent Publications, 1993. A do-it-yourself handbook offering many clear and simple steps to small-scale sustainable living.

WHEALY, KENT, and STEVE DEMUTH (eds.) *Fruit, Berry and Nut Inventory.* 2nd Edition. Decorah, IA: Seed Saver Publications, 1993. An invaluable reference source for growers living in the United States, listing all of the varieties of fruits, nuts, berries, and edible tropical plants available through U.S. mail-order nurseries.

WHITEFIELD, PATRICK. *How to Make a Forest Garden.* Clanfield, Hants.: Permanent Publications, 1996. A step-by-step guide to creating a low-maintenance food-producing garden designed using the ecological principles of a natural woodland.

___. *Permaculture in a Nutshell.* Clanfield, Hants.: Permanent Publications, 1993. An introduction to permaculture in temperate climates.

WRENCH, G.T. *Reconstruction by Way of the Soil.* London: Faber, 1946.

The U.S. distributor for permaculture books published by Tagari and Permanent Publications is Permaculture Resources, Inc., 56 Farmersville Road, Califon, NJ 07830; phone (800) 832-6285.

Recommended Suppliers in North America

General Suppliers

GARDENER'S SUPPLY CO., *128 Intervale Rd., Burlington, VT 05401;* *(800) 863-1700.*

PEACEFUL VALLEY FARM SUPPLY, *P.O. Box 2209, Grass Valley, CA 95945;* *(916) 272-4769.*

REAL GOODS TRADING CORPORATION, *Route 101, Hopland, CA 95449;* *(800) 762-7325.*

Mail-Order Nurseries: United States

Note: For a more complete list of mail-order nurseries in the U.S., as well as listings of all varieties of fruits, nuts, and berries offered by them, consult the *Fruit, Berry and Nut Inventory* (Seed Saver Publications, 1993), available for $22.00 softcover ($28.00 hardcover), plus $4.00 shipping and handling from Seed Savers Exchange, 3076 North Winn Rd., Decorah, IA 52101; (319) 382-5990.

ELMORE ROOTS NURSERY, *Apple Box 171, Lake Elmore, VT 05657; (802) 888-3305* (fruit trees, berry plants, and flowering shrubs for cold-climate regions).

A.I. EPPLER Ltd., *P.O. Box 16513, Seattle, WA 98116-0513; (206) 932-2211* (specializes in European gooseberries and black, white, and red currants).

FEDCO TREES, *Rt. 2, Box 275, Clinton, ME 04927; (207) 426-9005* (hardy trees and shrubs).

HENRY FIELD SEED & NURSERY, *415 N. Burnett St., Shenandoah, IA 51602.*

FOUNDATION PLANT MATERIALS SERVICE, *University of California, Davis, CA 95616-8600; (916) 752-3590.*

FOWLER NURSERIES, INC., *Garden Center, 525 Fowler Rd., Newcastle, CA 95658; (916) 645-8191.*

GIRARD NURSERIES, *P.O. Box 428, Geneva, OH 44041; (216) 466-2881* (rare and unusual plants, conifers and flowers).

JOHN GORDON NURSERY, *1385 Campbell Blvd., Amherst, NY 14228-1404* (specializes in hardy nut varieties).

GREENMANTLE NURSERY, *3010 Ettersburg Rd., Garberville, CA 95440; (707) 986-7504* (homestead fruits and chestnut seedlings).

HARMONY FARM SUPPLY, *P.O. Box 460, Graton, CA 95444; (707) 823-9125* (drought-tolerant bareroot fruits, nuts, and berries).

HARTMANN'S PLANTATION, INC., *310 60th St., P.O. Box E, Grand Junction, MI 49056; (616) 253-4281* (specializes in blueberries, raspberries, and hard-to-find fruits and other plants).

HIDDEN SPRINGS NURSERY, *170 Hidden Springs Lane, Cookville, TN 38501; (615) 268-9889* (unusual fruits and nuts; nitrogen-fixing shrubs).

HOLLYDALE NURSERY, *P.O. Box 26, Pelham, TN 37366; (615) 467-3600.*

LAWSON'S NURSERY, *Rt. 1, Box 472, Yellow Creek Rd., Ball Ground, GA 30107; (706) 893-2141* (old-fashioned and unusual varieties; heritage apples).

HENRY LEUTHARDT NURSERIES, INC., *Montauk Hwy., Box 666, East Moriches, Long Island, NY 11940; (516) 878-1387* (rare and choice old varieties).

LIVING TREE CENTRE, *Box 10082, Berkeley, CA 94709* ("dedicated to the reforestation of North America"; historic varieties).

J.E. MILLER NURSERIES, INC., *5060 West Lake Rd., Canandaigua, NY 14424; (800) 836-9630* (specializes in dwarf fruit trees).

MUSSER FORESTS, INC., *P.O. Box 340, Route 119 North, Indiana, PA 15701; (412) 465-5685* (evergreen and hardwood seedlings; ornamental shrubs and ground covers).

NEWARK NURSERIES, INC., *P.O. Box 578, Hartford, MI 49057; (616) 621-3135* (large selection of fruit trees).

NORTHWIND NURSERY & ORCHARDS, *7910 335th Ave., NW, Princeton, MN 55371; (612) 389-4920* (organically grown fruit trees and nursery stock for cold climates).

NORTHWOODS RETAIL NURSERY, *27635 S. Oglesby Rd., Canby, OR 97013; (503) 266-5432* (exotic fruits and nuts that are hardy and disease-resistant).

OIKOS TREE CROPS, *721 North Fletcher, Kalamazoo, MI 49007-3077; (616) 624-6233* (nuts, oaks, and native fruits).

OREGON EXOTICS, RARE FRUIT NURSERY, *1065 Messinger, Grants Pass, OR 97527; (503) 846-7578* (rare and unusual fruits and nuts from around the world).

RAINTREE NURSERY, *391 Butts Rd., Morton, WA 98356; (206) 496-6400.*

ST. LAWRENCE NURSERIES, *325 State Hwy. 345, Potsdam, NY 13676; (315) 265-6739* (fruits, nuts, and edible landscape plants for cold-climate gardens; excellent selection with several unique varieties).

SIERRA GOLD NURSERIES, *5320 Garden Hwy., Yuba City, CA 95991; (916) 674-1145.*

SMITH NURSERY, *270 West Briggs Ave., Lathrop, CA 95330; (209) 982-1276.*

SONOMA ANTIQUE APPLE NURSERY, *4395 Westside Rd., Healdsburg, CA 95448; (707) 433-6420* (large selection of organically grown heritage apples and other fruit trees).

SOUTHMEADOW FRUIT GARDENS, *Box SM, Lakeside, MI 49116; (616) 469-2865* (large selection of choice and unusual fruit varieties for home gardeners).

STARK BROTHERS NURSERY, *P.O. Box 10, Hwy. 54, Louisiana, MO 63353; (800) 325-4180.*

TELTANE FARM & NURSERY, *RR1, Box 3000, Monroe, ME 04951; (207) 525-7761* (unusual and heirloom apple and other fruit varieties for cold-climate areas).

VAN WELL NURSERY, *P.O. Box 1339, Wenatchee, WA 98801; (509) 663-8189.*

BOB WELLS NURSERY, *P.O. Box 606, Lindale, TX 75771; (903) 882-3550.*

WOMACK'S NURSERY, *Rt. 1, Box 80, De Leon, TX 76444; (817) 893-6497* (fruit and pecan trees; blackberries and grape vines).

M. WORLEY NURSERY, *98 Braggtown Rd., York Springs, PA 17372; (717) 528-4519* (fruit trees, including heritage apple varieties).

Mail-Order Nurseries: Canada

BOUGHEN NURSERIES *Valley River Ltd., Box 12, Valley River, Manitoba R0L 2B0* (organically grown, hardy fruit trees).

CAMPBERRY FARM, *RR 1, Niagara-on-the-Lake, Ontario L0S 1J0* (specializes in nut trees).

CORN HILL NURSERY, *RR 5, Petitcodiac, New Brunswick E0A 2H0* (hardy fruit trees, including heritage apples).

V. KRAUS NURSERIES, LTD., *Carlisle, Ontario L0R 1H0.*

MORDEN NURSERIES LTD., *Box 1270, Morden, Manitoba R0G 1J0* (prairie-hardy fruit trees).

NORTHERN KIWI NURSERY, *RR3, 181 Niven Rd., Niagara-on-the-Lake, Ontario L0S 1J0* (good selection of hardy kiwis).

SURSUM CORDA, *Scotstown, Quebec J0B 3B0* (organically grown fruit trees).

TSOLUM RIVER FRUIT TREES, *Box 68, Merville, British Columbia V0R 2M0* (organically grown fruit trees).

WESTERN ONTARIO FRUIT TESTING ASSOCIATION (WOFTA),

Agriculture Canada Research Station, Harrow, Ontario, N0R 1G0
(members can purchase new fruit varieties; nonmembers can purchase budwood or seeds).
WINDMILL POINT FARM & NURSERY, *2103 Blvd. Perrot, Notre-
Dame, Ile Perrot, Quebec J7V 5V6* (organically grown fruit trees).

Places to Visit

As of the time of printing, we know of the following forest gardens
that are open to the public. For a more extensive guide to visiting permaculture projects in the UK, refer to Simon Pratt's *The Permaculture
Plot* (see Suggested Further Reading).

Ken Fern's *Plants for a Future* (featured in the *Forest Gardening
with Robert Hart* video) will be open to the public on Sundays as of
March 1996. Their database of 6,800 species is currently available in PC
format. It takes up 21MB of disk space as a MS Access file, but can also
be supplied as a text file. By mid-1996 it will be available as a complete
program. They also sell plants by mail order and to personal callers.
Please write rather than phone wherever possible. *Plants for a Future,
Higher Penpol, Lostwithiel, Cornwall PL22 0NG. Tel 01208 873554.*

Green Adventure is a group which focuses on education through
practical permaculture design projects in the community. Their community orchard on a site in front of Camberwell Magistrates court
will open in early 1966. Contact *Stefania Stregg, Green Adventure, 2d
Peabody, Camberwell Green, London SE5 7BQ. Tel 0171 708 2151.*

Naturewise at Crouch Hill in north London has an inner-city forest
garden (started in 1991) which is open to the public. The address is *Crouch
Hill Recreation Centre, Hill Rise, London N19 3PT. Tel. 0171 281 3765.*

Nature's World in Middlesbrough has a forest garden (started in
1994) open to the public 11 AM to 4 PM all year round (longer in summer). Local volunteers needed. They also have work days about once a
month. The garden is at *Ladgate Lane, Acklam, Middlesbrough TS57YN.*

Tel 01642 594895.

At *Earthward* on the Scottish borders, the forest garden planted in the winter of 1994-95 is coming along, and a new agroforestry demonstration site is being established in a seven-acre field. There are plans to set up a UK Fruit Explorers Network to exchange information on fruit and nut species and cultivars suited to this climate, and a gene bank. Volunteers welcome. Open weekdays any time, and by appointment on weekends. For more information contact *Earthward, Tweed Horizons, Newtown St. Boswells, Roxburghshire TD6 OSG.*

Membership Organizations

AGROFORESTRY RESEARCH TRUST, *46 Hunter's Moon, Dartington, Totnes, Devon TQ9 6JT.*

The ART is setting up an experimental forest garden on the Dartington estate near Totnes, and will be holding open days from 1996 onwards. Their newsletter gives information about tree and shrub crops, fruit varieties to grow, and details about other agroforestry projects. They also have an extensive catalog of publications, and sell plants and seeds. Newsletter subscription is 18 pounds per year.

BIODYNAMIC FARMING and GARDENING ASSOCIATION, *P.O. Box 550, Kimberton, PA 19442; (215) 935-7797.*

A nonprofit corporation that advances the principles and practices of biodynamic agriculture. Publishes a bimonthly newsletter, "Biodynamics," as well as books.

CALIFORNIA RARE FRUIT GROWERS, INC., *Fullerton Arboretum, California State University, Fullerton, CA 92634.*

A nonprofit organization committed to the study and preservation of rare fruit varieties. Members receive "The Fruit Gardener," a bimonthly magazine.

ECOLOGY ACTION OF THE MIDPENINSULA, *5798 Ridgewood Rd., Willits, CA 95490; (707) 459-3390.*

Ecology Action is an environmental research and educational organization that focuses on "biointensive mini-farming," a method that emphasizes farm-generated fertility and other useful principles. Membership is $30 per year. In addition to offering workshops, Ecology Action offers a large number of research reports and booklets, and runs Bountiful Gardens, a mail-order seed source.

FRUIT TESTING ASSOCIATION NURSERY, *Inc., P.O. Box 462, North St., Geneva, NY 14456; (315) 787-2205.*

A nonprofit cooperative fruit nursery established in 1918 to introduce the most promising varieties developed at the New York State Agricultural Experiment Station at Geneva. Annual membership is $10; members receive a newsletter and can purchase from a catalog of new fruit varieties.

HENRY DOUBLEDAY RESEARCH ASSOCIATION (HDRA), *Ryton Gardens, Ryton-on-Dunsmore, Coventry CV8 3LG; telephone from the U.S. is 011-44-1203-303517.*

The HDRA is the leading center for organic gardening in the UK, and has a forest garden that is open to the public. HDRA also publishes an occasional "Friends of the Forest Garden Newsletter." Inquiries and contributions to Jane Powell c/o Earthward, Tweed Horizons, Newtown St. Boswells, Roxburghshire TD6 0SG.

HERITAGE SEED PROGRAM, *RR 3, Uxbridge, Ontario L9P 1R3 Canada.*

A grassroots seed exchange which searches out and preserves heirloom and endangered varieties of vegetables, fruits, grains, herbs, and flowers. Members receive a magazine, which comes out three times a year, and an annual Seed Listing. Regular membership is $15, fixed income $12, U.S. and foreign $18; supporting membership $20.

HOME ORCHARD SOCIETY, *P.O. Box 230192, Tigard, OR 97281-0192.*

A nonprofit educational organization formed to assist new and experienced fruit growers. Membership is $10 per year and includes a subscription to the quarterly journal "Home News."

THE INTERNATIONAL *RIBES* ASSOCIATION (TIRA), *707 Front St., Northumberland, PA 17857; (717) 473-9910; Edward Mashburn, President.*

Dedicated to furthering the cultivation and knowledge of currants, gooseberries, and jostaberries. Members receive the "Ribes Reporter" newsletter.

NORTH AMERICAN FRUIT EXPLORERS (NAFEX), *c/o Jill Vorbeck, RR 1, Box 94, Chapin, IL 62628.*

NAFEX has over 3,000 members who are committed to discovering and cultivating superior varieties of fruits and nuts. Membership is $8 per year, or $15 for two years. Members receive the informative quarterly journal, "Pomona."

NORTHERN NUT GROWERS ASSOCIATION, *4518 Holston Hills Road, Knoxville, TN 37914.*

SEED SAVERS EXCHANGE, *3076 North Winn Rd., Decorah, IA 52101.*

Seed Savers Exchange is one of the largest and best-known private organizations working to find and preserve traditional and heirloom varieties of edible plants. SSE operates Heritage Farm, where it grows out part of its large seed collection every year, and has planted a Heritage Orchard and vineyard filled with old and rare fruit varieties. Publications issued by SSE include the invaluable *Fruit, Berry and Nut Inventory,* which lists all varieties of fruits and nuts available from U.S. mail-order suppliers. The organization also publishes an annual Yearbook, in which members offer varieties that they are saving in their own home gardens. In recent years, SSE has started Seed Savers International to collect and preserve food-crop seeds from Eastern Europe and the former Soviet Union. Membership is $25 per year; send $1 to receive a color brochure describing SSE projects and member services.

THE SOIL ASSOCIATION, *86-88 Colston St., Bristol BS1 5BB; telephone from the U.S. is 011-44-1179-290661.*

The Soil Association campaigns to improve the quality of food, health, and the environment by promoting organic agriculture. It offers a membership that includes a newsletter subscription.

WORCESTER COUNTY HORTICULTURAL SOCIETY, *Tower Hill Botanic Garden, 11 French Drive, Boylston, MA 01505; (508) 869-6111.*

The society maintains the S. Lothrop Davenport Preservation Orchard, which contains over 115 pre-1900 apple varieties, and sells a limited amount of scionwood to members and to the public on a first-come, first-serve basis.

Index

Index

Index

FOREST GARDENING VIDEO
-NOW AVAILABLE-

A companion video for *Forest Gardening*
which shows three separate projects can now
be ordered from Chelsea Green. 45 minutes.
Produced by Malcom Baldwin.

*To order: call **1-800-639-4099** or call your
bookseller.*